A MEMOIR

smile for the camera

WITHDRAWN

kelle james

SIMON & SCHUSTER BFYR

Simon & Schuster Books for Young Readers

New York   London   Toronto   Sydney

SIMON & SCHUSTER BFYR

An imprint of Simon & Schuster Children's Publishing Division
1230 Avenue of the Americas, New York, New York 10020
This work is a memoir. It reflects the author's present recollections of her
experiences over a period of years. Certain names and identifying characteristics
have been changed.
SIMON & SCHUSTER BFYR is a trademark of Simon & Schuster, Inc.
For information about special discounts for bulk purchases, please contact
Simon & Schuster Special Sales at 1-866-506-1949 or
business@simonandschuster.com.
The Simon & Schuster Speakers Bureau can bring authors to your live event.
For more information or to book an event, contact the Simon & Schuster Speakers
Bureau at 1-866-248-3049 or visit our website at www.simonspeakers.com.
Book design by Lucy Ruth Cummins
The text for this book is set in Adobe Caslon Pro.
Manufactured in the United States of America
2 4 6 8 10 9 7 5 3 1
Library of Congress Cataloging-in-Publication Data
James, Kelle.
Smile for the camera / Kelle James.
p. cm.
ISBN 978-1-4424-0623-0
1. Models (Persons)—Juvenile literature. I. Title.
HD8039.M77J36 2010
746.9'2092—dc22
[B]
2009053000
ISBN 978-1-4424-0625-4 (eBook)

To Randy, for listening

ACKNOWLEDGMENTS

It all started with a unicorn.
    I wanted to write a happy little story for young girls about a unicorn. I joined a writing class led by Claudette Sutherland. As an exercise, she asked us to write a page or two about an emotional event in our lives. I read mine to the class.

That was the night *Smile for the Camera* was born.

Many thanks to Claudette and my Monday night classmates—it's good to have friends like you. Especially Shelley—you're the best cheerleader ever.

Countless thanks to my husband, Randy, who reads every single word I write, usually more than once, no matter how busy he is. I love you.

And my heartfelt thanks to:

My son Colton, for all his encouraging little sticky notes. I've saved them all. They make me smile.

My songwriting son Alex, who loves the written word and kindly helped me with mine.

My agent, Lydia Wills, whose creative mind and kind heart are true inspirations. Thanks for taking a chance on me.

My editor, Courtney Bongiolatti, who is so right for me and so very good with that red pen of hers. Thank you.

My brothers, Bob and Rick, and my sister, Kim. I'm so grateful for all your love and support. In so many ways, this is your story too.

Kathy and Susie, the best sisters-in-law a girl could have.

Yvette Melvin, who said, "You should write." Although I think she had journaling in mind when she said that. You're the best.

The always helpful Eric and Jan Elfman.

Francesca Lia Block, for her way with words.

Guinevere, for a-musing me.

And of course, thank you to Rayna—still best friends after all these years.

Oh, I haven't written that unicorn story yet, but I'm going to. . . .

smile for the camera

He's in my room. I know because I can smell his cigarette breath. I pull my leg under the covers and pretend that I'm asleep. Whenever I do that, I always make sure I move around a little. My brother Bob taught me that. He says sleeping people roll around, fakers don't. I always listen to Bob. He's my big brother.

I hear the whir and click of my fan as it moves from side to side on my nightstand. Every time it passes by, it pushes my father's air at me. I can feel him on my skin. I'm glad my windows are open.

I open my eyes just a tiny bit. I peek out. I see him. He's standing really close to my bed. A streetlamp shines behind him, through my window. The light flares around his dark form like a halo. He's got his gun in his hand.

I can't stand that gun.

I realize that I haven't moved in a while, so I make a little moaning noise and drop my arm over the edge of the mattress. My brother will be impressed when I tell him what I've done.

While I lie there and wait till it's time to move again, I try to imagine I'm surrounded by a powerful force field. If I do it right, it will keep bad things from getting to me. It's hard for me to do, though. I'm not as good at it as Bob is. Anytime I tell him that, he says, "Keep working on it."

Lately I've had lots of chances to practice.

I'm pretty sure I've waited long enough. I think it's safe to move again. I stretch my arm down over the side of my bed and tuck my hand between the mattress and the box spring. I curl my fingers around the short metal rod I hid there. I found it with my brothers' car stuff. It was the perfect size, so I cleaned it up and put it there, just in case.

Maybe I'm moving too much. I decide that I can't move again for at least five minutes. I press my face into the mattress. I lie really still.

My father starts making little hiccup sounds with his throat.

He's crying.

I've never heard him cry before.

The gun thing I'm used to. He does that for attention. But the crying has me worried.

I wish I could see his face, but it hasn't been five minutes yet. I wonder, *When it comes to armed and crying fathers, what's better, steel rods or force fields?* I go with the force field, the kind that sends bullets back where they came from. The harder I try, the louder my heart thumps. The sound fills my ears. I feel like I'm at the bottom of a really deep pool. My ears hurt, but I don't stop. I'm not a quitter.

I look out from under my hair.

My father's gone.

I roll over and stare up at the ceiling. I can't do this anymore. I have to get away. I just need to figure out how.

I climb the big Greyhound bus steps and look around. There's one window seat left. All the passengers are seated, so it's mine. As I hurry down the narrow aisle, my suitcase bumps a man's arm. He pulls his elbow in and gives me a dirty look.

Hot weather has a way of bringing out the worst in some people.

I slide into my seat and rest my legs on top of my suitcase. If I fall asleep during the long drive to the city, I'll know if someone tries to take it.

As the bus driver closes the doors, they make a loud shooshing sound. I look out the window. My father is standing where I left him when I got on the bus. I can tell he's waiting for me to look at him, so I do.

Our eyes meet.

Something about his expression bothers me. I lift my

hand up to the window and give him a little wave. He slowly nods back.

His eyes are quiet. His mouth is soft.

He's sad.

His sadness makes me feel strange, like my heart is too heavy for my chest. I don't understand. Is he sad because I'm leaving?

No. It's not possible.

He hates me. I'm the worst thing that ever happened to him. I'm not even allowed to speak to my mother in front of him.

Once, my brother told me that the reason my father hates me so much is because there's a rumor he's not my father. My uncle is. I like my uncle. I never saw him that much, but when I did, he was always nice to me.

My father waves as the bus pulls away.

I take a deep breath. I've never been to New York City before. I stare out the window and wonder what it will be like. I'm not very good with directions. I hope I'll be able to find my hotel.

I look back at the bus station. My father is still standing there. He hasn't moved. Maybe he doesn't hate me as much as I think he does. Maybe he wants to yell, "Don't go. You're a good girl. I love you. I'm sorry I chased you away like this. Come back. I'll make it up to you. I promise."

Maybe.

I lean my head against the window and close my eyes.

His not moving is the second-best thing he's ever done for me.

I think about the best thing.

It happened at the beach in Ocean City. We were on vacation. I can't remember how old I was. I was little.

I'm wearing my new blue bathing suit. It has a little heart cut out on the bum. I'm very excited about having a heart tanned onto my bottom. I'm lying on my towel really still so the cutout doesn't move—if I do, the heart won't tan right. My sister's radio crackles in the background. She always has her radio with her.

I'm bored. I roll over onto my back.

"Mom? Can Kim and I go put our toes in the ocean?"

My mother nods. "Stay in front of the umbrella, where I can see you," she says.

I take my big sister's hand and we walk to the edge of the water. The waves roll in one after the other. Shallow ripples of water wash up over our feet.

"The water's so cold," Kim says.

A jellyfish lies in a tangle of seaweed. I take Kim's elbow and pull her away from it. I don't want her to get stung.

"Jellyfish," I say.

"Oh," she says back.

Every wave washes the jellyfish closer to our ankles.

I keep pulling Kim farther down the beach.

"Do you think we've gone too far?" I ask.

"Can you still see our umbrella?"

"Yes."

"Is Mom sitting or is she walking over here?"

"She's sitting."

"We're okay, then," she says.

Around us little air bubbles pop up out of the wet sand.

"Sand crab bubbles!" I yell.

I kneel down, scoop a squiggling crab out of the sand, and put it into Kim's hand. It scrabbles at her palm. She laughs and lets it go.

The sun is hot on my back. My skin feels tight and itchy.

"I'm hot," I say.

"Let's go back, maybe Mom will take us in the water," Kim says.

"You ask."

I take Kim's arm and guide her across the hot sand back to our big blue umbrella. Sometimes we get too close to people lying on their towels and Kim almost steps on them. Before they yell at us, I look from their face to my sister's. When they see her clouded eyes, they stay quiet.

"Mom, can you take us in the ocean?" Kim asks.

My mother looks over at my father.

"Richard?" she says. "The waves are big today. The lifeguard's gone out a few times already. Do you think you can come out with me and the girls?"

He doesn't say anything, but he sits up. That means yes.

My mother takes my sister's hand and walks off toward the water. My father sits there staring out at the ocean. Finally he takes his sunglasses off, stands up, and heads off after them. His legs are longer than mine. I have to run to keep up with him.

Kim and my mother are already in the ocean. The water is up to my sister's waist. When a wave gets close, my mother says, "Jump." My sister jumps and laughs as the wave lifts her up off the sandy ocean floor.

My father holds his hand out and waits for me to take it. If I don't, I can't go in the ocean. My sister is having so much fun. I want to have fun too. My father is watching my mother. I'm glad he's not watching me. He'd know I don't want to hold his hand and he'd be mad.

I slide my hand into my father's. I don't remember ever holding his hand before. I'm sure I must have, I just don't remember it. His hand is big. It has lots of muscles.

My hand is small.

We walk out into the ocean. A wave comes and splashes the front of my swimsuit. It's really cold. I squeal and jump up in the air. When I land, the under-tow pulls at my legs. I can barely stand up.

My father takes me farther out into the water. It's up to my chest now. The ocean currents swirl around my body. As the water swells, I hop up and float down. I'm pretending I'm a spaceman drifting across the moon.

A lifeguard blows his whistle. That means someone is out too far.

Off in the distance I see a big wave building. The undertow pulls me really hard. I can't stand up. My father picks me up and sits me on his hip. I think he's taking me back to shore, but he's not. He's walking right toward the giant wave.

He's walking quickly. I wrap my legs around his waist and my arms around his neck. He feels so strong, fighting the undertow.

The wave is almost here.

My breath catches in my throat. I've never been this close to such a big one. The pull of the ocean roars in my ears.

My father hurries toward it. He's looking at the wave. He's holding me really tight. He won't let me go. He's protecting me. He's going to save me from the wave that's about to crash down on top of me and hold me under the water until all my air is gone.

The wave is right in front of us. The top curls over, spitting its frothy foam in our faces.

"Don't let go!" my father yells.

I squeeze myself against him.

Just as the wave crashes over us, my father jumps up through the water. The swell carries us up, up, up. Higher than I've ever been. And just as quickly we float down as the wave slams down behind us.

My heart thumps wildly and I start to laugh. My father laughs too as he quickly walks us back to shore.

I open my eyes, look out the bus window, and think about my father and that big wave.

I faced death for the first time in his arms. It wouldn't be the last.

By the time the bus pulls into Port Authority, I'm so nauseous I'm afraid I might throw up. The aisle is packed with people waiting to get out. When the bus stops, they sway forward like falling dominoes.

A woman wearing a business suit and sneakers is standing at the end of my row. I look at her, smile, and wait for her to let me out. Instead she looks at me like she's holding something sour in her mouth.

When the aisle finally clears, I hurry toward the door. I don't want the bus driver to have to wait for me.

"Thank you," I say as I walk past him.

The driver is a round-faced black man. His sideburns stand out because they're so gray compared to the rest of his curly dark hair. He smiles at me. His eyes crinkle up at the corners.

"Come here to model?" he asks.

"Yes, sir," I say.

"Good luck, then," he says with a wink.

He closes the bus doors.

I decide his words are a sign that I'm going to make lots of money.

"God willing," I say quietly to myself so God will overlook my pride. Then I add a "Touch wood." Just in case.

Holding my suitcase tightly against my chest, I follow the flow of people out to a long, long escalator that leads down to the hub of the station. I hold my foot over it and wait for the next full step to slide out from under the floor.

A short guy with thick arms pushes around me. "Fuckin' tourists," he says under his breath. As I watch him run down the escalator, I want to yell at him. I want to tell him that I'm not a tourist. That I'm here to stay. But I don't. When he gets to the bottom, he throws himself into the swarm of people and disappears.

I've never seen so many people in one place. As the escalator slowly delivers me toward the milling throng, I can't breathe right. My heart beats, *bump, bump, bump.* I don't know what to do. I want to run back up the moving steps and find the nice Greyhound bus man, but I can't, there're too many people behind me. And if I could, what would I do then?

As the escalator slides me into the rushing crowd, people knock into me and push me farther and farther toward the middle of the station. I can't see over their heads. My eyes dart and twitch. I'm like a leaf in the rapids and they're the river, rushing over and around me, pulling me along on their white-water ride. I feel swallowed up. I can't breathe.

Using my suitcase as a shield, I push it into the man ahead of me. He moves over a step. I squeeze past him. A shoulder knocks into my suitcase. It hits my lip. The metallic taste of blood leaks into my mouth.

My knees start to tremble and fold.

A hand reaches toward me. It clamps around my arm and drags me sideways through the crowd. The hand belongs to a man. I can only see his arm and his back as he muscles his way through the crush, hauling me off behind him. I'm too stunned to stop him.

He pulls me into a small coffee shop and sits me down at a table. He pats my hand and smiles. His gold tooth glints in the harsh coffee shop light.

"New in town?" he asks, his voice smooth and pleasant. I nod.

"Thought so."

He slides over to the counter and whispers something in the waitress's ear. She laughs and pushes his chest with her palm. He comes back with a soda and puts it down in front of me.

"Gotta keep your strength up," he says.

I wrap my hands around the icy-cold glass. I'm not allowed to drink soda. I take a sip. The fizz rises up and burns my nose.

He rests his hand across my bare forearm. "What's your name, sweetheart?"

I don't like him touching me. I pull my arm away.

He leans over the table. "You know, a young girl like you can get into trouble in a town like this." His breath smells like he needs to eat. "I can show you around. Introduce you to people." He cups his hand under my chin and grins.

I look at him flatly.

"No thanks," I say.

I put a dollar bill down on the table and leave.

I'm mad at myself. I don't have many dollars and I just wasted one.

The hallway is lined on both sides with little shops and places to eat. I glance back at the coffee shop. I'm not being followed. I duck into the first food place I see. It's a bagel shop. I've never had a bagel before. I haven't eaten all day and I'm hungry.

"One, please," I say to the bagel guy. He pulls a bagel out of the case and lays it down on a cutting board. He's got a big knife in his hand.

"Whadaya want on it?" he asks.

"Butter," I say.

"Toasted?"

"Ummmm . . ."

He lops the bagel in two and sticks it in the toaster. He's too busy for beginners like me who don't know how to order bagels properly.

I take my bagel and sit down. Little bits of onion, a half-chewed piece of smelly fish, and a bunch of crumbs lie scattered across the tabletop. I wipe it clean with my only napkin. I'd like another one, but I'm too afraid to ask. I don't think the bagel guy is having a good day.

As I take my first bite, the melted butter drips through my fingers and down my wrists.

The bagel guy lays a pile of napkins down on the table. "Here," he says.

I swallow my mouthful of bagel. "Oh, thank you."

"Hey." He looks down at his feet. His long, dark hair falls forward, covering his big, brown puppy-dog eyes. "Sorry I was an ass to you."

"That's okay."

He puts his hands on his hips and stares at me. "How old are you, anyways?" he asks.

I like how his lashes curl up at the ends.

"How old are you?" I say back.

"I'm nineteen," he answers.

I make a face. "I thought you were a lot older than that."

He crosses his arms in front of his chest. "I'm mature for my age," he says.

I nod. "I'm sixteen," I say.

"Really? I figured you for thirteen, tops." He shakes his head like he's amazed.

"I guess I'm immature for my age."

He laughs. "What's your name?"

"Kelle."

He pumps my buttery hand up and down. "Nice meetin' ya, Kelle. My name's Vince."

I hand him a napkin. "Vince? How do I get to 140 East Sixty-third Street?"

"Takin' the train?"

I shrug my shoulders. "Is that expensive?"

"Tell you what. I get off soon. I'll take you to the station and get you started."

"Really?"

"Yeah."

A sea of bobbing heads flow past the bagel shop window. When I squint my eyes, they blur together and become one long moving thing, reminding me of the dragons the Chinese use to celebrate their New Year. But my squinty-eye dragon isn't made of fabric, it's made of hundreds of heads that lift and thrust and sweep down the hallway in one long uninterrupted line.

I get tired of squinting. I open my eyes. A man presses his face against the window. He moves his thick, wet lips against the glass. He's saying something, but I can't tell what. He looks at me with his wild red eyes. I push my seat back.

Vince raps the glass. "Get the fuck outta here."

The man slinks back into the crowd.

"Keep away from that window," Vince says to me. "They like it when you look at 'em."

He waves his finger in my face. "Don't ever look them nuts in the eye. They'll be all over ya. Dumb bastards."

White and yellow spit slowly drips down the window. I move to a back table. I hope Vince can leave soon.

While I wait, I clean the tables around me with my leftover napkins. After a couple of minutes Vince walks over. He picks up my suitcase.

"Ready?" he asks.

I look up at him with big eyes. I'm nervous about the "people dragon." He reaches out and takes my hand.

"Come on, it'll be all right."

We take a few halting steps into the crowd.

Vince puts my suitcase down between his ankles. "Listen," he says. "You can't keep stopping every time some schmo walks past you." He cocks his head to the side. "You ever watch any boxing?"

"I have Sugar Ray Leonard's autograph," I say.

"A little thing like you got a boxer's autograph?" He laughs. For some reason he thinks that's funny.

He jabs his fists in the air really fast. "In crowds like this you gotta think like a boxer."

I make a face. I'm not sure what he means.

"You gotta tuck in your chin, keep your hands in front of you, be quick on your feet, and use the old bob, weave, slip, sway, and block as needed." He gives a quick demonstration of each move as he says it.

The crowd walks a wide path around his flailing

hands and feet. He points at the people, snaps his fingers, and gives me a double thumbs-up.

"Aaay," he says. "Let's go. The train's down this way."

As we walk, I practice my moves on the crowd. Vince watches me out of the corner of his eye. Every once in a while he nods his head and smiles.

A jowly, red-faced man totters up to me. He licks his lips. "Can you spare some change?" he says.

He smells like wet carpet. I back away from him.

Vince pulls me away. "I told ya, you gotta stop lookin' at 'em."

We get on a down escalator. When we reach the bottom, I look around. We're completely underground. There aren't any windows or anything.

"We're here," he says.

"Trains come down here?" I ask.

"Yeah, subway, train, same thing."

"Oh," I say.

I thought he was taking me to a real train, like an Amtrak or something. I look around. It's hot. It's dark. It smells. I'm not sure I'm ready for this. Everything I've heard about the subway is bad. Vince seems to think it's okay, though, so I don't say anything.

He leads me over to a turnstile. "I wrote you some directions." He hands me a bagel shop menu with writing on the back. "And oh yeah, before I forget, you gotta remember the three *L*s."

"Should I write them down?"

"Nah, you'll remember. It's easy. Don't loitah. Don't look lost. And don't look up."

"Don't loitah, don't look lost, and don't look up," I say.

I don't tell him that I don't know what "loitah" means. He might think I'm stupid or something.

"Oh, one more thing. Don't never walk on Forty-second Street neither. They'll make a meal out of ya there."

"Okay."

He lifts his shoulders. "I guess this is it, then."

"Yeah," I say quietly.

He puts two tokens in my hand. "One for now and one for later," he says.

I pick up my suitcase, drop a token in the turnstile, and push my way through the rotating bars. I turn around.

"Bye, Vince. Thank you."

"Bye, Kelle. Nice meetin' ya."

"I'll never forget you," I say.

He waves me off and smiles.

I look down the dark subway track and wish Vince didn't have to go.

When I look back, he's gone.

As I slowly walk toward the dimly lit platform, I hear a loud rushing sound coming from inside the tunnel. The concrete floor vibrates under my feet. The people around me walk forward, so I walk forward too. Some go right up to the edge of the platform. But I don't. Someone might push me.

I see a light. The train is coming. A strong draft blows my dress up. It billows around my waist like a parachute. I push it down and look to see if anybody saw. Luckily, no one seems interested in my blowing dress.

The train makes a really loud shrieking sound as it slowly comes to a stop. I'd cover my ears, but I'm too busy holding down my dress. The doors slide open with a whoosh. People jostle and push their way off and on the train. I wonder what their hurry is. Someone behind me pushes my back. I want to turn around and look to see who did it, but Vince told me not to. The doors slap at people's shoulders. Open, close. Open, close. I wonder if it hurts. I don't want to find out.

Open.

Someone pushes me. I stumble into the car.

Close.

I look around. It's completely packed. People sit, stand, and hold on to metal poles. Their arms are everywhere. Reaching over and under one another in awkward angles and positions, like they're playing a game of Twister. They don't dare let their poles go. If they do, they'll lose their place.

The train takes off. I rock backward into the woman behind me; she rocks into the man behind her. We don't fall, though. The train is too full.

I peek under a pole-holder's arm. I see an empty seat. When the train pulls up to the next station, I slip through the crowd and claim it. I put my suitcase on the floor between my knees and look forward. I feel very smart.

As the train moves forward, I notice that it's not as crowded as it was before. The space right in front of me is clear.

I turn my bagel shop menu over and look at Vince's handwriting. All his letters curve up at the end like they're smiling. I run my fingers over the ink.

It's strange. Even though I just met him, I miss Vince. There's a little Vince soft spot on my heart. Like a small bruise, it hurts. But that'll fade. And when it does, I won't remember the good-bye part anymore; I'll just remember the hello part.

Sometimes it's not that easy, though. Some feelings cut so deep that my heart bleeds. It's bleeding now. If people could see inside of me, they'd know my heart's not well. They'd know it's all leaks and scabs. But they can't. All they see is my smile. The smile that says everything's perfect. Nothing's wrong.

But something is wrong.

Because while this has been the most exciting day of my life—it's also been the worst.

Tendrils of a thick, wet mist float around me like tattered sheets. When I hold my arm out straight, I can barely see my fingertips. I like the fog.

At the barn door I stop and take a deep breath. I quietly open the door. The horses nicker.

I turn on the light. The horses stare out at me with blinking eyes. I walk into the feed room and grab a scoop. The sweet feed is stored in an old oil drum. It's running low, so I'll have to lean way into the barrel to get to it.

It's dark in the bottom of the barrel. I hope there aren't any mice in there. I don't like it when they run up my arm.

I get the flashlight off the shelf, flick it on, and shine it into the barrel. Squirming around on top of the grain are a bunch of baby mice. I carefully lay the drum on its side. The babies fall forward with the feed. I pick them up with the scoop and hide them behind some bales of hay. Hopefully their mother will find them before the cat does.

I fill a wheelbarrow with feed and roll it out to the horses. Sweetheart twitches her tail and bangs her bucket with her knees. I'm never fast enough for her.

I reach out to pat her, but she runs to the back of the stall and quivers.

I bite my lip.

My father's been in the barn again.

"It's okay, Sweetheart. I'm not going to hurt you," I say. As soon as she hears the grain hit the bottom of her bucket, she trots over and starts to eat.

"Back, girl," I say to Windy. She moves just enough for me to lean over her door and pour her breakfast into her feeder. She shoves her head in and eats like she's starving.

Next it's Muffet's turn.

"Hi, Muff Puff Cream Puff," I say. When I fill her bucket, she doesn't eat. Instead she turns around and pushes her rump up against the stall door. She wants me to scratch her, so I do.

"That's enough," I say after a few minutes. I pat her rump. She turns around. While I watch her eat, I hold my knuckles to my nose. They smell like molasses and Muffet.

I pull back her door latch and walk in. I bedded her

stall with lots of straw yesterday. Much more than I'm allowed. But I don't care.

Muffet reaches around to my back pocket and pulls out her carrot. I hold the end of it while she takes one little bite at a time. When she gets to the end piece, I hold my palm out flat and she gently picks it up with her lips. She's always careful not to bite me.

When she finishes her treat, she puffs her carrot breath in my face. Her breath is warm. Her whiskers tickle.

Outside, the car door closes.

Muffet looks at me with her big brown eyes. She's the only pony I've ever known who never once in her whole life had a single bad thought.

I wrap my arms around her and bury my face in her neck. I squeeze her really hard. She doesn't mind, though; she stands really still and lets me do it.

Outside, the car engine starts.

"I love you, Muffet," I say quietly.

She moves back a step and nuzzles my salty cheek. She licks me with her rough tongue.

Outside, the car pulls up to the barn.

I look down at my watch. I'm not supposed to leave for fifteen more minutes. I want my fifteen minutes. But I can't have them. He won't wait; he never does.

I lock Muffet's door. She hangs her head over the side and reaches her nose out to me.

She doesn't understand.

She doesn't know that I'm never going to see her again.

I want to open her door and set her free. But I can't. She wouldn't get very far. She's afraid of shadows. She thinks they're holes in the ground. She won't walk through one without me to tell her it's okay.

It's always been my job to protect her. I've stood in front of his lashing whip for her. I've covered her quaking body with mine to protect her from his belt.

I would do almost anything for her.

But I can't stay for her.

Outside, the car horn beeps.

I kiss Muffet's forehead and walk outside.

I fold up Vince's menu and put it in my pocket. To my left is a door that leads out to the next car. A man pushes a button and walks outside. The wind rushes in. Little bits of paper and dirt swirl around my feet. Suddenly the air smells strange. I hold my hand over my nose and wait for the door to close.

When it does, I lower my hand. But the smell's still there. It's so bad it makes me want to throw up. It reminds me of body odor, bad breath, urine, and death.

I hear a little clicking noise.

Click. Click.

A pole-holder stares at me. I look at him out of the

corner of my eye. He shakes his head and looks down at the floor.

Click. Click.

The sound is coming from the lady sitting next to me.

I look down at her feet. She's not wearing any shoes. Her feet are black. The ends of her toenails twist like curlicues.

Click. Click.

I look up at her hands. She's making that noise with her thick yellow fingernails. She pokes them into her matted hair and digs around. She stops scratching and grins.

She doesn't have any teeth.

She pulls her hand out of her hair.

She's holding something between her thumb and third finger. She holds it up to her nose and stares at it. I stare at it along with her. It's a sesame-seed-size bug. It has short, stumpy legs that wiggle in the air.

Click. She cuts it in half.

Click. She flicks it onto the floor.

I jump away from my seat with a jerk.

Little lice bodies drift across the swaying floor.

I grab the end of my suitcase and drag it over to one of the poles. Everybody moves away from me.

I can't help myself. I look the bug lady in the eyes. When she sees me staring at her, she lifts her chin and laughs.

The hotel juts up from the street like a big, tall ship. I lean my head way back and look up. If Vince were here, he'd be wagging his finger in my face, reminding me of the three *L*s. But I can't help myself. I've never seen anything like it. Its high towers poke up into the blue sky like ocean liner smokestacks.

The doorman pinches the brim of his cap.

"Welcome to the Barbizon Hotel for Women," he says.

"Thank you very much," I reply.

A bellboy rushes over. His uniform shirt hangs off his bony frame like a muumuu. I look at him and wonder how anybody who lives in a town with bagels can be so skinny.

He reaches for my suitcase. "Can I take that for you, miss?"

"No, no thank you," I say.

If he carries my suitcase, I'll have to give him money, and I don't want to waste any more of my dollars.

He shrugs and walks away.

I lightly tap the front desk bell. A woman walks out. Her high heels go *clackity-clack* on the worn marble floor.

"Checking in?"

"Yes, please."

She opens the reservation book. I point at my name. "That's me," I say.

"Staying one week, correct?"

"I think so. Can I stay longer if I haven't found a place to live by then?" I bite my lip. I said "can" instead of "may." I hope she didn't notice.

She nods and hands me two keys. "Eleventh floor, room eleven ten. The smaller key is for the shower room at the end of the hall. And under no circumstances are men allowed above the ground floor."

I want to say, "Except for the bellboy," but I don't think she'd think that was very funny.

Her no-men-above-the-ground-floor rule doesn't make any sense to me. If a guy and a girl really want to do it, they can always find a way. Besides, these aren't the only beds in town. And even if they were, a lot of people don't just do it on a bed. They do it anywhere they can. Back home I find my brothers' used condoms in the hayloft all the time. I scoop them up with a shovel and bury them in the manure pile.

One time I complained to my mother about it.

She rolled her eyes. "Kelle, they're men, that's what men do."

"But can't they throw them away afterward, Mom? Do they have to leave them behind? That's Muffet's hay."

She ignored me and walked away.

Girls rush in and out of the hotel's reception area. Some look like they're expecting good news any minute, and others look like they've already gotten their news and it was bad. Their eyes are puffy. Their mascara is smudged. They look down at their toes. I turn my head away from them.

Bad thoughts have a way of spreading.

I look around the big hotel lobby. Everything is polished up and well cared for, in that strict-English-boarding-school kind of way. I pull my shoulders back and walk across the dust-bunny-free floor.

The old-fashioned elevator nears the landing in stops and starts as the attendant lines it up with the lobby floor. He folds the scissor gate back. It makes a loud clattering sound. He's got short white gloves on his hands. I've never seen a man wearing gloves like that before. He looks silly.

He points down. "Watch your step," he says.

The elevator floor sits two inches up from the lobby's. I step up onto it.

"Eleventh floor, please," I say.

A girl runs toward us. "Hold the elevator, please," she calls out.

The attendant points down again. "Watch your step," he says to the girl. "Ninth floor?" he asks her.

She doesn't look at him. "Yes, thank you." She has long, thick hair and bright green eyes.

He closes the door and pulls a lever, and up we go.

The attendant jogs the control. The elevator stops. He looks up from the landing and smiles. The elevator and hallway floors are perfectly even.

The green-eyed girl steps off the elevator.

The elevator slowly lifts upward.

Suddenly it stops.

We're stuck between floors.

I look over at the attendant.

"I like the way your bottom lip makes you look like you're pouting," he says. He stares at me with hungry eyes.

I suck my lip up under my front teeth. I'm not sure what to say. I don't want to make him mad.

I hear a loud ringing sound. Someone's calling for the elevator.

The attendant yanks the control lever.

The elevator lurches upward.

"Eleventh floor. Watch your step," he says under his breath.

I hop down onto the landing.

He shuts the door behind me.

I unclench my hand. The room key has left a perfect imprint in my palm.

I think I'll take the stairs from now on.

Grace Kelly, Gene Tierney, and Ali McGraw all stayed at the Barbizon Hotel. They're my favorite actresses. I don't really like any of Ali McGraw's movies, but a lot of people tell me I look like her, so I put her on the list anyway.

I read that Grace Kelly once danced down the hotel hallway in her skivvies. What exactly are skivvies, I wonder? And why would she dance down the hall in them?

Room 1110. That's my room. I pretend it was Grace Kelly's room too. I take the big key and stick it in the lock, but it won't go in. I've never opened a door with a key before. At home we never lock the doors. We don't have to. We have big dogs and my father's temper to protect us.

I turn the key over and try again. This time it slips neatly into the slot. I drop my suitcase and run to the window. I hold on to the sill and look down. The people on the street look really small. I get a funny feeling when I look at them. Like I don't matter. Like I'm just another speck on the sidewalk.

Concrete. Asphalt. Granite. Stone.

The city's so hard. I'm so soft.

I turn away. I don't like city windows. I like country windows.

I stick my chin out.

I'll get used to it. I have to.

I'm never going back.

Ever.

My mother tells me I'm stubborn.

She's right.

I look around my room. It's got a dresser, a desk, an end table, a bed, and very little floor space. Now I know why Grace Kelly did her dancing in the hallway.

I open the desk drawer. When I let its little brass handle go, it makes a soft jangling sound. The drawer is stocked with stationery. I pick up an envelope and turn it over. "The Barbizon Hotel for Women" is printed on the back flap in bright pink letters. I like pink. It's my favorite color. I'm going to write my mother later. She'll be so impressed when she sees my fancy stationery.

My belly button itches. I remember my money. Before I left home, I put all my money in an envelope and sewed it to my panties. I pull my dress up and look down at my underwear. The thread has broken loose. The edge of the envelope is pushing up into my belly button. There's a big red mark on my stomach where the envelope used to be.

Looking at my stomach makes me hungry. I open up my suitcase and pull out an electric skillet, a small pan, a can opener, and a can of SpaghettiOs. I love SpaghettiOs.

While I wait for the skillet to heat up, I sit on the floor by my suitcase and look at myself in the small mirror glued inside the lid. My ponytail has come loose. Short bits of hair curl around my forehead and temples. I flatten them down, but they spring right back up like tiny pig tails.

I run my fingers over my lips. My bottom lip really does stick out. I wonder how come I never noticed before. I think about my mother saying, "That's what men do." I know she's not just talking about my father and two brothers when she says that. She's talking about elevator attendants and bus station men with shiny gold teeth, too.

Men are strange. I don't think I like them very much. My friend Tina used to say the same thing, until my father changed her mind one night.

I like my brother Bob, though. He isn't strange. He tells me lots of funny stories.

As I think about Bob and his stories, I catch a glimpse of myself in my suitcase mirror. I'm smiling. It's a great big smile. The kind you can't fake. Until I saw myself, I had no idea I was doing that. I have the feeling I smile more than I think I do.

'Cause not all my secrets are scary ones.

I have lots of funny ones too.

Like Bob's suckling calf story. It's his favorite. It's my favorite too.

Bob and I agree on a lot of things, and this story is one of them. . . .

On the farm we always have a big steer and a little steer. My father doesn't believe in supermarket meat, so we raise our own. When the little steer gets big, the bigger steer goes right to the butcher. Then we get a new little steer.

They're just little babies when they first come to us. Still nursing. We mix formula powder in water with our hands and pour it into a special bucket with a long nipple on the end that looks just like a cow's udder. The formula smells really good, like a vanilla milk shake. I always wanted to taste it, but I never did. I got in big trouble once for tasting mare's milk. My friend Holly talked me into it. I told my mother that I didn't swallow it, I just held it in my mouth, but she didn't believe me. She said, "Shame on you, Kelle." She only says that when she's really, really mad.

My brothers are close. They're less than a year apart in age. They do a lot of stuff together.

Bob told me about the night they were all standing around feeding the new calf when a friend of theirs stopped by. It's really nice to mix the formula and watch the calf nurse from the bucket. He gets so excited. His twitchy little tail wags back and forth. He's so happy. You get all puffed up watching him. You've made an animal happy. You've done a good thing. You don't think about what's going to happen later when he becomes the bigger steer and the butcher's big box van comes calling.

So, while the friend watches the calf, my brothers watch the friend. He's not from the country, so he's never seen a calf nursing from a formula bucket.

"Would you look at that," my brother Rick says.

"Yeah," the friend says. He can't take his eyes off the calf.

"Our old man needs us for about a half hour. Want to wait for us here?"

The friend nods.

My brothers make a show of leaving the barn. Then they hide and watch the friend through their knotty pine peepholes.

The friend rubs his pant leg. The formula is running low.

He opens the stall door. Being careful not to step in any liquidy cow pies, he walks over to the calf.

"Nice girl," he says. He rubs the calf's outstretched neck. The calf ignores him.

He stands there summoning up his courage. A minute later his pants and boxers are down around his knees and his talleywhacker is in the calf's mouth.

The calf happily latches on. His formula bucket is empty and he wants more milk.

He gives the friend a bump.

"Easy, girl." The friend pats the little steer's head.

About this time the calf realizes that he's got his mouth wrapped around another empty nipple. He tightens his jaw and yanks down hard on the empty "udder." The friend doubles over. The calf is mad now. He pulls back on the "udder," shakes his head, and rams the friend in the stomach. The friend falls to the floor, writhing in agony.

My brothers run back into the barn.

"What happened? What's going on? Why are your pants around your ankles?" they shout.

They drape the friend's arms over their shoulders and drag him out of the stall. He's covered in liquidy cow pie.

They spray him down with cold hose water.

"Sorry, man, what happened in there? That calf go after you or something?" they ask with serious faces.

The friend nods.

"Man, we're sorry, he's still a bull, he hasn't been cut yet."

"Bull?" the friend says. His eyes roll back in his head.

My brothers can barely contain themselves. They elbow each other and bite their cheeks. They won't forget this story anytime soon.

I love that story. I push my suitcase back and smile.

I run my fingers over the agency's small brass door plaque. So this is it. I take a deep breath, push the door open, and walk in. Inside, the agency looks just like a doctor's office. If it weren't for all the framed magazine covers everywhere, I'd think I had walked into the wrong place. Somehow that makes me feel better.

The receptionist doesn't look at me. She slides a clipboard across the counter. "Sign in and take a seat," she says.

"Excuse me, where's your bathroom?"

She flicks her hand at me. "Down the hall, to the left."

"Ummmm . . . do you have a pen I could use to sign in?"

She slaps one down on the counter.

"How long do you think the wait will be?"

She looks up. Her thick bangs hang down over her eyes.

"Go," she says.

I turn around. I hope she doesn't tell her boss what a bother I am.

I stare at myself in the bathroom mirror. My lips aren't shiny enough. I open my gloss, get its sticky little rolly ball started, and roll it over my lips. They glisten in the bright bathroom light. When I lick them, they taste just like strawberries.

I'm wearing my new lucky dress. My mother bought it for me. I feel very grown-up in it. It's a baby-doll dress. When I asked my mother why it's called that, she said that it's named after a famous old movie. When I asked her what movie, she said she couldn't remember.

It's got pretty blue ribbons that tie at the shoulders. When I move my shoulders back and forth, the soft white skirting lifts and twirls around me.

The waiting room is full of girls. They sit side by side without speaking. There are no empty chairs, so I lean against the wall. Portfolio books sit in laps and rest against chair legs. I don't have a portfolio book. I wonder if I should leave and go get one. I'd ask the reception desk lady, but I'm afraid of her stink eye.

A tall lady walks into the waiting room. Everybody sits up.

"Kelle?" she calls out. Her voice is sharp. Like I've done something wrong. Maybe the receptionist told her about me.

I hurry over to her.

When she sees me, she tosses her chin and spins

around. Her long blond hair flips down her back, rippling like wheat in the wind.

I follow her into a small office.

"Where are you from?"

"Maryland," I say.

That's good, I think. *She must be interested.*

She points at the wall. "Shoes off."

I set my ballet flats off to the side, making sure to line the heels up properly so she can see that I'm a tidy person.

She taps her toes. I think she's waiting for me to do something, but I don't know what. I'm wasting her minutes.

She picks up an old hardware store measuring stick. "Back against the wall," she says.

I press my heels against the baseboard and my head against the dirty white wall.

She swings the measuring stick over my head. I flinch. Her eyes narrow.

She lays the stick on top of my head.

"You're too short," she says.

"Too short?"

"You've got to be at least five seven."

"But I just want to model in photographs. I'm not interested in runway."

She stares at me. "Do yourself a favor, Kelle. Go back home to Virginia. You will never work in this town. Ever."

I want to tell her that I'm from Maryland, not Virginia, but I can't get my words out.

I try to squeeze my feet back into my shoes but I can't—they're too tight. My feet are puffy from walking.

The Ford lady puts her hands on her hips.

I go out into the hallway where she can't see me and force my shoes up over my heels.

I stumble toward the front door. The girls look up. Their eyes shine when they see me. They don't have to worry about me messing up their dreams now.

A few pity me and look away.

I don't know which is worse.

The hot sidewalk heats my thin-soled shoes all the way through to my feet. Blisters form on my heels. If I cared, it would be hard to walk. But I don't care. I look down at my toes and walk. When people stop in front of me, I stop. When they walk, I walk. I don't look up.

I can't go back. I can't go back, I say to myself.

My head hurts with thinking.

I'm not afraid of walking the streets now. I'm not afraid of getting lost. I hope I get lost. I want to get lost.

When I was little and my father did something bad to me, I would go outside and run around the pastures. I would run and run and run until I couldn't take another step. I would fall down, wet with sweat, and look up at the sky while the world spun around me. Sometimes my pony would walk over and puff her grass breath into my face. I'd smile.

"Kelle, get up off the ground before you get trampled," my mother would yell.

I want to do that now. I want to walk till I fall down. Then I'll lie there on the concrete until someone comes along, breathes life into me, and makes me smile.

There's a clearing in the crowd. I stop and look up. I'm standing in front of a long, wide bank of steps. People are sitting on them. Eating. Laughing. Talking. The steps lead up to a big marble building. It looks like the kind of building that only really smart people are allowed into. I'm surprised regular people are allowed to sit on the steps.

I want to sit on them too. Making my way around all the happy people, I find an empty spot and sit down.

My dress floats up over my knees. I hold it down so people can't see my underwear. I shouldn't have called it lucky until I was sure it was.

People rush up and down the jam-packed sidewalk. They all have a place to go. The only place I have to go is home. The blond lady said so. My chest rises and falls. Up, down, up, down. I can't go home. I can't. I'd die first. I would, too.

I think about my poor brothers. How they work for no money laying carpet for my father. How they can't leave because they work for no money laying carpet for my father. Poor Rick. Poor Bob. Poor Muffet. I think about my blind sister. Poor Kim. Stuck there. Feeling her way through life. Never knowing what she's missing.

Kim used to have a fluffy white Persian cat. His name was Nicky. She loved that cat so much. She brushed him and kissed him. And he warmed her with his throaty purrs.

One day he went missing. Nobody could find him. As soon as I got home from school, Kim asked me to look for him. She knew how good I was at finding lost things.

I really tried to find him, but I couldn't. It was so hot out. I wanted a Popsicle. I went to our big freezer chest to get one. I opened the lid. And there was Nicky, lying on top of a stack of sirloins, frozen stiff. It was Kim's job to get the dinner meat out to thaw. Nicky must have jumped in while she was feeling around for the pork chops.

My brothers tried to defrost him. They thought if they did it right, he might come back to life. But it didn't work. I never told Kim what happened. And neither did anyone else. Sometimes it's better not to know.

I feel something wet on my cheek. I hold my palm to the sky and feel for raindrops. It's not raining. It's me. I'm leaking. I tell myself it's okay to cry for Nicky. I lean forward and wipe my nose with the hem of my dress.

Someone taps my shoulder. It's a guy. He reminds me of my brother Bob. It's not that he looks like him. It's just something about his face. If I were lost in a crowd, he'd be the one I'd go to for help. His jaw is square, with deep, straight dimples that run down the sides like they were drawn on with a ruler. He's beautiful.

He looks at me. "Mind if I sit here?" he says.

I wipe my cheeks with the back of my hand and nod.
He sits down.

"What's the matter?"

I shrug.

"Tell me," he says.

"My sister's cat died."

He squints his eyes and smiles. He knows I'm lying.

The hot sun flares behind him. I cup my fingers over my eyes and look up at his face. The bright light surrounds him like a stained-glass saint.

"Tell me," he says again.

I nod. "Okay."

And I do.

"So it's hopeless," I say at the end of my story.

He doesn't say anything for a minute.

Then he points up at the big marble building. "See those two stone lions?"

"Yes."

"Do you know what their names are?"

I shake my head.

"Patience sits on the left and Fortitude sits on the right."

"Oh."

"They've had those names since the Great Depression."

My eyes grow large.

"You're sitting at the feet of Patience and Fortitude. You're exactly where you need to be."

I look into his crystal blue eyes and smile.

He writes something down on an index card and hands it to me. "You're going to be fine," he says. "Remember your new friends here."

I look at the lions and nod.

As I watch him walk away, I think about God. God heard me talking. I know it. Because when I fell, he sent an angel to breathe life into me and make me smile.

I close my eyes and whisper, "Thank you, God. Thank you, angel. Thank you, Patience and Fortitude."

I look down at the index card. Three names and addresses are written on it. The first two—Marge McDermott Enterprises and William Schuller Talent— have little stars and the words "children's agency" printed next to them.

Why would he give me those names? I wonder. *I'm sixteen. I'm not a child.*

The last one, My Fair Lady, is more than forty blocks away.

I look down at my feet and sigh.

A sudden, strong breeze lifts my hair. An old newspaper whirs open. *Tck, tck, tck, tck.* One by one its pages come loose, blowing toward me, sliding slowly down the steps. I catch one with my toe. I pick it up, rip it into strips, and tuck it around the blistery parts of my feet.

I look back at the lions. I want to touch them, but they're too high up for me, so I wave instead. "Bye, Patience. Bye, Fortitude," I say out loud. Nobody seems to care that I'm talking to a couple of lion statues.

I check the street signs and step down onto the side-walk. The crowd closes around me. I walk fast to keep up with them. I walk and walk. Counting down the blocks.

Finally I see it: 155 East Eighty-fourth Street. It's a seven-story redbrick building. A man is out front, hosing the sidewalk. The air smells good, like damp concrete.

"Excuse me. Do you know what floor My Fair Lady is on?" I ask the man.

He points. "It's right there. Ground floor," he says.

When I see the big My Fair Lady sign, I thump my forehead with my palm. "How'd I miss that?"

He looks up and smiles.

His shaggy hair and big, bushy mustache remind me of our Old English sheepdog, Cornelius.

I always liked Cornelius.

The agency sits a little bit below street level.
I walk down a couple of brick steps and in through the
open door. A pretty girl sits on a high stool behind the
reception counter. When I walk in, her blue eyes widen.

"Hi," I say.

She rests her chin on the palms of her hands and
looks at me.

"Are you interviewing new girls today?" I ask.

She shakes her head. "We see girls tomorrow, not
today."

"Oh."

I wiggle my sore toes around inside my shoes.

"It's just that I walked so far," I say softly.

She leans over the counter, looks down at my feet,
and laughs. It's a nice laugh, not the kind that makes
you mad.

I wish I had dimples like hers.

She points at my newspaper Band-Aids. "Well, I've never seen that before," she says.

I shrug. "It's all I could find."

She reaches out. "Hi, I'm Melanie."

We shake hands.

"Hi, I'm Kelle."

With her blond hair, apple cheeks, and dimples, she's everything I imagine a model should look like. She's the prettiest girl I've ever seen in my life.

When I look at her, I realize that the Ford Modeling Agency lady was right. I'll never work in this town. I feel ashamed for even trying.

I look up at her. "You're so pretty. How come you're not a model?"

She smiles. "Oh, I am."

On the wall next to her hang three framed magazine covers: *Cosmopolitan, Redbook,* and *Seventeen.*

"Is that you?" I ask.

She nods.

"How come you work here, then?"

"This is my agency. I own and run it with my partner."

She cups her hands around her mouth. "Buddy, come here a minute," she calls out in a loud voice.

The brown-eyed janitor pops his head in. "Yeah, babe?"

"This is Kelle. She's . . ." She looks at me. "How old are you?"

"Sixteen."

"She's sixteen but looks thirteen. She's got a great look for commercials, don't you think?"

"Yep," Buddy says.

I lift up on my toes. "Really?" I say.

Melanie hands me a My Fair Lady business card. "If you need anything, anything at all, call this number. Buddy and I live in the building. Seventh floor. The number rings here"—she points down—"and there." She points up.

"Thanks," I say.

Buddy gestures across the street. "Why don't you come have dinner with us at that little Italian joint tonight. Eight o'clock."

"Tonight? Sure," I say. "I'll see you at eight."

Around the corner is a phone booth. I walk in and close the door. Phone booths are weird. Even though they're made of glass, once that door is closed, it feels so private. I drop a dime in the slot and dial home. When an automated voice tells me to deposit more money, I do. The phone rings.

Bob, please pick up, please pick up, I say to myself.

If my father answers, I'm going to hang up.

"Hello," a voice says.

"Bob, thank goodness," I say.

"I thought it'd be you," he says. "How's it going? Got an agent yet?"

"It's not that easy," I say as sadly as I can. "The woman at Ford said no. I'm too short."

Silence.

"Don't give up," he says softly, sounding like I dashed his dream.

"Buuuut . . . ," I say, drawing the word out dramatically.

"But what?"

"The girl at My Fair Lady said yes!" I squeal.

"I knew it," he says. "That's great. Really great."

"Thanks, Bob. You're the best big brother in the world, you know."

"Ahhhhh," he says.

I laugh.

He laughs.

The automated voice comes back on, telling me to put more money in or my call will be disconnected.

"Bob, I don't have any more change."

"Yeah," he says quietly.

I don't want to hang up.

I wish he were here.

I miss him.

"Bye, Bob."

"Bye," he says.

The phone cuts off.

I hang up the receiver.

I'm so lucky to have a brother like Bob.

He thinks I'm great. My dreams are his.

The whole way back to the hotel I smile and sing songs. When people stare at me, I pretend it's because they know I'm a model.

I'm supposed to meet Melanie and Buddy at eight o'clock. The sidewalk is crowded with people. I'm afraid I'm going to be late. I step onto a wide metal sidewalk grate. It shifts and clanks under my feet. I try to lift myself up a little so I weigh less. The guy next to me looks down and steps around it. Below me a fast-moving train hisses and squeals as it winds its way beneath the city. It pushes a strong blast of air up through the grate. The air's as hot as teacup steam.

Dry lightning flickers across the dark city sky.

A big, splashy raindrop hits the back of my neck. It runs down under my blouse.

Lightning flashes. "One, two—"

Thunder cracks.

It starts to pour.

I put my head down and make a run for the restaurant. I yank the door open and rush inside. The little hairs on my arms stand up. I'm cold. I'm not used to air-conditioning. My parents don't believe in it. My father says it makes you soft, and my mother says it makes you sick. I cross my arms and give them a good rub. One side of my blouse drops down over my shoulder.

A small, dark-haired man walks over to me. "Can I help you?"

He looks at my bare shoulder. I cover it.

"I'm having dinner with Melanie . . ."

I stop. I don't know Melanie's last name.

"Follow me, please," the dark-haired man says.

He leads me past a wall of signed book jackets. I read the names: Mario Puzo, Peter Maas, Gay Talese. I've never heard of any of them.

The waiter stands next to a large table in the middle of the room. He pulls out a chair and waits for me to sit down. Everybody stares at me.

"Would you like a glass of wine? Maybe a mixed drink?" he asks as soon as I sit down.

"I, a . . ."

"How about you let me choose something for you?"

"Okay," I say quietly, in case someone is listening.

I lean forward and study my napkin. It's folded up just like a fan. I've never seen that before. It's very fancy.

Polished brass railings run along the restaurant's wood-paneled walls. The lighting is soft.

When people look at me, I smile at them. Some smile back, but most look down at their plates like I've done something wrong. If they don't want to be smiled at, they shouldn't stare.

Hanging on the wall next to the table is Melanie's *Cosmopolitan* cover. It's signed, "To Nicky, Best Joint in Town. Love, Melanie." Melanie's arms are crossed and her smoky eyes stare out at me like a dare. Her lips poke forward, all pink and pouty. Bright orange sweater sleeves hang down over her shoulders, barely covering her naked breasts. If I didn't know for sure that it was her, I wouldn't believe it.

The waiter leads a girl over to the table. He pulls out the chair next to mine and she sits down.

She looks at me.

"Don't I know you?" she asks.

I shake my head. "I don't think so. I'm new here."

"Are you staying at the Barbizon?"

"Yes."

"I saw you in the elevator yesterday."

"Oh my gosh," I say in a loud voice.

A woman at the next table gives me a dirty look.

"That elevator guy's creepy," she says. "He's always rolling his tongue around in his mouth and looking at me weird."

I make a face. She laughs.

"Hi. My name is Rayna."

"Nice to meet you. I'm Kelle."

The waiter puts a drink down in front of me. "Your sloe gin fizz," he says.

"Thank you."

I widen my eyes at Rayna and point at my sloe gin fizz. "Can you believe it?"

She nods. "Nicky doesn't care. He owns the place. He'll give you whatever you want."

I blow the paper wrapper off my straw. It floats up and lands under Rayna's chair.

I take a tiny sip of my drink. It's tart. My mouth gets all puckery.

Rayna raises her eyebrows. "Well? What do you think?" she says.

I quickly drink some water. "I like it," I say.

She smiles.

I'm glad Rayna is here. She knows things.

"I like your green eyes," I say. "How old are you?"

"Seventeen."

The restaurant's front door swings open. Melanie and Buddy walk in.

"Sit up," Rayna whispers. "You'll look taller that way."

We both sit up.

Melanie's ponytail swings back and forth as she rushes over to the table.

"Sorry we're late," she says.

Her face is shiny and pink, like she just scrubbed it clean. Plain green pants cover her long thoroughbred legs, and her plaid shirt is snapped closed right up to her throat. I guess she saves her cleavage for the camera.

Three pretty girls trail Buddy to the table. When they sit down with us, I'm surprised. I didn't expect so many people.

Buddy pretty much looks like he did when I first saw him. His shaggy hair hangs down over his forehead. My brother Rick has hair like that, the kind that sticks out all over the place. There's not much hope for that kind of hair. No matter what you do, it springs back to its natural form. Buddy probably gave up on it a long time ago.

Buddy looks up at me.

I look down at the menu. I think he knows I was staring at him. Everything's so expensive. I bite my lip.

I lean over and whisper into Rayna's ear. "Do we have to pay?"

She shakes her head.

A round-tummied waiter sets a frosty glass of Coke down in front of Rayna. A bright red cherry floats on top of the bubbly liquid. She pops it in her mouth and lays the stem down on the side of her bread dish. One of the pretty girls picks it up and twirls it around in her fingers. I guess she doesn't worry about cooties the way that I do.

Her eyes glint. "I can tie this cherry stem with my tongue." She looks over at Buddy.

Buddy shakes his head and smiles. Melanie doesn't say anything. Her back goes rigid.

"Really?" I say.

The pretty girl ignores me.

"I want to see," I say.

I don't believe someone can really do that. My cherry stem is gone, so I can't try.

Rayna bumps my leg with her knee. I'm new to the group. Maybe I'm not supposed to talk.

"Jill, how'd your Alexander's shoot go today?" Melanie asks one of the other girls.

"Really well. We shot their winter catalog. I still have some of that fake snow in my hair."

I wish I had winter-catalog snow in my hair.

Rayna nudges my arm with her elbow.

Everybody is staring at me. Two of the pretty girls have their hands over their mouths, giggling.

"Kelle, don't do that at the table," Buddy says with a grin.

I look at Rayna. I don't understand. She opens her eyes a little bit and looks at my lap.

I look down.

I'm really cold. My hands are stuck between my legs.

I look back at Rayna. I still don't understand.

"What?" I say really softly. The pretty girls stop giggling and start laughing. I shake my head. I'm doing something funny, not good funny, and I don't know what.

"Buddy, stop teasing her," Melanie says. Her eyes flash at the pretty girls. They go back to their drinks.

They're making fun of me. They think I'm a stupid country girl.

Maybe I am a stupid country girl.

"Excuse me," I say. "I need to find the ladies' room."

I hurry away from the table.

Rayna chases after me into the bathroom.

"What did I do? Why are they laughing?" I ask her.

"They're making a joke, like you're, you know, touching yourself."

"What do you mean?"

"Like you're masturbating."

I sit down on the bathroom floor and cover my face with my hands. I'm not going to leave until Melanie and Buddy and the three pretty girls all go home. I'll sit here all night if I have to.

"Rayna, I can't go back out there."

"You have to," she says. By the way she says it, I know it's true.

She takes my hand and pulls me to my feet. "Come on. We'll pretend it never happened. Those girls are stupid. They probably already forgot about it anyway."

I follow her back out to the dining room.

I'm glad I did, because as soon as we sit down, plates brimming with food are set down on the table. I'm trying to save money, so I haven't eaten in a long time. I'm starving. My hunger takes my mind off my troubles.

I offer some of my chicken parmigiana to Rayna, but she says no, she's on a diet. All the girls are eating salads except for me. Every once in a while I catch them looking at my big plate of food. They don't know what they're missing.

I'm so full my stomach sticks out like a baby's belly. I can only finish half my dessert. I'd unsnap my jeans, but after the whole touching-myself thing, I don't think that's a good idea.

I push my cheesecake plate to the middle of the table. I was the only one who ordered dessert. "Anybody want some?" I ask. Everybody digs in.

I yawn and rub my eyes. It's late. I'm used to early nights and early mornings.

"Let me get you a cab," Buddy says.

"No, oh no, I can walk. I don't mind."

"Don't be ridiculous." He sounds irritated.

Rayna stands up. "We can share," she says.

The three of us walk outside together. It isn't raining anymore. The air is thick. Lightning flashes.

We look up.

"I don't think it's over yet," Rayna says.

"I think it's just beginning," I say with a smile.

Rayna lies on her stomach across my once-tidy Barbizon bed, kicking her bum with the heels of her feet. Even though we only just met a few days ago, it feels like we've been friends forever.

"What else does she say?" Rayna asks.

I look down at the letter my mom just sent me. "'Lil Stink bit me again. I'm going to smack him one if he doesn't stop it.'" I laugh.

"Is that your dog?"

"Yeah. He's a Yorkie. He only weighs two and a half pounds."

"What kind of a name is Lil Stink?"

"It's the kind of name you give a dog that runs under a big sheepdog every time he lifts his leg."

"Does he sleep in your bed?"

"Yeah."

"You won't share a glass of water with anybody, but you'll sleep with a urine-soaked dog?"

I nod. "It doesn't make sense. I know."

"Read more. Your mother's funny."

"'We had a flood from the rain. The entire basement has about two inches of water in it. The propane tank outside floated out of its hole, and the boys were riding it to try to keep it down. Everything is pretty wet.'"

"Wow," Rayna says.

"Oh, listen, there's more about Lil Stink." I scooch in next to Rayna. "'Lil Stink trapped himself a rather large baby owl. He was quite proud of himself.'"

"I've got to see this dog. Do you think I can go home with you sometime?"

"Maybe," I say. I don't want to tell her that my family looks better on paper.

"Here, let me read the rest." Rayna takes the letter out of my hands. I roll over onto my back and stare up at the ceiling.

"'We have all new chickens. You should have been here to help me put the old ones in the freezer. Very entertaining. We went to the boat, and a duck had laid her eggs on the sofa and kept flying aboard while we were there. I went down to turn the stereo on and was pressing around looking for the button when it occurred to me it was gone. The boat was ripped off—radio, tape player, TVs. No more good news for now. Have fun, Mom.'"

"Oh no," I say.

"Wait, I'm not done," she laughs. "'P.S. Don't work too hard, not worth it. P.P.S. Remember, don't push your hair behind your ears, dummy. P.P.P.S. Call me once in a while.'" Rayna waves the letter at me. "Oh my gosh, Kelle, where are you from?"

"You don't want to know," I say.

"Stuff like that never happens at my house," she says. "It sounds so exciting."

Rayna's very enthusiastic. I like that about her.

"I heard you on the phone with your parents earlier, they sound nice," I say.

Rayna's eyes grow soft. "They are nice," she says. "They'd do anything for me."

I look over at her. "Rayna?"

"Yeah?"

"Why did those girls at Nicola's laugh at me like that?"

Rayna pulls at a piece of yarn on the chenille bedspread. "It's because you're young."

"They didn't laugh at you."

"I'm not innocent like you are."

I don't say anything.

"Rayna?"

"Yeah?"

"Have you done it yet?"

She shakes her head. "No, not yet. Pretty close, though."

She rolls over. We both stare at the ceiling.

"Do you like being with a boy like that?" I ask.

She closes her eyes and smiles. "Uh-huh," she says.

"I don't think I'm ever going to like it."

"Oh, you will too."

"You really think so?"

"Yeah, you just have to meet the right guy. That's all." She sits up. "Want to go to the pool?"

"No. They make you wear swim caps."

"I didn't know that. Forget it, then."

"Is that your portfolio?" I point at a leather case sitting by the door.

She nods.

"Can I see it?"

"Sure."

I sit down on the floor and look at it.

"Wow. You've worked a lot."

"Just in Georgia. That doesn't really count."

"I think it counts."

"I'm hungry," Rayna says. "Let's go do something so I don't eat."

"Like what?"

She thinks. "I know. Let's go see a porno. It'll be educational."

"A porno!" I cover my face with my hands.

She stands up. "Come on, let's go!"

"I don't know. . . ."

Rayna takes my hand and pulls me out the door.

"You better know what you're doing," I say.

She laughs.

I don't like the sound of that. "You do, don't you?"

She laughs some more.

Something tells me I'm going to regret this.

"*R*ayna, *I think that man* just patted my butt."

"Walk faster," she says.

"Rayna, we're on Forty-second Street. Vince told me never to walk on Forty-second Street. I'm scared."

"Walk faster," she says again.

The air smells really bad. Like people pee. I hold my breath so I don't breathe it in. I only make it half a block before I have to breathe again. It's a bad technique. Catch-up breaths are much worse than regular ones.

"Here, let's go to this one." Rayna points at a little theater. Three red *X*s run across the front of it. It looks just like the twenty other *X*-decorated theaters we've walked by.

"Why this one?"

"Looks cleaner."

"Have you ever done this before?"

"No."

"Oh," I say.

A man sits behind a window in a little booth. Rayna slides a ten-dollar bill under the partition. I peek over her shoulder at him. His hair is neat. His face is clean. He's got all his teeth. At least all the front ones.

I whisper in Rayna's ear, "The sign says 'Must be over eighteen to enter.' I think we should go. We might get in trouble."

"Two, please," she says.

The man pushes two tickets and some change back under the window. He grins at Rayna. I step behind her. I don't want him looking at me. If I ever get famous, he might tell someone I went to see a porno and my career will be ruined.

"Enjoy the show," the ticket man says.

Rayna takes my hand. "Come on."

Inside, the theater is dingy and dank. The movie is already playing. The screen light flickers brightly in the darkness. I don't look, though. I'm not ready yet.

"We should go," I say. "The movie's already started."

"It's not the kind of movie you have to watch from the beginning," she says.

I wonder how Rayna knows these things.

"Don't look!" she says loudly.

I look.

I put my hand up over my mouth. I start to gag.

"I told you not to look," she whispers. "Here, sit down.

Keep your eyes closed. I'll tell you when it's safe." She pushes me into a seat.

Closing my eyes makes my nose work better.

"It smells funny in here. Why's it smell so funny in here?"

"Quiet."

While I sit there waiting for Rayna to tell me it's safe to open my eyes, I smell the funny smell. It smells like really bad morning breath mixed with curdled milk. I've never smelled anything like it.

The actors aren't talking anymore. They're moaning. During the short period of time when my eyes were open, I counted five men in the audience. And now it's like some sort of crazy camp sing-along. Apparently, audience participation is acceptable, because they're moaning louder than the stars of the movie.

"Okay, look," Rayna says.

But as soon as I go to open my eyes, Rayna yells, "Don't look!"

I think the movie is making her nervous.

All of a sudden the theater lights come on.

"You can open your eyes. The movie's over."

"Just like that?" I say. I look around the theater. All five men are staring at us. One is rubbing his pant leg. His mouth hangs open in the shape of a big *O*.

"Yeah. I don't think it was about the plot."

"Your forehead is all sweaty," I say.

Rayna looks shaken up. I feel like she's just taken a bullet for me.

"Let's get out of here," I say.

When we stand up, my bum feels funny. I brush the back of my jeans with my hands. There's something wet there. It feels like sticky glue.

I look at my gooey hand. It smells funny, like the theater.

"Rayna! What's on my hand?"

I stick my hand in front of her face.

She shrieks. Her eyes are scary-movie big.

She grabs my clean hand and out we run.

After three long showers I finally feel clean again. I stand on the hotel's eighteenth-floor terrace looking out at the nighttime skyline. Multicolored lights wink and blink like an overdecorated Christmas tree. Down on the street a doorman blows a whistle.

I put my elbows on the banister and rest my chin on the palms of my hands. They smell like Fels-Naptha soap. I was going to use bleach, but Rayna said that Fels-Naptha was better. I think it's a Southern thing.

My hair is tied up in a high ponytail. A warm breeze lifts the loose hair at the back of my neck. I like it when that happens. It tickles in a good kind of way. Below, a car horn honks. Traffic sounds rise and fall like ocean swells. I close my eyes.

I hear better that way.

No longer made by nature, my life's soundtrack is now made by man.

Off in the distance some unseen siren wails. Police car? Fire engine? Is there a difference, I wonder? I don't know about siren sounds or doormen's whistles or honking horns. I know the sound my horses' hooves make on the hard-packed summer soil. I know the crackle of autumn's papery leaves under my thick-soled barn boots. I know the hushed whoosh of my father's windblown wheat fields. . . .

Rick jumps into the big red combine. A gust of hot air blows my curly hair around. Ripe golden heads of wheat rustle and wave in the breeze. It gives me goose bumps.

"Daddy, why do you keep doing that?"

My father stands on the edge of our big wheat field rolling a piece of grain between his fingers. When he's done rolling it around, he taps it with his front teeth, looks at it, tosses it on the ground, and starts the process all over again on a fresh piece of grain.

"Rick, start her up. It's dead ripe. Time to bring it in."

My father picks me up and sits me next to Rick on the operator's deck. My mom's at work. It's my father's job to watch me. I hop up and down on the padded seat. I like it, it's springy.

"Sit," my father says.

I sit.

Rick starts her up. I put my hands over my ears.

"Hold on to the wheel," Rick yells. "You can help me steer."

When we start to move, it shakes and vibrates so hard I'm afraid I might be thrown out of the seat. I curl my fingers tightly around the steering wheel. I'm glad Rick is letting me help steer.

Rick heads straight toward a row of wheat. As he runs into it, I scrunch my eyes shut. When I open them back up, Rick is smiling. I guess he likes running into three-foot-tall walls of wheat. In front of us the long wheel with sharp metal teeth goes round and round. Chain belts twirl. Parts spin. Bars jab back and forth. My hands are really little compared to Rick's.

When we get to the end of the row, Rick spins the steering wheel around. My arms aren't long enough to keep holding on. I have to let go. I hold on to the front of the seat. My teeth knock together like one of those windup chattering-teeth toys.

As soon as Rick makes the turn, I see where we've been. I point and gasp. The tall, bushy-topped wheat stalks are lying flat on the ground now. The big red machine has killed them. I know because their heads are gone. They're not going to make that nice sound in the wind anymore. I really like that sound. *Shush*, the wheat whispers in the night. *Shush*. I listen and they help me sleep. My eyes grow wet.

I don't want Rick to know about my wet eyes. I wave my hand around in front of my face. "It's really dusty," I yell. I rub my eyes with the back of my fist.

Rick laughs. He nods at the flat gold field. "We'll bale that up later for the horses. That's straw."

"It is?"

"Yep."

I smile. My pony likes lots of straw in her stall. She likes to eat it. That's why she's so fat.

My father drives toward us in a big, long truck. The back part is covered over with a canvas tarp held up on long poles. Rick stops the combine and waits. My father lines up the bed of the truck with the long metal chute that sticks up out of the side of the combine. Rick does something and suddenly a bunch of grain pours out of the chute into the back of the truck.

We do this over and over and over. The vibrating makes me sleepy. I try to stay awake. I don't want to fall out of the combine. But I can't help it. I lay my head against Rick's shoulder and fall asleep.

Rick shakes me.

"We're almost done. One last dump," he says.

My father lifts me up and carries me over to the bed of the big truck. He climbs up the side and lowers me onto the top of the grain. It's cool under the canvas. I sit on top of the big pile of wheat and slide my feet down through it until they're covered up to my knees.

"Close your mouth and breathe through your nose," my father says. He gives Rick a signal. I look up at the big, openmouthed chute just in time to see the grain start pouring out. I hold my hands out and feel the little grains pattering against my hands. I move a little bit closer. The seeds plink off the top of my head. It's better than a head scratch. When the grain stops coming, I lie on my tummy and pretend I'm swimming in the sea. Only, this is better. Much better. The grain feels cool on my skin. I roll onto my back and make grain angels. I could stay here all day. I lift handfuls of the light-colored seeds and watch them sift through my fingers, framed by the light of the setting sun. I don't have goose bumps. I am a goose bump.

Over in the corner a big black beetle climbs up the side of the truck. I look over at my father. He holds out his arms. I climb over to him, laughing.

As he lifts me out, he says, "Don't tell your mother."

I walk down the sidewalk, close my eyes, and pretend that I'm my sister. One step, two steps, three steps.

"Hey, watch it," a guy yells. Then, just in case I didn't hear him, he bumps me really hard with his shoulder. I roll my eyes.

New York, New York. So nice they named it twice.

I have one twenty-dollar bill, three quarters, four dimes, two nickels, and a lucky penny in my pocket. I check to make sure it's all still there. I do that whenever I get bumped into.

The guy next to me has a small tape player in his hand and big earphones on his head. The volume's turned way up. He's bobbing his head up and down, walking to the beat of his music. I walk beside him, pretending that it's my music too.

The singer's words leak through his earphones. "Ahhhhh, love to love you, baby. Ahhhhh."

The way she whimpers and sighs and says the word "ahhhhh" is kind of embarrassing. I wonder if the music guy knows I'm listening.

I stop at the crosswalk and wait for the DON'T WALK light to change. The music guy doesn't stop. He walks right out into the busy street. I'd follow him, but I'm too afraid of the moving cars.

A car inches forward, blocking his way. He smashes his fist down on its hood.

The driver blares his horn.

The music guy gives him the finger. "Fuck you, asshole," he yells.

"Fuck you," the driver yells back.

Then, like it's nothing, the music guy climbs up on top of the car, walks across its hood, and hops down on the other side. He quickly disappears into the crowd, taking my music with him.

I'm glad I don't have a car.

A frowny-faced girl comes up and hands me a flyer. I don't think she likes her job very much. The sidewalk is covered with her flyers. She doesn't pick them up. She doesn't care if anybody reads them. Her job is to give them away. That's all she cares about.

To make her feel better, I make a show of my interest in it. It's a flyer for a restaurant called Healthworks. The last flyer I got was for a nude modeling agency.

When I look up, the girl is gone. Her stack of flyers is in the trash can.

I walk around the corner to the restaurant, push the door open, and walk in. It's clean, colorful, and brightly lit inside. A lady pushes her tray down a long stainless steel counter. When she sees a salad she likes, she stops and points at it. The server scoops some up onto a small plate and hands it to her.

Yes, I say to myself. *I can do that. I can dish up salads.*

I breathe in the lettuce and peanut smells. My stomach gurgles and growls. I give it a comforting pat. "Soon, soon," I tell it. It's half past one and I haven't eaten all day. I'm trying not to, so I can save money. I'm doing pretty well. As long as I don't smell good things, I can go a long time.

I walk up to the girl at the cash register. She's got short, curly hair, brown eyes, and a nose that rounds up at the bridge like a half penny. She doesn't look anything like the people I grew up with. She's very exotic looking.

"Excuse me. Do you know if the restaurant is hiring?" I ask.

She nods, reaches into a box under the cash register, and hands me a form to fill out.

"Do you have a pen I could borrow?"

I have my own, but I like using other people's pens. I don't know why.

"Here. Make sure you bring it back, though. It's the

only one I have." The clip part of it is bent back at a funny angle. It bothers me.

"Excuse me." I hold the pen up. "Why's the clippy part bent like this?"

"It keeps people from stealing them," she says.

"Really?"

"Yeah."

"Wow," I say.

She points at an empty table near the back of the restaurant. "You can sit over there if you want."

"Thank you," I say.

When I'm done, I give her the application and the pen. She looks at the pen and smiles.

"Joey," she calls out.

A round-faced guy with blond hair and blue eyes walks over.

"This is . . ." She looks down at the application. "Kelle. She's looking for work."

He looks at me.

"Great," he says. "You want to start now?"

"Now?" I say. "You mean right now?"

He nods.

"Okay, sure," I say.

"Come on, then, we'll get you a uniform."

I follow him through a door and down a long, steep staircase. The steps are damp. Little bits of lettuce and shredded carrots stick to them. I walk slowly so I don't slip. Joey walks fast. He's used to them.

He opens a closet door, pulls out a bright cherry red jumpsuit, and hands it to me. "Here. You can change in the bathroom there." He motions at it with his elbow.

It's a unisex bathroom. I don't like unisex bathrooms. When I walk in, my sneakers stick to the urine-soaked floor like I'm walking on a smear of honey. I put a handful of paper towels down on the floor, take my shoes off, and step onto them.

I get changed and look at myself in the mirror. I like my new uniform. I think it's almost as cute as my lucky dress.

When I walk out, Joey smiles and holds his thumbs up. "You look great," he says.

"Thank you," I say. "I really like it."

"The restaurant hired some big designer to make them. I don't remember his name, though."

I smile. I've been in New York less than a week, and already I'm wearing designer clothes.

Joey takes me behind the counter and teaches me how to dish up and weigh all the different salads. I'm a server. That's my job. Joey says someday I'll work the cash register. But not yet. That's an advanced position.

"My name's Beth," the curly-haired girl says to me after my lesson is over. "Joey's my boyfriend. He's the day manager."

She looks up at the clock. "Ken should be here soon. He's the night manager. If you work till closing for me, I can go home early. What do you think?"

"Sure. No problem," I say.

As soon as Ken shows up, Joey and Beth introduce me to him and leave. He's small, thin, and tightly strung. He reminds me of a whippet. I think he's about thirty, but I'm much better at comparing people to dogs than guessing their ages.

It's really boring standing for hours behind the big bowls of salad, waiting for someone to serve. When Ken asks me to sweep and clean up the dining area, I'm happy to have something to do.

"Let's wrap it up. It's closing time," he says.

He locks the front door.

I put my rag and spray bottle behind the counter just like he taught me.

"Come help me bring some stuff up from down-stairs," he says.

"Okay."

As we walk down the stairs, he shakes his head and points at the lettuce-and-carrot-covered steps. "Careful," he says. "This is ridiculous. Joey needs to make sure this gets cleaned up during the day."

He's on the railing side. I'm not. I feel like I'm walking on butter. I reach out and grab his arm so I don't fall.

He pats my hand. "Just take your time," he says.

He's so nice.

"What do you want me to do?" I ask when we finally get to the bottom.

He opens the closet door where the uniforms are stored.

"I'll tell you what I want you to do," he says in a low voice.

He takes me by the shoulders, pushes me inside the closet, shoves my back up against the wall, and closes the door behind us.

It's dark. I can't see anything. Uniforms hang down in my face. I can't breathe. He sweeps them aside. Empty hangers rattle above my head.

He pushes his mouth up close to my ear. "How old are you, Kelle?" he whispers.

I don't move away from his wet lips or his warm air that stays in my ear even after his words are gone. I stay still. I stay still and wait. I can get out of this. I know I can. My brother taught me what to do. A quick knee to the groin, he'll bend forward, then another thrust to his face and I'm free.

Free and jobless.

"Sixteen," I say.

He touches my lips. His fingers are damp. They taste like salt.

"Fsssssssh . . ." He sucks air in through his teeth.

"Awwwww . . ." He lets it out with a moan.

I feel nothing.

He kisses my neck and pulls at my bottom lip with his teeth.

His breath smells like spearmint. I wonder what kind of gum he chews.

He lifts up on his toes. His lips smash down on mine.

He rocks up against me and groans into my mouth. He's hard against my leg.

I got this job. I can get another one, I tell myself.

I don't say anything. I just push him off of me, open the door, and walk out. I make sure to close the door behind me. I think he needs a minute.

"Hey, what are you doing down here?" It's Joey. He's back. Beth stands behind him.

"Ken asked me to take some stuff upstairs," I say.

Beth gives Joey a look. "Where is he?" she asks.

I shrug and walk upstairs.

There's a knock on my door. I grab my purse and open it. It's Rayna.

"Ready?" she says.

"Ready," I say.

Whenever the creepy elevator guy's on duty, Rayna and I take the elevator together. Rayna got his hours from the desk clerk, who's from Georgia. People with Southern accents stick together like that. I wouldn't be surprised if they even had a secret handshake. They feel all noble about it, like they're Knight Templars or something.

We walk outside.

I point at my mood ring. "Look. It's blue," I say. "That's a good sign."

Rayna laughs. "That or it's hot," she says.

I stick my tongue out at her.

I look down at Rayna's little high-heeled feet.

"I can't believe you're still scooting around town in those things," I say.

"Every inch counts," she tells me.

"Is the apartment far from here?" I ask.

"No, it's really close."

"How'd you find out about it?"

"I told Buddy if I didn't find a cheap place to rent soon, I was going to have to go back home. He said this girl Gina is looking for a roommate and gave me her number."

"Does she know I'm coming too?"

"No. It's better if she meets us first."

"How many bedrooms?" I ask.

"None. It's a studio," Rayna says.

I pretend I know what a studio is. Sounds very artsy.

We stand in front of the building's directory. Rayna runs her pointer finger down the list of tenants, finds Gina's name, and rings the buzzer. When she doesn't buzz us in, Rayna pushes the button again.

"Are you looking for Gina?"

A tall black girl looks over our shoulders. She's wearing short shorts. If I had her legs, I'd wear short shorts too.

"Oh. Are you Gina?" Rayna asks.

"No. I'm here to look at her apartment."

"So are we," Rayna says.

The girl pushes her lips out in a puckery knot. She doesn't scare us. We were here first. I rest my hand on the doorknob. Rayna rings the bell again.

A girl's voice comes over the loudspeaker. Her words are slurry. I think we woke her up.

"Who is it?" she says.

"It's Rayna."

"Who?"

"Rayna. I've come to look at your apartment with my friend. I have a two o'clock appointment."

There's a long pause.

Finally she buzzes us in.

We walk up to the third floor. I hope the apartment is as nice as the stairwell. It's very clean. Rayna and I make sure that we get to Gina's door first. We don't have to knock. It's wide open. Gina is inside sitting on the toilet.

The apartment is nothing more than a small rectangle-shaped room with one window, a small bathroom, and a kitchen that runs along one of the walls.

Now I know what a studio is.

There's a sleeping bag on the floor and a dark brown sheet stretched across the window. That's it. No chairs, no bed, no table. Nothing.

Gina flushes the toilet. She walks into the living room tugging at her panties. Her legs are vampire white. Her nightshirt is wrinkled and stained.

She stares at the three of us. Her long black hair falls over her glacier blue eyes. With her high cheekbones, full red lips, and delicate heart-shaped face, she's the most stunning-looking girl I've ever seen in my life. And that's without makeup. She must work a lot.

She frowns. "I thought you said you and *a* friend," she says.

"This is my friend Kelle," Rayna says.

I hold out my hand.

Gina crosses her arms. She looks over at the black girl.

"I'm Sharon. You told me to come at two also."

Gina rubs her head and nods. "Yeah, yeah, yeah," she says.

Rayna looks at me and then Gina. "Gina, if you have room for one more, Kelle and I would like to share the apartment with you. We could split the rent and expenses three ways."

Sharon clears her throat. "If you let me move in too, we can split it four ways."

Gina doesn't say anything. She grabs an open soda can off the kitchen counter and takes a swig. She makes a face. "I hate warm soda," she says. She throws the can into the sink. Soda splashes out across the wall.

She wipes her mouth with the back of her hand. "Fine. Move in," she says.

We're all teenagers. We're all new to the city. And we all want to be models.

We were made for each other.

By the end of the night we're settled in. Our newly purchased sleeping bags are spread out over the floor.

"Let's practice auditioning," I say.

"That's a good idea," Sharon says.

Gina lets out a long *You're boring me* sigh. "My manager told me I don't need any practice," she says.

Rayna remembers a commercial she likes and writes the words down on a piece of notebook paper. She's going first. Sharon's auditioned a few times already, so she's the director.

"Slate your name," Sharon says.

"Rayna."

"Let's start over. Say 'Hi, I'm Rayna' and smile. They want to see your personality."

Rayna bubbles through the rest of her "audition." She's really good. I'm too nervous to go next, so Sharon does. Rayna stops her a few times and gives her some notes. Now it's my turn.

"Hi, I'm Kelle," I say.

"That's great," Rayna says. "You look really cute. Keep going."

"I forgot my lines," I say.

Gina laughs. It's not a nice laugh. She's being mean. I'm terrible at this.

Rayna shows me the paper. "Got it?"

"I think so."

"Okay. Action." Rayna claps her hands together.

I sniff my wrist and smile dreamily. "Love's Baby Soft. Because innocence is sexier than you think."

"I loved it!" Rayna cheers.

"Me too," Sharon says. "I especially liked the wrist-sniffing part."

Gina doesn't say anything. She's got her eyes locked on me. I know that look. It's the one girls give me when I win first place at a horse show.

Every night we practice. Who needs to pay for acting classes when we've got each other? Gina's not around very much. She goes out every night, comes home in the morning, sleeps a few hours, and disappears. She doesn't tell us where she's going. She's stick thin. Dark circles lie under her eyes like smudges of purple ink. If she were a horse, I'd say she looks like she was ridden hard and put away wet. She looks used up. She barely resembles the beautiful girl I met just four weeks ago. "Pretty is as pretty does," my mother always says. If that's true, it looks like Gina's outsides have finally caught up with her insides.

"She's doing drugs," Sharon says.

"You think so?" Rayna asks.

"Yeah, that's why she never sleeps. And look at all the weight she's lost. Do any of you have her family's phone number? We should call them."

"No," I say. "She never talks about her family."

"Remember that man she took me to meet when we first moved in? He told me she's a call girl," Sharon says.

"I don't believe that. She's only sixteen," I say.

"I didn't believe it then either. But now I'm starting to."

Maybe she has been ridden hard and put away wet.

"I have to be at work early tomorrow. Joey changed

my schedule so I don't have to be around Ken anymore. I'm going to bed now."

"Yeah, me too," Rayna says.

"I'm going to go see *Grease* with my cousin. See you guys later. I'll be quiet coming in," Sharon says.

"Have fun," we say.

I pull my sleeping bag up over my head and fall right to sleep.

"What are you doing?!" Sharon yells.

I roll over. There's a shadow over me. I wipe the sleep out of my eyes and try to focus. Sharon turns the overhead light on. I blink. It's Gina. She's the shadow. Her eyes are wild. She's got the end of my ponytail in one hand and a pair of scissors in the other. I scream and throw myself backward. She yanks my hair. Sharon grabs her wrist. Gina won't let go. Sharon hits her as hard as she can with her shoulder. Gina falls down. The scissors clatter to the floor. Rayna kicks them over toward the kitchen.

Sharon sits down on top of Gina. Gina starts shrieking like a crazy person. She's making up words.

"She's on PCP," Sharon says.

I'd ask what PCP is, but I don't think it's a good time. Rayna dials the police.

While Sharon sits on Gina, we pack everything up. Since we're living out of our suitcases, it only takes a few minutes.

Gina isn't making up words anymore. Now she's using real ones. She's calling Sharon all kinds of terrible things. Racist things. She says if she ever sees us again, she'll kill us. I believe her.

We're ready. We look at Sharon. To keep Gina from scratching her face, she's holding her hands down with her knees. "I can't get off her now. She'll go crazy on me. You guys go. I'll stay here till the police come. You can reach me through that manager guy, Walter."

"Where are you going to go?" I ask.

"I can stay with my cousin."

"Okay, we'll find you later."

We hurry out into the hallway. Rayna heads toward the elevator.

I open the stairwell door. "This'll be faster," I say. "If Gina gets loose, she might come after me again. That girl's nuts."

Rayna nods.

We run down the steps.

"Do you think she was trying to stab me?" I ask, taking two steps at a time.

"No. She was trying to cut your hair off," Rayna pants.

"My hair!" An icy chill darts up my back. For some reason that sounds much worse than getting stabbed.

As we rush out of the building, the cops rush in. Rayna holds the door open for them.

It's raining out. We huddle together under a sidewalk tree.

"Rayna, I forgot my skillet. My mom's going to be mad. Should I go back for it?"

"No, I don't think you should go back for it."

"What are we going to do now?"

Rayna's eyes light up. "The Barbizon!"

"We can't afford that."

"We'll sleep in the TV room. They'll never know."

We walk up to the hotel doorman. Rayna drapes her arm around my shoulder and leans hard against me.

"Kelwe," she says loudly. "That was some party."

"Uh-huh, that was some party," I repeat. I give the doorman a look. He opens the door.

We're supposed to show our room key when we come in after hours. The desk clerk is waiting.

"Let's get you to your room," I say.

Rayna slaps her leg. "No bed. Television," she yells. When I make a move toward the desk clerk, Rayna loses her balance and staggers back a step. I look at the desk clerk and shake my head. She motions to the elevator.

"Eighteenth floor, please," I say to the elevator man as we get on. I haven't seen him before, he must be new. He pulls the lever. The elevator lurches upward.

Rayna slumps against me. Her eyes are closed.

A moment later the elevator stops. "Eighteenth floor. Mind your step," the elevator man says.

"Thank you," I say.

As I drag her off the elevator, Rayna blows the elevator man a kiss.

The elevator doors close. Rayna lifts her head and smiles.

"Told ya it would work," she says.

"I can't believe it. My heart was pounding so hard!"

It's nearly one o'clock in the morning. The television room is empty. Rayna shuts the door and locks it. The place is ours. At least for now.

We stretch out across the couch. Rayna's feet are in my face and my feet are in hers. We're too tired to care.

"Rayna, what if somebody tries to come in and catches us? The door isn't supposed to be closed."

"If we're up before six, we should be okay," she says.

"Night, Rayna."

"Night, Kelwe." Rayna giggles.

I shake Rayna's shoulder.

"Rayna, wake up."

Rayna pulls the sofa pillow over her head. "Too early," she says.

"Rayna, it's five thirty. Somebody just rattled the doorknob. We've got to get out of here."

She takes the pillow off her head. "I forgot where I was for a minute. The couch feels so good."

We grab our stuff and make a run for the stairwell.

"Now what?" I say.

"Well, we're here. We might as well get cleaned up."

We go to my old floor and wait outside the shower room. You need a special key to get in. The door swings open. A girl walks out with a towel twisted around her head. Rayna catches the door, and just like that we're in.

"Like stealing candy from a baby," she says.

A half an hour later we're back out on the street.

"Let's go to My Fair Lady. Maybe Judy will let us keep our suitcases there," Rayna says.

"Who's Judy?"

"She's the agency's booker. She's really nice. You'll like her."

We walk up to the agency. Buddy is already out hosing down the sidewalk. The sun is behind him. A hose-spray rainbow is in front of him. I love hose-spray rainbows.

"Hi, Buddy," I say.

"Hey, babe."

Nobody's ever called me "babe" before. I like it.

He points at our suitcases. "What's up?"

I look at Rayna. She's the talker.

"We were wondering if we could keep our suitcases here for a little bit. We're homeless."

It's strange to hear her say "we're homeless." For some reason it doesn't feel as bad as it sounds.

Buddy jams his hands in his pockets and looks down at his feet. "You can put your stuff in the storage room. Come on."

He takes us to a small, windowless room in the back of the agency.

"You can stay here till you find a place. You just have to be out when the agency's open. On the weekends the place is yours. Don't tell anybody you're here. And if the phone rings more than three times, answer it."

"Thanks, Buddy!" we say.

He shyly shrugs his shoulders and walks away.

I really like Buddy. He lets me be with his agency even though I'm short. He feeds me good Italian food. He gives me a place to stay when I've got nowhere to go. And all I have to do is answer the phone if it rings more than three times.

If my father had been that kind to me, I never would have left home.

By the time I get back from work, it's late. The agency is dark. I use the side entrance so I don't attract any attention. I don't think I'm supposed to turn on any lights. I have to feel my way back to the storage room. Rayna has our sleeping bags stretched out across the storage room floor. The corners are folded back and our nightgowns are sitting where our pillows would sit if we had any.

"How was work?" Rayna asks.

"Okay, I guess. Joey was out sick. I had to slap Ken's hands a few times. I swear, he's worse than a horny teenager. His face is even breaking out."

"A horny middle-aged man with a face full of pimples. I don't know how you resist him," Rayna says.

"I'm a pillar of strength." I laugh.

"I talked to Sharon. She's going to be at that manager's office tomorrow if you want to see her," Rayna says.

"Sounds good," I say. "I'll need to grab a shower at the Barbizon first, though. My hair smells like satay sauce."

I hold my ponytail under Rayna's nose.

"Get away!" She laughs.

We change into our pajamas and climb into our sleeping bags. Our new home is clean and it's air-conditioned.

"Aren't we lucky?" I say.

"Yeah," Rayna says softly.

"Buddy's so nice."

Rayna doesn't say anything.

"Rayna?" I whisper.

"Hmmm?" she says.

"Nothing. Go to sleep."

I lie in the dark listening to the steady rhythm of Rayna's breath. She's my sleepy-time metronome. I feel so safe, so at home. I want to stay here forever. I haven't felt like that in a long time. A little voice in the back of my head says, *Don't think about it, you'll jinx it.*

The last time I felt like this, it didn't last long.

My father saw to that.

It's five o'clock in the morning. My bed sits next to a narrow, wavy-paned window. The window's open. My thin curtains rise and fall in the gently blowing breeze. They sweep over me, lightly touching my face and bare arms. Before this house I had to share a room with my sister. I really like having my own room. It's airy and bright. It's everything I want it to be.

I don't want to get up yet, but I have to. As it is, I'll have just enough time to feed the horses, clean their stalls, and ride before I have to leave for school.

I hop out of bed, get dressed, and head down the hallway. As I walk by Bob's door, he quietly calls out to me. "Kelle," he says. "Come here." His voice is low.

I walk into his room. He closes the door behind me. His room is dark.

"Sit down," he says.

I sit on the edge of his bed. His sheets are dirty. They smell like stinky feet. "I can do your laundry after school if you want," I say.

"Kelle, listen to me." He says it so fast it sounds like one long word.

"Okay," I say.

He leans his ear against the door.

I link my fingers together. My forefingers point up like a church steeple.

My brother comes away from the door and sits down next to me.

I pull my shoulders up and wait.

"I'm not supposed to tell you this," he says to the floor.

I sit really still.

He pushes off the bed with a jerk and paces back and forth.

I open my church steeple and wiggle my fingers around.

Bob stops his pacing. He stoops down in front of me.

"Kelle, today while you're at school, Dad's going to burn the house down."

I'm quiet.

I feel like my throat is filled with cotton balls.

"Put the junk you want to keep in different places in the barn. Lay some spiderwebs and stuff over it so it looks like it's been out there a long time. Not too much, though. And no photos."

I think about all my pony pictures. "No photos?" My breath catches in my throat.

Bob shakes his head. "No. If there's an investigation and they find photos, it would look suspicious."

"What about the dogs?"

"He's going to let them out of the house before he does it."

"Even Hooty and Alfie?"

My father doesn't like them.

"I'll make sure they get out," he says.

"Promise?"

He lays his hand on top of my church-steeple fingers. "I promise. Now go. Don't let anybody see you."

I go to the barn first. The horses are hungry. I have to feed them. While I'm there, I look for good places to put my stuff. I don't clean the stalls. I have too much to do.

I go back to my bedroom. I open my closet door. I pull everything out of it. Everything. My floor is covered in clothes, photo albums, prize lists, blue ribbons, everything that's important to me.

It looks messy. I have to organize it. I sort my memory things into subjects and carefully lay them in my old blue milk crate. I make my clothes look neat on their hangers and put them back in the closet, arranged by color. I line my shoes up in tidy rows. When I'm finished, my closet looks so nice I wonder why I've never done it before.

I like it so much I decide I'm going to do my drawers, too.

There's a light tapping at my door. It's Bob. He points at the piles on my floor. "What the fuck are you doing?"

"Sorting," I say.

He shakes his head. "Hurry up," he says.

He walks away.

I put my clothes back into my dresser drawers. I could have folded better. Some of the T-shirt neck holes aren't centered. It really bothers me. Oh, well. It'll have to do. I stand back and look at what I've done. My room is perfect now.

Maybe my father will change his mind.

I look outside. The sun is coming up. I go to my closet and pull out my photo album. I pick out three pictures. One of Misty, one of Cricket, and one of Muffet. I put my pony pictures in my back pocket and head out to the barn.

I pull the lid of my tack trunk open by the hasp and prop it open with a short crop. I'm careful not to get any fingerprints on the dusty lid. I reach inside, feeling my way through the horse bits, leather lead reins, halters, and horse blankets. I keep going until my fingers touch the wallpaper-lined bottom. I lift the wallpaper up and slide my pictures under it. Holding the lid up by the hasp, I take out the crop and close it.

I smile. No one will ever know what I've done. Not even Bob.

The third-period bell rings, signaling the start of my history class. Sister Ignacio comes in a few minutes later with a small pink note in her hand.

"Kelle, the principal would like to see you," she says.

Everybody turns and stares at me. I've never been called to the principal's office before.

Brenda and Connie raise their eyebrows and grin. They don't like me.

As I walk down the long corridor toward the office, I feel really strange. Light-headed. Like my soul has sprung a leak. I listen to the sound of my footsteps and tell myself to focus.

As soon as I walk into the front office, the school secretary knocks on the principal's door. The principal steps right out and gestures for me to come in.

"Kelle, sit down, please." Mrs. Roberts points at the big oak chair in front of her desk.

Her voice is stern.

I sit down.

I look at her with big eyes. My heart thumps through to my back.

"Kelle, your mother called. You need to go right home. Your house is on fire." She pauses between each sentence. Like she's waiting for my brain to catch up to her words.

"Your brother will be here soon. Go to your locker and get your things so you're ready when he gets here."

I hold my quivering lip still with my front teeth. I don't want to cry in front of Mrs. Roberts. If my father found out, I'd get in trouble. I'm not allowed to cry. Ever. I pinch the side of my leg really hard. My eyes glaze with the tears I won't let fall.

Mrs. Roberts holds out a tissue. When I don't take it, she lays it down on her desk.

Her face softens and she tilts her head to the side. "Go on now," she says.

"Thank you, Mrs. Roberts," I whisper.

I don't go to my locker.

Instead I sit out on the curb and wait for my brother to come.

I think about the textbooks I left behind.

It'll be nice not to have any homework for a change.

When I don't get right out of the car, my brother comes around and opens the passenger-side door. I'm staring at the house. I can't move.

The outside walls are still standing, but inside the house is completely gutted. If I didn't know better, it wouldn't have surprised me to see a meteor sitting where the basement used to be.

My father did a good job.

Firemen, newsmen, and nosy neighbors move around the property like busy ants. Waterlogged clothes and household items cover the yard. A lace curtain blows through a busted-out window, glowing orange with licking flames. Firemen wet down the barn with their big hoses. The horses in the upper pasture bump into one another and kick out nervously.

My brother takes me by the hand and pulls me out of the car.

The smoky air smells like fireplace wood but with a tang to it. A sharpness, a bite, that stays in my nose, making it itch and burn. I lift my arm and breathe into my sleeve.

Pieces of ash float around me like little feathers. I look at them and wonder if they're my blue ribbons, or school reports, or stuffed animals coming back to visit me one last time. They comfort me.

Thank you, ashes. Good-bye, I say to myself.

My mother's up ahead. She's holding our toy poodles in her arms. She's looking out over Hooty's topknot, staring blankly at our ash-feather house.

My father is over with the firemen, waving his arms around, pulling at his hair, making a show of his devastation. Making a show of his loss.

It was such a beautiful old house. It had sat empty for decades and was almost condemned before we bought it. We all worked so hard to fix it up. We lived in tents and showered under cold hoses for months. We put in plumbing and repaired rotting floorboards. We painted. We cleaned. We did it justice.

It was three stories tall, with big pillars reaching all the way up to the roof. Smartly dressed jockey statues held lanterns that lit the pathway to the house. My father told people it was the oldest house in the county, that it was a historic landmark. I'm not sure, though; sometimes he makes things up.

"Mom," I say.

Alfie hears my voice. He pushes his paws against my mother and whines. She puts him down and he runs to me. When I pick him up, he leans his nose against my neck and shivers.

"It's okay, boy, I've got you," I say. He feels so good in my arms.

My mother doesn't look at me. She just coos in Hooty's ear. "Shush, shush, shush," she says like people talk to crying babies.

Alfie and I stand next to her. I push my shoulder up against hers. I want her to know I'm there. I feel sorry for her. I don't know how she stays with my father. I guess she has to.

For us.

"Do you want to make it the fast way or the slow way?" the man behind the desk asks me. Measle-size balls of sweat cover his forehead. He's a squat, fat-bodied man with short legs and a bumpy complexion. His dry gray skin hangs off his body in loosely swinging folds. He reminds me of a toad.

I think I know what he's getting at. When I don't answer, he smiles. I nudge Rayna with my elbow. She looks down and smooths the wrinkles on her skirt. Sharon laughs. She's heard it all before.

I cross my fingers behind my back. Lies don't count if your fingers are crossed.

"Slow," I say.

If I say "fast," he might get the wrong impression.

"You'll change your mind," he says.

I press my back against his leatherette couch. It

makes little crinkling sounds. He fixes his dark, colorless eyes on me. I wonder who will turn away first. He swallows. His Adam's apple bobs up and down. He blinks.

Game's over. I win.

He swings his head toward the busty blonde sitting to his right. His baggy neck wags back and forth. "Any problems last night?" he asks her.

He calls himself a manager. I wonder what he's managing.

She smiles at him with sleepy eyes. "Went great, Walter," she says. She slides a fat envelope toward him.

He pushes back from his desk and stands up. "Excuse me," he says.

As he passes in front of me, I get a whiff of his cologne. It's horrible. I take another sniff just to be sure it's as bad as I thought it was. It smells like a product of science, not nature. I think some of it is stuck to my nose hairs now, because the bad smell won't go away. I can't stand it when that happens.

He leaves the room.

"Tissue," I say to Rayna.

She gets one out of her purse and hands it to me. I give my nose a soft little blow.

I tilt my head back. "Clean?"

Rayna looks and nods.

Walter comes back into the office. He waddles over to his desk and sits down. The long journey across the office floor has exhausted him. I bump the foot of the couch with my heels. Walter writes a name and number down on a scrap of paper.

"Here." He flips the paper at me. "Come see me after you get some photos. This guy is looking for models to do test shots with. His name is Perry."

The paper is sweaty-palm damp. "Thank you," I say.

He looks at the three of us. "I have to ask you girls to leave now. I have some business to discuss with Vickie."

Vickie leans back in her chair. She uncrosses then recrosses her legs. Her skirt hikes up her perfect thighs. She runs her fingers along the top of her breast and smiles lazily at Walter.

I wonder how long Vickie's been "making it the fast way" with him.

I stand up. "Okay, then," I say.

Rayna and Sharon get up and follow me to the door.

Rayna turns back. "Bye, Walter," she says.

He doesn't even look at her.

"Nice meeting you," she says anyway.

I guess she can't help herself. Politeness runs in her blood.

The hot sun blazes straight down out of the sky. Drips of sweat roll down my neck and back. My satin blouse sticks to my skin like a Band-Aid. I pull it out and wave it back and forth. A church bell tolls. One long, deep, hollow note, repeating. The sound feels good in my ears.

Up ahead a huge arc of water spews from the mouth of an open fire hydrant. The water fans out, wide and long, across the street and sidewalk. Along the edges it lands in soft, splashy sprinkles. Toddlers patter back and forth under the cooling spray. Their little bare feet go *slap slap* on the puddly concrete.

Teenage boys turn their backs to the powerful center blast. They back into it in a game of who can get to the hydrant first. The force of the water pushes their chins down onto their chests.

Water washes up over the clogged gutters and spills

out onto the sidewalk. A boom box sits on the hood of a rusty old car. Dark-haired girls sway to the rhythm of the thumping drumbeat and smooth Spanish words. They smile at the boys and tap their brightly painted toes in the moving swirl of water. They lift their chins and lean their chests under the spray of water. The boys stop and stare.

"Hey, *chica*, *chica*," a shirtless boy calls out. He wiggles his fingers at one of the dark-haired girls. He wants her to walk under the water with him. She throws her head back and laughs. Her lips are full and red. Her teeth are straight and white. The shirtless boy grabs her and pulls her in with him. She stands behind him with her arms wrapped around his waist and her head resting against his back. The water pours over them like a waterfall.

I cross to the other side of the street. That photographer, Perry, is taking test shots of me today. If my hair gets wet, it'll turn all frizzy.

A patrol car slowly makes its way toward the open fire hydrant. The siren blips. *Whoop. Whoop.* Out steps one of New York's finest. He's got a big wrench in his hand. When he closes down the hydrant, the toddlers pull at their mothers' skirts and cry.

My ankle hurts. I slip my shoe off my heel and push my soggy Band-Aid back down over my oozing blister. It slithers off, landing on a glob of something I'm not touching. I pull a tissue out of my pocket, fold it into a rectangle, and use that instead.

Even though my blister-limp slows me down, I still get to Perry's right on time. His assistant, a pretty Asian girl with glossy, butt-length hair, takes me to the dressing room. When I come back out, she directs me to a spot in front of the camera.

Perry walks out. "Hi, Kelle," he says like he's happy to meet me.

He's so cute. My cheeks feel warm. "Hi," I say.

The pretty Asian girl puts on some music, says goodbye, and leaves.

Perry points at a little masking-tape X on the floor. "Do you think you can kneel right there on that X?" he asks politely.

I drop right down on my knees. It hurts, but I don't complain. I'm a model now. I'd stay like this all day if he wanted me to. That's the kind of stuff models do. I read it in a magazine.

"Fix your collar," he says.

I move it around a little.

"Here, let me help you." Perry moves from behind his tripod, stoops down, and gently slides one of my buttons out of its hole. Then, with his green eyes still shining down on me, he undoes one more. As he turns to go back to his camera, his hand brushes against my breast. I don't know what to do, so I smile.

Back behind the camera, he rests his hands on his hips. His lips turn down. I stare at him and wonder what I've done wrong.

He disappears for a minute. When he comes back, he's carrying a big fan. He puts it down in front of me and turns it on. He fidgets around with the airflow and direction, and then, finally happy, he goes back behind his tripod.

He runs his fingers through his tousled honey blond hair. "Face your body toward the fan and stretch forward," he says softly. His eyes and his emerald green, crocodile-clad polo shirt are a perfect match.

If the photos he takes look as good as he does, I'm going to be in great shape.

I stretch my arms across the floor and stare up at his camera. With every click and flash, I change my expression slightly. I can tell he likes me, because his strobe is on overdrive.

"Very good," he says when we finish. He smiles.

I'm happy that he's pleased.

When I finally look down from his camera, I see my shirt gaping open. I'm so ashamed. I swallow down the rising bile and fumble with my buttons.

"Don't worry, that just happened," Perry says.

But I can tell he's lying.

He pulls me to my feet, leans his hips against me, and slowly draws his thumb across my lips. "How would you like to go to Studio Fifty-four?"

"I'm sixteen," I say. I turn away slightly so I don't have to breathe in his air.

"I can get you in," he says.

"Okay, when?" I say.

"I'll leave a message with your service." He squeezes the tip of my nose.

I don't believe him.

I go to the dressing room and pack up my things.

When I come out, he's waiting for me. His arm rubs against my body as we walk toward the door. I move a tiny bit away. He frowns.

"Thanks, Perry," I say when we get to the door.

"Yeah, thanks," he says. His voice sounds different now, harder.

I open the door and walk outside. The streetlights are sputtering; it's almost dark out.

It's hot. My skirt sticks to my body. I pull the damp cotton up off my legs as I step around an overflowing trash can. The air around it smells like rotting food and dog urine. Two men with rough faces and dirty hands stand on the street corner and coo, "Hey, baby, baby . . . whatcha doin'?" at me. They click their tongues and moan. I fix my eyes across the street and pretend someone is waiting for me. Finally they give up and go back to drinking their paper-bag beverages.

Suddenly it seems like I'm catnip to every borderline pedophile in Manhattan. I can't wait to take a shower.

"254 *West Fifty-fourth Street,*" I say to the cabdriver. He looks at me in his rearview mirror. I check to make sure the door lock is the kind that can be opened by hand. Rayna lent me cab money. She didn't think I was dressed appropriately for walking.

She picked up my outfit at some cheap sidewalk shop. She said it was perfect for a night at Studio 54. I've never worn anything like it.

"You can't go wrong with a little black dress," she said.

"Little" is an understatement. It barely covers my butt. And it fits like glue. She even got me a pair of spiky black heels to go with it. Every once in a while my ankle gives out and I nearly fall over.

"Don't worry, you'll get used to it," Rayna says.

She put a lot of makeup on my face too, but I looked like Brooke Shields in the *Pretty Baby* platter scene, so I washed it all off.

There's a huge crowd of people milling around in front of the club. How am I ever going to find Perry? What if I don't recognize him? What if he doesn't recognize me? I should have thought this through. I was just so excited when he called and asked me to go, I said yes without thinking about it.

I find a place to stand where people won't bump into me.

A guy wearing tight white pants, a shiny half-buttoned shirt, and two gold chains yells out from the back of the crowd, "Hey, Mark, it's me!" The doorman doesn't even look at him.

All of a sudden the crowd parts. An odd-looking man with white hair and thick glasses walks past the doorman and into the club. A bunch of pretty girls and good-looking men follow him.

"That was Andy Warhol," the girl next to me says to her friend.

I don't know who Andy Warhol is, but he must be important. Only an important person would have the nerve to look like that.

Up front a girl pleads with the doorman. "Come on, let me in," she says.

"Maybe later," he tells her.

"Aw, come on. Will you let me in if I take all my clothes off?"

He smiles. "If you take all your clothes off, I'll let you in."

"Promise?"

"I promise."

She takes her clothes off. Mark unhooks the rope. She grabs her clothes and runs inside.

I hope Perry doesn't think I'm going to take my clothes off.

"Kelle, over here!"

It's Perry. He's standing over near the front of the club. I squeeze through the crowd. When he holds out his hand, I take it. He pulls me up to the doorman.

"Hey, Mark," he says.

"Hey, Perry. Who's this?"

"This is Kelle."

Mark unhooks the rope. "Have fun, Kelle," he says.

The crowd groans. They don't know why we get to go in and they don't. I don't know either.

It's like all of a sudden I'm one of the cool girls. All it took was a short black dress, spiky heels, and a well-connected man.

Perry stares me up and down. "Do you know how hot you are in that dress?" he says. His eyes look funny. The black part has taken over the green part. He rests his arm across the top of my butt. His fingers drape down across the front of my thigh. He gives my leg a squeeze. It tickles. I pat his hand and place it on my hip.

"Behave yourself," I say.

He laughs. I guess he likes being talked to like he's a child.

A big fog machine belches out clouds in the wide hallway that leads to the dance floor. Donna Summer's

"Last Dance" is playing. Perry's perfect blond hair falls down over one eye like a pirate's patch. He's really handsome. He's tall and thin. I bet he's a runner. His jeans rest loosely across his hips. I want to hook my thumb in them. I look up at him and smile.

We walk into the fog. Perry stops and pulls me up close to him. I let him. He holds my face between his hands and leans down to kiss me. This is the most romantic moment of my life.

Something grabs my leg.

I jump away. "What was that?" I yell.

"What was what?"

"Something grabbed my leg."

Perry waves his arms. The fog clears enough for us to see a long row of cages. Inside the cages are little kids. They can't be older than eight or nine. They're crawling around on their hands and knees pretending they're wild animals. Growling, barking, purring. They have makeup on their faces. One of the "lions" takes another swipe at my leg. I put my hand up over my mouth.

Perry takes my hand and walks me farther down the hallway toward the dance floor. Everywhere I look is another cage filled with little-kid animals. I push my face into Perry's chest. As we walk onto the dance floor, "Boogie Oogie Oogie" comes on. I feel like I'm in a movie.

"Let's get a drink," Perry yells into my ear.

I nod. A drink would be nice.

He waves over the crowd at one of the shirtless bartenders. He holds up two fingers. The bartender nods. Being tall is good for more than modeling. By the time we get up to the bar, two glasses of white wine are poured and waiting.

Perry clinks my glass. I take a quick sip. "Let's dance," he says. He puts our glasses down on the bar and we're off to the dance floor. The music is fast and fun and I love it. My feet are working especially well, considering the heels. Perry's such a good dancer. I really like him. Maybe he'll give me the negatives to those photos he took the other night.

Next to us a girl opens her arms and spins in slow-motion circles. I used to do that when I was little, only I did it really fast until I fell down. Then, with my back on the ground, I would look up at the sky and watch the clouds go round.

A girl jumps up on a furry-chested man. She wraps her legs around him. He grabs her waist. She leans her head way back. They spin around.

Above my head sparkly disco balls twinkle and shine. Bright flashes of white light hit my eyes like lightning bolts. Perry points up. Hundreds of balloons fall down from the ceiling. The dancers bat them around. They lift and float across the room. This is better than Disneyland.

Perry talks in my ear. "Come on," he says.

I'm having so much fun. I don't want to leave. But Perry wants to, so I do. I follow him to a dark staircase.

Two guys are making out on the second step. Two top-less girls and a guy are making out on the fifth step. My stomach twists. If this is happening down here, what's happening up there? I don't want to find out. I stop. I look at Perry.

"I want to go back and dance," I say.

"I've got a surprise for you," he says.

"A surprise?" I ask.

"Yeah. Want some candy, little girl?" he teases.

"Candy?"

"Nose candy." He makes little sniffing sounds.

My eyes grow big.

He holds out his hand. "You'll like it."

I shake my head. "I'll wait down here for you."

He shrugs. "Okay. Suit yourself," he says.

I go back to the dance floor. I'm afraid to dance by myself, so I lean against the wall and watch every-body having fun. Eight guys in black thong underwear gyrate on eight tall pedestals. A girl with bright orange hair dances in a swinging wrought-iron cage. When I look at her, she sticks her tongue out and runs it around her lips.

There's a loud pop. White powder floats down over the dance floor. I hope Perry comes back soon. The music is really loud. My ears hurt. It's so crowded. People keep bumping into me. When I look at them, they laugh.

A man puts his hand on my shoulder. "Want to dance?" he yells.

"I'm with somebody," I yell back.

At least, I think I am, I say to myself.

A huge man-in-the-moon sculpture looks down over the dance floor. When a large spoon swings under its nose, it lights up.

I wonder what's taking Perry so long. A girl and guy fall down in front of me. I guess they've been spinning too much. They kiss and grind against each other. People dance around them like they aren't there.

A guy walks up to me. "What's a nice girl like you doing in a place like this?" he slurs.

"I'm here with—"

He grabs my breasts and squeezes them. Hard. I lunge backward. My head hits the wall behind me. He cages me in with his arms and grins.

I look him over from tip to toe, slowly, smiling sweetly. My eyes rest on his groin. I look back up, nodding appreciatively.

He quivers.

Oh, sweet justice.

I push my body up close to his, trail my fingers down his belly, right on down to his crotch. I cup my hand around his private area. He widens his stance and closes his eyes.

I whisper in his ear, "How's this feel, baby?"

Before he can answer, I close my hand and yank his package upward. For good measure I add a little twist at the end. He drops to the ground.

I stand over him.

"What's the matter, big boy? Cat got your tongue?" I say.

I've had enough for one night. It's time for me to go home.

As soon as Nicky puts our sodas down, Rayna takes out the cherry and pops it in her mouth.

"Who's coming tonight?" I ask.

"I think just Buddy and his brothers," she says.

The cherry makes the side of her face stick out funny. I poke her cheek with my finger. "I didn't know Buddy had any brothers."

She swallows. The cherry bump disappears. "Me neither," she says.

The front door opens. "There they are!" she yells.

"Hey," Buddy says. He points at his brothers. "Doug. David." He points at us. "Rayna. Kelle." Doug sits down next to me.

"Hi," I say.

He looks at me. "Haven't I met you before?"

"No, people always think they've met me before. I guess I look like a lot of different people."

He laughs. His hair is dark. His eyes are big. His face is round and sweet.

"How old are you?" I ask.

Buddy looks over at us.

Doug snaps his napkin open. "Seventeen."

David looks just like Buddy, only a lot younger. He's small, thin, and handsome in an odd sort of way. I can tell he's good at something. There's an air about him. A confidence. Since he and Buddy sat down, they haven't stopped moving. It's always something—their mouths, their fingers, their feet. They're like sharks in shallow water.

"Let's order," Buddy says.

David rubs his stomach. "Yeah, I'm starving."

Recognizing the time-to-order tummy rub, the waiter hurries over. He drops a big basket of crusty bread down on the table. As soon as we tell him what we want, he rushes back to the kitchen.

Buddy hands me the bread.

I tear off a hunk and pass it to Rayna.

"I heard you two are living in the back of the agency. How's that going?" David asks.

"It's going great. We love it," Rayna says.

"They shower at the Barbizon," Buddy says. He sounds proud of us.

Buddy likes resourceful people.

"The Barbizon? How?" Doug asks.

"We're in there so much the staff thinks we're still guests!"

Doug's knee touches mine. As soon as he realizes it's my leg he's bumping into, he moves it away.

Two plate-laden waiters set our piping-hot, sauce-covered meals down in front of us.

"Who wants to try some of my chicken?" I ask.

"I do," says Doug.

"I do," says Buddy.

I cut two big pieces off and put them on their plates.

"Want some of my pasta?" Doug asks.

I tip my bread plate under his dish, and he pushes some of his pasta onto it. "More?" he asks.

"No thanks. That's perfect."

The table grows quiet. Everybody eats. I really like Buddy and his brothers. I feel like we're a real family having a big Sunday dinner. I can talk if I want to. I don't have to say anything smart or funny. I let out a happy sigh. Buddy looks at me and smiles. Buddy doesn't miss anything. He's really smart that way.

Rayna looks at my empty Shirley Temple glass. "Do you want your cherry?"

"You can have it in a minute," I say. "I want to show you guys something first."

She raises her eyebrows. "What?"

"It's a surprise," I say.

She taps her glass with her spoon. "Kelle wants to show us something."

Everybody looks at me. I get nervous. "I don't know if I can do it with everybody staring at me," I say.

"Come on," David says.

"All right. I'll try."

I lean my glass over slightly. The cherry falls forward. I pull it out by its stem. I open my mouth really wide and stick out my tongue.

I point into my mouth. "Ahing en hah."

Buddy's, David's, and Doug's foreheads wrinkle up.

I give the cherry to Rayna and keep the stem for myself. It's nice and long. I hold it out for all to see.

I put it in my mouth and softly close my lips. I hope I don't mess up. It's important to look casual. The less lip movement the better. My heart is racing. I hold one end of the stem between my teeth and push the other end around with my tongue. I think I've done it. I can't be sure until I see it, though. I push it out of my mouth and into the palm of my hand. Everybody leans forward. My perfectly tied cherry stem is a beauty. Tight. Even. It's my best one yet.

Buddy slaps the table and laughs. David blushes.

"No way," Doug says.

"I've been practicing," I say.

Everybody smiles. They look so happy.

When dinner is over, we all stand up to leave.

"Buddy," David says. "Do you have any money? Doug and I only have a hundred dollars to get through the weekend."

Rayna bumps me with her elbow. I bump her back. We're on a three-dollar-a-day budget, and that includes food. If Joey didn't let me bring food home from Healthworks, we'd starve.

Buddy pulls a wad of bills out of his pocket. He peels off two hundred-dollar bills and hands them to David. David shoves them in his pocket.

"Thanks," he says.

"Let me walk you ladies home," Doug says.

He called us ladies. He called it home.

We walk across the street.

Rayna punches in the combination.

"I'm moving in with Buddy in a few days," Doug says.

"You are?"

He nods.

"Cool," I say.

He pushes a dry leaf around with the toe of his shoe. "So I guess I'll be seeing you around."

Rayna holds the door for me.

"I gotta go. Night, Doug," I say.

"Yeah. See ya," he says.

Rayna closes the door behind us.

"He likes you," she says.

"He does not."

She tugs my ponytail. "Does too."

I roll my eyes. "He's too young for me," I say.

Rayna shakes her head and laughs.

"I'm serious."

"I know you are," she says. "That's why I'm laughing."

I push my empty plate back and rub my stomach. "They make the best corn muffins here."

"That's because they fry them in butter," Rayna says.

"I loooove butter," I say.

Every once in a while we go crazy and eat fried corn muffins at the G&M. It's a splurge, but it's worth it. They fill my stomach up for a long time.

And any day without hunger pains is a good one.

I pick up the menu. "G&M Luncheonette. Luncheonette. That's a funny word. Luncheonette. Say it."

"Luncheonette," Rayna says.

My legs are stuck to the Naugahyde. I lift them up a little and look outside. A little kid pees on a lamppost while his older brother keeps guard. My muffin plate has little drips of melted butter on it. I'm glad I'm done eating. "Do you think it's safe to go home now?"

Rayna looks down at her watch. "Way safe. The agency should have closed a half hour ago."

I lay two one-dollar bills down on the table.

Rayna narrows her eyes. "I'm paying," she says.

"You always pay. It's my turn." I push my money toward the edge of the table.

She shoves it back. "My parents help me. Yours don't," she says.

I cross my arms. "Bob helps me. He gave me three hundred dollars."

"Which you spent. It's not the same, anyway. You've got to pay him back."

I put my hands on my hips. "He says I don't."

She smiles up at the ceiling. She knows I'm going to. Someday.

It might take a while, though. It's hard to save money when you serve salads for a living.

The waitress walks over. Rayna hands her a five. "Can I have two dollars back, please?"

Rayna's a really big tipper.

The waitress shakes her head. "Your bill's been paid already."

"What?" Rayna says.

"By who?" I ask.

The waitress nods behind us. "By the man in the next booth."

Our heads spin around. There's no one there.

"He just left. He heard you talking and wanted to help."

Rayna and I stare at each other.

Some feelings are too good for words.

We put our money in our pockets and walk outside. A dribble of sweat runs down the back of my leg. "Can you believe this heat?" I say.

Rayna wipes her forehead. "It's hotter than a burning stump out here."

She gets a little spray bottle out of her purse and gives my face a spritz.

I look at her purse. "What else do you have in there?"

Rayna points toward My Fair Lady. "Uh-oh," she says.

Buddy and Melanie are sitting on the agency's stoop. Buddy's arms are clasped across his chest. Melanie is crying.

"We better wait till they leave," Rayna says.

I nod.

Buddy calls Melanie "the girl with a thousand faces." If that's true, then this is her sad face. She's all red. Her eyes are puffy. She wipes her nose with the underside of her T-shirt.

Buddy puts his arm around her shoulder. She leans her head against him. He strokes her hair. After a couple of minutes they get up and go into the building.

We run across the street. While Rayna unlocks the door, I peek around and make sure the elevator stays on the seventh floor. It does. That's Buddy and Melanie's floor. I don't think Melanie knows about us being in the back room. I don't want her to see us.

The phone rings. Buddy's apartment and My Fair Lady share the same number. Buddy usually picks up on the first ring.

"Should I get it?" I ask.

"Yeah. Buddy and Melanie must be talking," Rayna says.

I pick up a pen and pad. "My Fair Lady Modeling Agency, how may I help you?" I say in a low voice. I sound very professional.

"Budd Zzzyp?"

"Excuse me?" I say.

"Is Budd Zzzyp there?" a girl asks.

"I think you have the wrong number."

The girl hangs up. The dial tone hums loud in my ear. I stare at the phone.

"Who was that?" Rayna asks.

"A girl asking for Budd Zzzyp."

Rayna makes a face. "Write it down. We'll ask Buddy about it in the morning."

I write it down. The pen has "My Fair Lady" printed on it. I want a My Fair Lady pen. Maybe Buddy will let me have one.

Melanie named the agency after her favorite musical. If it were my agency, I'd name it after one of my favorite ponies: Misty Models. Muffet Management. Cricket's Coterie.

Rayna walks up behind me. "It's getting dark. We have to get in the back before someone sees us."

"How many models does the agency have?"

"About twenty," Rayna says.

"Does that include us?"

"No. Not yet. After we build up our books it will."

Someone taps on the front door. Rayna and I duck down beneath the counter.

"What do we do?" Rayna asks.

"Stay here till they go away."

Whoever it is knocks again, only this time the person knocks, *Da-da-dada-da.* There's a pause. *Da-da.*

I look up over the counter. It's Doug. He's laughing. I walk over and unlock the door.

"You scared us," I say.

"Sorry."

"You don't look sorry."

"Sorry."

"We're supposed to be a secret."

"I know. Sorry." He bites his lip and tries not to laugh.

"I guess we have to be more careful."

I show him the pen. "Do you think your brother would mind if I took this?"

"No. He doesn't care about stuff like that."

I put the pen in my back pocket. I'm still going to ask Buddy, though. Just to be sure.

"I'm almost all moved in," Doug says. "I'm gonna help Buddy renovate the Park East building."

"Park East building?"

"Yeah. Buddy's a real estate developer. The agency's just a side thing. He opened it for Melanie."

"Oh," I say.

He sticks his hands in his pockets. "You want to go out to dinner on Friday?"

"At Nicola's?"

"No. That's my pop's place. We're going to a restaurant that David and his girlfriend like to go to. Nothing fancy. It'd be the four of us."

"That sounds fun," I say. "I didn't know your father ate at Nicola's. How come I haven't met him?"

Without answering my question, Doug spins around and hurries out the door. "So I'll see you Friday at eight, then," he calls out over his shoulder.

"Okay," I yell back.

I press my lips together.

What was that all about?

I shrug.

I guess he's just really shy.

"Rayna, come look!" I yell.

"I'll be right there. Let me brush my teeth first."

I get into position and wait for her to come back to the storage room.

"We have to hurry. It's almost seven thirty," Rayna says as she walks into the room. She stops. "What the heck are you doing?"

I'm lying on my back with my head tilted so my face is upside down. I've drawn two eyes, a nose, and a big mustache on my chin. A T-shirt covers the rest of my face.

"So, I hear you want to be a bartender," I say. I move my mouth around like Mister Ed when I talk. It's funnier that way.

"I hope that marker isn't permanent," she says.

I take the T-shirt off my face and sit up. "You mean you hope your eyeliner isn't permanent."

She shakes her head, fishes a little bottle out of her makeup kit, and hands it to me.

"What?" I say.

She rolls her eyes. "It's makeup remover. Don't you know anything? Clean that mess off your face. We gotta get out of here."

We walk outside. Buddy is watering the sidewalk tree. Some of Rayna's eyeliner is still on my chin. It looks like freckles, though. I don't think he'll notice.

Rayna looks up at the sky. "It's hotter than a two-dollar pistol on the Fourth of July," she says.

"Sure is," I say. You never know what's going to come out of Rayna's mouth next. I don't make a big deal of it. I'm afraid if I do, she'll stop.

I hold the My Fair Lady pen out in front of me. "Buddy? Doug said you wouldn't mind if I use this pen."

He looks at me. "Use or take?"

"Ummm. Take."

"You can take all you want." He pauses. "But next time say what you mean."

"Thanks, Buddy." I tap my sneaker in a little puddle. Water splashes up on my leg.

Buddy looks at Rayna. "Jack tells me you're meeting him later today at the All Ireland. He's a nice guy. You'll like him."

"Thanks for setting that up, Buddy. I don't want to keep asking my parents for money."

"Oh. I almost forgot," I say. "A girl called last night.

She asked for Budd Zzzyp and hung up. I think it was a prank call."

Buddy waves his hand at me and smiles. "Budd Zzzyp's the last number in the phone book. If somebody needs my number and they don't have a pen, I say it's easy to find, I'm the last number in the book."

"Oh," I say.

Only Buddy would think of something like that.

I wait on the corner of Eighty-first and Third while Rayna has her job interview.

It doesn't take long.

"Well, how'd it go?" I ask when she comes out.

Rayna opens her arms and spins around in a circle. "I got the job!"

"You did?!"

"Yeah. Jack was really cool. When I told him I didn't know much about mixing drinks, he said it's mostly a beer joint and if anybody orders something I don't know how to make, I can ask what's in it. If they don't know, then they shouldn't be drinking it."

"My kind of boss," I say.

"He lives in our building, you know. Right across from Buddy and Melanie."

"Maybe I've seen him. What's he look like?" I ask.

"Hmmmm." Rayna pulls her mouth to the side. "I think he used to be a wrestler."

"I know exactly who he is!" I say.

"You do?"

"No!" I say.

Rayna laughs. "He's one of those big, beefy Queens kind of guys. You know, with the accent and all."

"Like John Travolta?"

She shakes her head. "Tupper's old. He's in his thirties." She stops for a second. "Oh, and he combs his hair funny."

I look at her.

"You know. Swooped over the top of his head."

I wrinkle up my nose. "I thought just the Greek deli guys did that. Why do they do that? It's not right."

"I'll introduce you. You can ask him."

I laugh. Rayna's so funny sometimes.

The *All Ireland* is the kind of bar you smell from way out on the street. I push the door open and walk in. It's very dark. The place is empty. Rayna stands behind the counter moving liquor bottles around on a shelf. Her face lights up when she sees me.

"Oh, hey!"

"Ready to go?" I ask.

"Yeah, let me tell Jack."

The pinball machine is the only bright thing in the room. I walk over and stand in front of it. The flipper buttons are dirty-finger filthy. The old jukebox in the corner is quiet. The pool table's faded green felt has little circular burn marks all over it.

This is a man's bar. It reeks of stale beer and cigarettes. I don't like cigarettes. My stomach feels funny. Like something bad's about to happen. I tell myself it's not true. That it's the smells that are scaring me.

They remind me of my father's bedroom. . . .

My mother hands me a great big serving tray. "Take this upstairs," she says.

I look down at the tomato-soup-filled bowl and packet of saltines. I grip the upturned tray edges and turn away. Some soup sloshes out of the bowl onto the crackers. I take in a sharp breath. Spilling is not allowed. I look up the long, steep staircase. I bite my lip. I remember what Bob told me. He told me not to look at the bowl when I take it to my father. He said I would spill less that way. I look ahead and start to climb the dark staircase. I really want to look at the bowl, to see how I'm doing. But Bob told me not to and I always listen to him.

Outside my father's bedroom door I slowly stoop down and place the tray on the carpet. I can't handle opening the door and holding the tray at the same time. More soup spills over the bowl rim and onto the crackers. I'm not wearing any shoes. I pull one sock off inside out and wipe the cracker packet clean. I right my sock and put it back on my foot. Now he won't know I spilled.

I open the door a crack. Even through the tiny opening the smell of cigarettes manages to fill up the hallway.

"Daddy. I have your soup. Can I come in?"

I press my ear against the door. I can hear him moving.

I can hear his headboard creaking. He's sitting up, getting ready to be served.

I wait.

"Come in."

My heart thumps in my chest. It swells up inside me. Being careful not to look at the bowl, I pick up the tray and push the door open with my moist tomato-soup sock.

The room is black. The air is stale. It smells like cigarettes, body odor, and bad breath.

"Bring it here."

My father pats the pillow he has placed on his lap. I slowly lower the tray onto his belly. His breathing is soft and regular. I did a good job. He isn't angry. He doesn't know some of his soup is on my sock.

"Daddy?"

"Hmmmm?"

"Daddy, can I have one of your candies?"

My father always keeps a stash of caramel creams in his nightstand. Once a week my mother buys a new bag for him. I really like caramel creams. My brothers and my sister wouldn't have asked; they aren't as brave as me.

"You can have one." His voice is flat.

"Should I get it myself?"

"Yes, but you can only have one."

I open the drawer of his nightstand. The bottom drawer, where he keeps his favorite things. Inside are his caramel creams, his magazines with the strange pictures that I don't understand, and his gun. I pull out one candy and shut the drawer.

"Thanks, Daddy."

He doesn't say anything.

I close the door behind me.

Rayna runs a spotty dishtowel around the rim of a tall beer glass. "Guess what?"

"What?"

"Buddy just called. He asked me if I wanted to watch TV with him tonight while you're out with Doug and David."

"Neat! What about Melanie?"

Rayna shrugs. "He didn't say."

"How's your food?" Doug asks me.

"Perfect. Want some?"

"No thanks."

"You Italian guys sure do eat a lot of pasta."

"We're not Italian," David says.

"You're not? I thought Buddy said he was Italian."

"Pass the salt," Doug says.

"I can't eat another bite," David's girlfriend says. She lays her hand on David's thigh. He looks at her and smiles.

They really love each other. I like that about them.

After we finish, Doug walks me to the agency. "Thanks, Doug. I had a really good time."

He leans toward me. Rayna opens the door.

"Oh, hey. I didn't know you were out here," she says.

"I'll see you later, Doug. Thanks again."

I close the door. I put my hand up over my eyes. "That was a close one. I thought he was going to try to kiss me!"

"I heard you guys walk up. I figured you'd need saving."

We run back to our room. "So, tell me about your night," I say.

"Well, first off, Buddy and Melanie broke up."

"What! You're kidding."

"No. And you're not going to believe this. She moved in right across the hall from Buddy—with my boss!"

"She moved in with Jack Tupper?"

"Yeah."

"Are they just friends?"

"No. Melanie told Buddy they're engaged."

"What! Engaged?! She just broke up with Buddy and she's already engaged to Jack? How's Buddy taking it?"

"He seems okay. Mostly lonely. We watched *Patton*. He slept through most of it. He looked so sweet. Like a little boy."

"Wait a minute. Did Buddy get you the job with Jack before or after Melanie left?"

"After."

"So Jack and Buddy are still friends?"

Rayna nods. "I guess so."

"That's cuckoo," I say.

Rayna opens her umbrella. "Ready?" she asks. Dark gray dots cover the sidewalk. I sniff the air. City rain smells almost as good as country rain. At least, uptown rain does.

"Want to get under with me?" she asks.

"No, my hair's ruined anyway."

She looks at my head. When she doesn't say anything, I know it's true.

I catch raindrops with my tongue.

It starts to pour. I jump under Rayna's umbrella. I hold my hand out. The rain runs down my arm and under my shirt. It tickles my armpit. Rayna walks around the puddles. I walk through them. I stomp my feet. The water splashes around us.

Rayna links her arm in mine and starts to sing. "'Singin' in the rain, just singin' in the rain. What a glorious feeling . . .'"

I sing the next line with her. "'I'm happy again.'"

People stare at us, but we don't care.

I leave Rayna at Alexander's. Sunday spent in a department store is not my idea of a good time. "I'll meet you back home," I say.

As I walk away, the sun breaks through a patch of clouds. Rain falls around me like glitter. It's magical. It only lasts a minute, though. Before I know it, the clouds are covering the sun again. I guess New York minutes apply to sparkly raindrops, too.

With the clouds comes another hard rain. I duck under a narrow blue awning. Three people join me. We're all so close. Everybody's touching somebody somewhere. Nobody says hello or excuse me, though. Everybody looks straight ahead. Elevator etiquette is the rule here. As long as no one acknowledges the fact that we're touching, it doesn't count.

A little boy in a bright yellow raincoat walks by. His hood has fallen down. His dark curls hang limply over his face. His chin juts forward. His little hands rest on his hips. He walks quickly. Like he's late for an appointment. The red DON'T WALK sign flashes. He stops and waits for the light to change. A sea of bobbing umbrellas moves around him.

I step away from the awning. When the light changes, the boy crosses the street. I follow him. Maybe he lives nearby. Maybe New York mothers let their little boys walk alone. I'm new here. I don't know.

I want to see his face. I walk up next to him. I look down at him and smile. He ignores me. His round little cheeks jiggle with his footsteps. He can't be more than four. He walks faster. I think he knows I'm following him. I don't want to scare him, so I drop back behind him.

We've walked ten blocks. Maybe he's almost home. My sneakers are sopping wet. My feet hurt.

The boy keeps walking.

This can't be right. His little head is soaking wet. I want to help him with his hood.

I walk up next to him.

"Hey, little man."

My voice surprises him. He looks over at me. That's when I see it. I know that face. I've made it before. Lots of times. He's pretending he's not afraid.

I take his little fist off his hip and pull him out of the flow of traffic. I stoop down and tie his hood strings in a neat bow. He looks at me with big eyes.

"Are you lost?" I ask.

He nods.

I touch his cheek.

"*Mamá*," he says. He has a Spanish accent.

"Don't worry. We'll find your mama."

He starts to cry. I put my arms around him. He clasps his arms around my neck and squeezes me tightly. "*Mamá*," he says into my neck.

"Can I pick you up?"

He scrambles up my leg. I lift him up and sit him on my hip.

He stops crying.

We walk back to the place I first saw him. I lean against a building and we wait. He plays with a strand of my hair. Other than that, he doesn't move. He just looks at the people walking by.

Forty minutes pass.

He kicks his legs and bounces up and down.

"*Mamá*," he whispers.

A small woman runs toward us. "Anthony!" she yells. Two little girls hold on to her skirt.

Anthony leans forward with his arms outstretched.

When she grabs him, his hood falls back. She smooths his hair. "*Mi hijo. Mi hijo,*" she murmurs in his ear. Her cheek pushes up against his.

She looks at me. She's crying. "*Gracias,*" she says. "*Gracias.*" She squeezes my hand.

I kiss Anthony's soft cheek. He smiles.

She doesn't speak English. I don't speak Spanish.

I don't think it matters.

I have my foot in the bathroom sink.

Rayna pops her head around the corner. "Hi," she says.

I can tell by her voice that she's in a good mood. "Where have you been all day?"

"You'll see," she says mysteriously.

I hold on to the sink with one hand and rub my soapy foot with the other.

"Ouch, that stings!" I say. "My blisters are really bad. Look."

Rayna leans over the sink and looks at my blisters with me. She points at a dime-sized flap of skin that's hanging off my toe. The area under it is all red and fleshy looking. It's the best one.

"It just popped," I say.

Rayna makes a little shiver movement. "That's nasty," she says.

I turn off the water and dry my foot with a paper towel.

"Wait till you see what I got." Rayna pulls me into the hallway.

Leaning against the wall is a great big piece of foam rubber.

"Oh my gosh!" I clap my hands. "Where'd you get that?"

"I got it at a sofa bed store. Someone returned it because it has a rip in it." She points at the rip.

"Was it expensive?"

"They gave it to me. They were going to throw it away. And guess what else?"

"What?"

"They offered me a job."

"A job? You already have a job. What did you say?"

"I said yes. I don't make enough at the bar anyway. I'm going to be a salesgirl. It's perfect."

I point at the piece of foam. "We have to hide it during the day, you know."

"I know. If we move some stuff around, I think it'll fit in the closet."

As we carry it back to our room, the telephone rings. We look at each other. Neither one of us wants to answer it, so we don't.

I sit down on the floor and shove a tall stack of shoe boxes back against the wall with my feet. Rayna puts her hands on top so they don't topple over. There must be a hundred of them.

"Rayna, have you ever asked Buddy why there are so many shoe boxes in here?"

She nods. "All he said was that someone owed him money."

Rayna asks Buddy questions all the time. She doesn't know that it irritates him.

I take the lid off one of the boxes. Inside is a flat, brown Capezio shoe. Size 9. I put that one back and open the box that sits under it. Inside is the exact same shoe.

"Rayna, go open one from that pile." I point at a stack that's a few rows away.

She goes over and opens up a couple of boxes. "They're all the same!" she says. "And they're all ugly."

Rayna knows a lot about shoes, so I believe her.

We turn back to our new twin-size foam pad. We each take an end and lay it down between the shoes. It just fits.

"Perfect," I say.

We flop down on our backs and look up at the ceiling. The foam rubber fills all my hollows. After so many weeks on a hard floor, it feels really nice.

For the first time I'm aware of the radio. A guy is singing about a hot child in the city who's running wild and looking pretty.

"I love this song," Rayna says. She turns the volume up.

While Rayna sings, I change into my nightgown. It has a satin ribbon and an Empire waist. When I wear it,

I feel like I'm a ballet dancer. I try to spin in a circle, but my feet won't turn on the foam pad, so I jump up and down instead. Rayna stops singing and we jump around together. We throw our heads back and laugh.

Boom. Boom. Boom.

We stop jumping and stare blankly at the storage-room door.

Boom. Boom. Boom.

"Did you lock it?" I ask.

Rayna shakes her head. Her eyes are really big.

Together we step back. I feel the shoe boxes at my heels.

There's no place to go. We're trapped.

I stare forward. Frozen.

The doorknob turns. The door opens. In the hallway stands a man. He has a gun. It's pointed at me.

Melanie squeezes past the man with the gun. She fixes her eyes on me. She's mad.

"Where's Buddy?" she asks. Her eyes are wild. Her shrill voice hurts my ears.

"I don't know," I say.

Rayna holds on to my elbow. The man with the gun is a police officer. I can tell by the baton and handcuffs hanging off his wide black belt.

"Melanie! We didn't break in. I swear. Buddy told us we could stay here until we find a place to live. Are we in trouble?"

"Buddy killed Jack!" she screams.

I've heard the words "Dad killed your dog, he was barking too much," "Dad killed your goat, he was knocking down the fences," "Dad killed your bunnies, he was tired of looking at them." But I've never heard the words "Buddy killed Jack" before. They aren't going into my brain right. I think I heard wrong.

I mouth the word "What?" My voice isn't working.

"Jack is dead. Buddy did it. We need to find him."

My bottom lip shakes. I look at our new mattress. "Does this mean we have to leave?"

Melanie puts her hand on my shoulder. "Go back home to Virginia, Kelle."

I lean against Rayna. I close my wet eyes.

"Kelle, there's a roomful of armed police officers waiting outside that door. You have to leave now. And don't come back. Ever."

I open my eyes. I look at Melanie. "I'm from Maryland," I say.

Rayna runs to the closet and throws some things into a suitcase. She pulls at my arm. "Come on, let's go."

I tug at the skirt of my nightgown. "I can't go out like this." Rayna hands me a pair of jeans and a T-shirt. I put them on over my pajamas.

A bunch of reporters and men with television cameras are across the street in front of Nicola's. When we walk out, their camera lights flash in our eyes. I put my head down. Rayna looks right at them.

I take the suitcase out of Rayna's hands. It's better if I carry it. If I keep my body busy, maybe my mind will stay quiet. I'm stronger than Rayna anyway.

We don't talk. We don't have to. We know where we're going.

Back to the Barbizon.

Rayna and I sit side by side on the edge of the television-room couch. It's six o'clock in the morning. My water-stained sneakers seem so far away.

"I'm tired," I say.

Rayna stares out at some speck that only she can see. "Me too."

"I have to get ready for work," I say.

"Me too," Rayna says.

I look at her. She stares back at me. She means her new job.

"Do you believe it?" I ask.

She shakes her head. "Uh-uh."

"Me neither."

We leave the Barbizon. It's cool outside. The sky is blue. The city is washed clean.

"See you after work," Rayna says softly.

I give her a little wave.

A page of the *New York Post* lies on the sidewalk. A black-and-white Buddy looks up at me. People have been stepping on him. Stupid *New York Post*. I crumple the paper up and throw it in a trash can. That's where it belongs, in the trash can with the dog poop. I go *La-la-la* in my brain. That's what I do when I don't want to think about something.

But it's not working.

Snapshotlike visions flash through my brain. Sweet-natured steers that I named even though I wasn't supposed to, returning home in neatly wrapped white paper bundles. Shrieking chickens panicked by the headless mates that went before them. Wild deer tied to a truck top. Frog legs in the freezer. The images spin round and round until finally, like a roulette ball landing on red, the one that haunts me most rolls to the forefront. If the others were snapshots, then this one's a movie. . . .

"Stay behind me," my mother says.

She's riding Frosty. I'm riding Misty. Misty's fluffy white mane blows back in the breeze. I put one hand on my hip and hold the reins with my other. That's what the big girls always do.

I lean my head way back and look straight up at the treetops. Beams of sunlight filter through the leaves. Birds flit and chirp. Squirrels chatter.

"Kelle, keep up," my mother says.

I close my legs around Misty's round stomach. We trot up to Frosty. Misty sticks her nose in Frosty's butt. He swishes his tail.

My mother looks back at me. "Don't let her do that."

I squint my eyes. "Mom, what's that?"

She doesn't look. She's busy tightening Frosty's girth. "I don't know," she says without looking.

Up ahead is a big tree. One of its long branches reaches over the trail. In a couple more steps we'll be under it.

I stop Misty. "Mom!" I scream.

She looks up. She yanks on Frosty's reins. "Turn around," she says.

I can't.

"Now!" she yells.

It's too late. I've seen it.

A small dog. Skinned and hanging from the tree branch. Under it, a puddle of blood.

I stand in front of Healthworks wondering how I got there. Joey waves at me through the window. I start to cry.

ABANDONED

I hand Rayna a *Healthworks* doggie bag. She raises her eyebrows. "Salad and carrot cake," I say.

"At least we're eating well," she says.

"How was work?"

"It went really well. Michael says I'm a natural. The sofas are nice. They sell themselves," she says.

"Well, that's good news."

She rubs her hands together. "I've got more good news."

"You do? What?"

"On the way here I stopped at a coffee shop to get a Coke, and I was telling the waiter about us needing a place to live, and he told me that there was an empty apartment right above the restaurant. The owner of the building isn't renting it because he wants to get every-body out and turn it into a co-op."

I take a bite of carrot cake. It's made with lots of

oil. It's really good. "So how is this good news for us?" I ask her.

"Well. He said we can crash there if we want to. He won't tell anybody."

"Did you go look at it?"

"I didn't have time. He said the bathroom's pretty torn up and the shower doesn't work. But I told him we're used to that."

"Less to clean," I say.

"Want to stop by the Barbizon and get our suitcase first? That way we won't have to get it later."

"Good idea," I say.

We pick up our suitcase, which we stashed in the television room behind a fake curtain.

"Bye-bye, Barbizon," I say as we walk past the doorman. He frowns.

"Kelle, careful. I think he heard you."

By the time we get to the new place, it's dark. The building's front door is held open with a brick. We walk up the stairs to the second floor. The hallway light fixture has so many dead bugs in it, barely any light comes out.

"Which apartment?" I whisper.

"Two C," Rayna says.

This isn't like any apartment building I've ever been in. There's no cooking smells. No television sounds. No light behind the peepholes.

"This is it," Rayna says.

Something's written on the door. I can't tell what it says, though. It's too dark.

Rayna turns the doorknob.

Nothing happens.

I look at Rayna. "Now what?"

"It's not supposed to be locked. Maybe it's just stuck." When she pushes her shoulder against it, the door falls right off its hinges. It lands on the floor with a loud crack. We jump backward.

I hold my hand over my heart. "Oh dear."

"It's open," Rayna says.

"Yes it is," I say.

Rayna stands on the door and runs her hand along the inside wall. "Found it," she says. She flips the switch. It doesn't work.

"Oh dear," I say again.

"Stop saying that," Rayna says in a high voice. She's getting testy.

Inside the apartment a shaft of light comes through what looks to be curtains.

I make my way over to the window. I keep my feet flat like I'm skiing. I learned that from my sister. You just kind of bulldoze things out of the way. It keeps you from falling over stuff.

I pull the curtains back. "That's a little better," I say. My hands feel chalky. I rub them on my pants.

I turn around. All I can see are Rayna's eyes. They glint like cat eyes. "Let's get this door propped up," she says.

We push the door back up against the jamb.

"I have to go to the bathroom," Rayna says.

"I'd hold it if I were you."

"I can go down to the coffee shop."

"You can't leave me here. We don't want them to know we're in here anyway. We can't lock the door."

"I think I can hold it," she says.

"Do you want to go back to the Barbizon?" I ask.

"No. I think the door guy's onto us."

We lay some of our clothes down on the floor. With T-shirts for pillows, we huddle up together.

We face each other.

"What's that smell?" I say.

"I don't smell anything."

"I know that smell. What is it?"

"Night," Rayna says.

It's been a long day. We fall asleep.

I wake up. It's still dark out.

"Rayna, something just touched me."

"Ghosts," she mumbles.

"Rayna. I know what that smell is now."

She nestles her face into the T-shirt.

"Rayna. It's rat poop."

She sits up. "Rat poop? Specifically rat poop?"

"Okay. Rodent poop."

"So it could be a mouse."

"If that makes you feel better."

"Do you think it might bite us?"

"Yes."

"I'm afraid to sleep now."

"Me too."

We sit back-to-back. We can't see the rats. But we can hear them. They're in the Healthworks bag. They're dragging it across the floor. The plastic lid makes a popping sound. They've got the salad container open. While some eat the lettuce, others work on the carrot cake. They pat and claw the tinfoil. Rayna and I lean against each other tightly.

The food must be gone. The rats' claws make little scratching sounds as they run across the wood floor. The room grows quiet. I'm so tired. I fall asleep.

I blink my eyes in the bright morning sun. I don't know where I am. Dust particles lift and spin in the light. I feel Rayna at my back. Her head leans against mine. If I move my head, she'll wake up. I stay still. She needs her sleep.

The Healthworks bag is lying in the corner. A small pile of radish shreddings is next to it. A thick layer of dust covers the floor. Rat trails lead in and out of the room. Some of the trails come right up to Rayna and me. I look down at my feet. There are bite marks on the soles of my shoes. There's a mound of black poop on my T-shirt pillow. Now I have to throw it away.

A fat rat waddles into the room. He's come for the radish shreddings. I kick my foot out at him. He ignores me. I cluck my tongue. Rayna moves her head.

"Rayna?"

"Yeah?"

"Open your eyes."

"Oh . . ." She jumps up to her feet.

I jump up with her. I don't want to be the only one on the floor. The rat scurries away.

The floor is a sea of rat feces, dead bugs, syringes, dried vomit, and who knows what else. I've seen enough.

"Let's get out of here," I say.

We squeeze through the door and take off down the steps. We stand outside looking up at our window.

"We forgot our suitcase," Rayna says.

"Oh, man," I say. "I don't want to go back in there."

"Me neither," she says.

"Let's get it after work. I have an early day today. Meet me here at two."

Rayna sighs. "Looks like we're homeless again."

I smile. "Oh well, less to clean."

As soon as I get off work, I walk to the apartment. Rayna isn't there yet. I sit down on the curb and rest my chin on my hands. I don't want to go in there by myself. My stomach hurts just thinking about it.

"Kelle, come on up."

I turn around. It's Rayna. She's calling me from the apartment window. I can't believe she went up there without me.

The staircase is even scarier during the day. The walls are covered in graffiti. Not the creative kind. The four-letter kind. Maybe Rayna's almost done packing us up. In case she isn't, I walk a little slower. I hope she doesn't let the floor clothes touch the suitcase clothes. She doesn't think about stuff like that.

I squeeze through the hingeless door. Rayna's transistor radio is on. She's singing "Stayin' Alive." She's got a red bandana on her head and a paintbrush in her hand.

She shows me the greenish blue bristles. "Do you like it? Teal's my favorite color," she says.

"I'm going to break a rule here," I say.

Rayna stares at me.

"What the fuck are you doing?"

Rayna smiles. "We can make this work."

I shake my head. "No effing way," I say.

"Stop cursing. It's not attractive."

"I said 'effing.'"

She puts her paintbrush down. "Just listen. We can clean the place up. Look, I already bought us some flashlights." She waves two yellow flashlights around. "We can take sponge baths and wash each other's hair in the coffeeshop sink. Don't be a pantywaist. It'll be an adventure."

"What's a sponge bath?"

"Kelle, come on."

"I don't know, Rayna. What about the rats?"

"We can take turns doing rat duty." She taps her lip with her finger. "Maybe we should get a cat."

I ignore the cat comment. "What about the door?"

"The door is a good thing. If somebody tries to break in, it'll fall over. We have a built-in alarm system."

"This is crazy."

She levels her eyes at me. "The bottom line is, we don't have a choice and you know it. We're going to get caught at the Barbizon. We don't have any money and this is better than the street."

I look at her. I know she's right.

"Home sweet home," I say.

"Just don't go near the bathroom," Rayna says. "Trust me."

I trust her.

She hands me a paintbrush. I look at the walls. Our graffiti artist didn't stop at the hallway. He decorated the apartment, too. Rayna's teal paint covers most of the words. She hasn't gotten to the Kama Sutra–posed stick figures yet.

The paint can sits on today's *New York Times*. Next to a big picture of Melanie is a picture of a girl I've never seen before. She's holding a camera. Her head is tilted back Farrah Fawcett style. She's got a big smile on her face.

I point at the article. "Nice drop cloth," I say.

I stoop down, wipe a glob of paint off the paper with my finger, and tear out the article. I read the headline to myself: POSSIBILITY OF LINK IN 2 DEATHS STUDIED. NEW YORK POLICE FIND CONNECTIONS BETWEEN MODEL KILLED IN A FALL AND A SLAIN RESTAURATEUR.

"Rayna, listen to this. 'At two thirty a.m. last Sunday morning, a twenty-year-old fashion model and a male friend plunged seventeen stories from his apartment balcony on Manhattan's East Side when a metal railing gave way. The women died. About twelve hours later, the beaten and bullet-torn body of a thirty-four-year-old former restaurant owner was found in a wooden crate that had been dumped in a vacant lot in the Bronx and set afire. Miss Corey and Mr. Topper . . .'" I stop. "Isn't his last name Tupper?"

"Typo," Rayna says.

"'Miss Corey and Mr. Topper had lived in the same building at 155 East Eighty-fourth Street on different floors. Miss Corey worked for the My Fair Lady model agency, also located at 155 East Eighty-fourth.'" I look at Rayna. "Oh my gosh. How horrible. They think Buddy had something to do with this!"

"Another paper said My Fair Lady was nothing but a high-priced call-girl operation. They talked about Buddy's luxurious penthouse apartment." Rayna rolls her eyes. "It's not luxurious. I know. I've been there," she says.

"Her poor parents. Did you ever meet her?"

"I saw her picture on Judy's desk. Her name was Cheryl. I think she worked a lot." She pauses. "Hey. I'm going down to the pay phone to call David in a minute. I want to see how Buddy's doing. Maybe David'll let us get our stuff out of the storage room. Want to come?"

"Sure."

She puts her brush down and out we go.

We squish together in the phone booth. I hold my ear up to hers. The phone rings once. David picks up. "Yep," he says.

"Hi, David. It's Rayna. How's Buddy?"

"Oh, hey. I'm glad you called," David says. "Buddy wants to know if you girls would be interested in running the building while he gets things sorted out. I can't do it. I've gotta work at the track, and Doug's back home with our mother. Four C is yours if you want it. Rent-free. It's up to you."

I squeal into my hands.

Rayna keeps her voice calm. "How soon?" she says.

"I'd say a week."

"I guess we'll see you in a week, then."

Rayna hangs up the phone. "How about that!" she says.

"*Oh, Rayna! Can you believe it?*"
We stand in the foyer of our new apartment with our mouths hanging open.

After an exhausting week in our abandoned, rat-infested, half-painted den of iniquity, we're more than ready to enjoy the finer things in life. Topping the list: electricity, running water, and a door that opens and shuts.

"A floral print with a soft-rose-colored background would go so nicely with the brick." Rayna clasps her hands at her chest and smiles.

We've been in the apartment for ten seconds and already Rayna's decorating the place.

We run outside onto the balcony and look down at the street. "We've even got our own balcony," I say. "I feel like such a grown-up."

Two men in business suits walk under us. They stop

and point up at Buddy's apartment. "That's where that murderer lives."

Rayna and I go back inside. We don't say anything about the two men. We don't want to ruin our day.

Rayna opens the refrigerator door and puts a big bottle of Coke inside. She kisses the fridge door. That's how much she loves Coke.

"Buddy told me caffeine stunts your growth," I say.

"I'm done growing," Rayna says.

"I'm not."

"Yes you are."

"No I'm not. You wait and see."

Rayna gets a pencil out of her purse. "Take your shoes off and stand here."

"Okay." I back up against the wall.

"No slouching. That's cheating."

"I'm not slouching."

She holds the pencil on top of my head and makes a little line on the wall. She writes "August 1978" across from it. She taps the date with her pencil point. "We'll measure you again in six months."

"Let's go check out the bedroom."

We walk down a short hall and into the bedroom. Rayna's eyes lock on the curtainless window. She mumbles and counts on her fingers. She's doing curtain math. I can tell.

I open the closet door. "Oh, look. David brought all our stuff up for us."

I pull out the foam mattress and lay it across the floor. We sit down on it. Right across from the bedroom is the bathroom. I lie back on the mattress. "No more sponge baths," I say.

"Hallelujah," Rayna says.

There's a loud knock at the door. Rayna and I jump to our feet. My blood pumps so hard my ears ring. We look at each other. I tiptoe over to the door and look through the peephole.

"It's a girl," I whisper to Rayna.

"Say something," Rayna whispers back.

"Hello?" I say.

"Hi. I'm your neighbor. I live across the hall," the girl says.

I open the door.

"Hi," she says. "My name is Donna." Donna has long, curly hair and a face full of freckles.

"Hi, Donna. I'm Kelle. This is Rayna. Want to come in?"

Donna nods and walks into our foyer.

I point at our empty living room. "Sorry there's nothing to sit on. We don't have any furniture."

She looks around the apartment. When she blinks, her eyes stay shut for longer than they should. Little crinkles form in the corners of her eyes. She looks like she's in pain, like she's got a butter burn. That's what my mother calls her cooking burns. Butter burns.

Donna holds a small box out for me to take. "I want you two to have this."

"You brought us a housewarming present?"

"No. Not really. It's just something I don't need anymore. I saw your suitcase. Figured you were the new girls." She looks over at the wall. Her eyes linger on my height chart. She sighs. "I don't know."

She seems so sad. Her neck has a bunch of big red splotches on it.

"Are you okay?" I ask.

"Yeah. My boyfriend, Ted, doesn't think I'm safe here. I'm moving back home in the morning. Looks like I'm going to get married, move to Connecticut, and have babies." She looks down at her feet. "Just like my mother did."

My stomach hurts for her.

She presses the box into my hands. "Ted gave me this. Now that I'm moving, there's no reason to keep it. Don't tell anybody where you got it, though. If anybody found out, he'd get in big trouble. He's a police officer."

I push the box back at her. "It's not a gun, is it?"

"It's a tear gas gun," she says.

"Oh," I say.

It's not a gun gun. How bad could it be? I take it.

"Well, I gotta go finish packing. Good luck. I hope things go well for you guys."

"Thanks, Donna. You too."

As the door swings shut, she catches it. She runs her fingers over its combination-lock buttons. "One more thing," she says. "Don't trust this. Every door in the building uses the exact same numbers. Buddy won't let you change it either, so don't bother asking." She looks down at the gun box. "You can't be too careful," she says.

She sighs and turns away.

"Bye, Donna. Thanks." As soon as she's back in her apartment, I close the door.

Rayna and I sit down on the living-room floor. The box sits between us.

"Open it," Rayna says.

I'm afraid to shake the box around too much. I don't know if the safety is on. I slowly take the lid off. Rayna rocks forward and looks into the box.

"There she is," I say.

"She" is a small four-by-three-inch Mondial tear gas gun. No fuss. Just form. I pick it up.

"And she's a beauty," I say.

Rayna scooches back. She doesn't want to get too close.

I hold it out to her. She leans against the rough brick wall. "Watch your shirt," I say. "You might get snags."

I hold the gun flat in the palm of my hand. I raise my hand up and down. "You gotta feel this. It's like expensive silverware. Weighty. Well balanced. It's amazing." The silverware part gets Rayna's attention. She leans forward.

Stamped into the steel barrel is a five-pointed star with tiny, round bullets at the ends of its points. I like that. It shows creativity.

I hold up a little plastic container.

"What's that?" Rayna asks.

"That would be our ammunition." I read the orange label that holds the container closed: TEAR GAS CARTRIDGES. CAL. .22. MADE IN GERMANY.

I tear the label off the container and open it up. I pick out one of the small, pellet-size bullets. "Let's try it out."

Rayna puts her hand up over her mouth. "I don't think that's a good idea," she says through her fingers.

"Come on, Reindeer. What good is it if we don't know how to use it?"

She smiles. "Reindeer?"

"I just came up with that." I'm very proud of myself. I'm good at coming up with nicknames.

"I like that," Rayna says.

I knew she would.

"Come on," I say.

Rayna follows me into the bedroom. I open the window just enough for the barrel of the gun to fit through. I put the bullet in the magazine and slide it into the chamber.

"Ready?"

Rayna nods her head up and down.

I take off the safety. "Here goes nothing!"

I stick the gun barrel out the window. I pull the trigger. *BANG!* It's loud. Earplug loud. My ears ring.

Right outside our window is a thick cloud of tear gas smoke. I slam the window shut.

Rayna throws herself down on the floor.

"Rayna, what are you doing?"

"Hiding."

"Rayna, come here."

She crawls over to the window and peeks up over the windowsill. The cloud is almost gone. If you didn't know someone just shot off a military-issue tear gas gun, you wouldn't even notice it. You'd think it was steam or something. We look down at the street. It's empty.

"If the police don't come in the next hour, we should be okay," I say.

Rayna looks down at her watch. "Well, that was the longest hour of my life," she says.

She pulls the handle on a frosty metal ice tray. The cubes break loose. They crackle and pop. She picks out a couple and plops them into a tall glass.

Her hand shakes as she pours out a few glugs of soda. "I found a couple of glasses in the cabinet," she says. Her little pinkie sticks straight up like she's serving tea.

"Want to go outside and sit on the agency's stoop?" I ask.

"Yeah. I'll take my soda with us. Want some?"

I shake my head.

"It'll be nice not having to sneak around anymore," I say.

Rayna goes out to get the elevator while I pour a glass of water.

"Kelle, hurry up. I'm holding the door."

I turn off the faucet and hurry out to meet her.

The elevator is really tiny. Rayna and I stand shoulder to shoulder, holding our glasses with both hands. Her pinkies stick out like meerkat tails. The elevator stops at the third floor. A guy steps in.

"Did you guys hear that loud bang earlier?" he asks.

I look at Rayna. She looks at me. We shake our heads. If we don't answer out loud, it's not lying.

The elevator door opens. The guy lets us out first. We push our heads together and giggle as we rush out the lobby door. We sit down on the stoop. The sun is going down. The sky is gold. The air is warm. Little breezes lift and ripple my shirtsleeves. I lean back and close my eyes.

"I haven't seen you two before. Are you new to the building?"

I open my eyes. A nice-looking man in a dark blue suit is talking to Rayna. His hair is blond and neatly cut. His eyes are blue. He's got dimples. He's gorgeous.

"We just moved in today," Rayna says.

"I hear most of the girls moved out."

"Their loss, our gain," Rayna says. Her words are soft and lazy. She leans back on one hand and flicks her hair over her shoulder. She's becoming more Southern by the minute.

"Are you two roommates?"

Rayna nods.

"What's the rent?" he asks.

"Four seventy-five a month."

I wonder why she doesn't tell him we're staying here for free.

"One bedroom or two?"

"One."

He raises his eyebrows. I don't like that.

Rayna talked to him first. She can have him. She's got first dibs anyway. I walk out to the middle of the sidewalk and look at the building. I want to find our balcony. I look up at the fourth floor. Our apartment is on the right. Twirly white wrought-iron railings frame the balcony's floor. It's so pretty. I can't believe it's mine.

"Are you here to model too?" the blond-haired man says.

I think he's talking to me. "Excuse me?" I ask just to be sure.

"Are you here to model too?" he says again.

I can't take my eyes off his dimples.

I decide to forgive him for his raised eyebrows. I walk back and sit down next to Rayna. "Hopefully," I say.

He smiles at me. "Want to go see a movie with me sometime?" he asks.

Rayna presses her elbow into mine.

My heart thumps. I try not to smile. "Sure," I say.

"This Friday?"

"Sure."

"Seven o'clock good?"

"Sure."

"Seven o'clock it is, then." He makes a little bow and winks at us. "Enjoy your night."

As soon as he gets around the corner, I bury my head in my hands. "What have I done? He's got to be at least thirty years old. Why didn't you stop me?"

Rayna laughs. "It's just a date. You're not marrying him."

I make a face. "What if he tries to kiss me?"

"What if he does?" She bumps me with her shoulder. "He's an attorney, you know. And he's cuter than a speckled pup in a red wagon. You got yourself a good one."

A long shadow takes the spark out of Rayna's bright green eyes. At the foot of the shadow are two men. One is tall and thin. The other is small and round. They walk up to us. The round one flips open his wallet and holds it out for us to see. He's a police officer.

Rayna and I shrink back. Someone must have seen the tear gas cloud. They're going to take us away. The new apartment was too good to be true. I knew it wouldn't last. Good things never do. That's why you have to remember them. It keeps them alive in your head.

"Were you girls here the night of the murder?" one of the detectives asks.

We nod.

"We have a few questions to ask you."

I take in a deep breath. We're not in trouble. I'm so relieved.

One of the detectives takes Rayna inside the building. I hear the elevator door open. I think they're going up to our apartment. The other one sits down with me on the stoop. I feel hot. The wind blows. A paper cup bumps up against the agency's front door.

"What apartment do you live in?"

"Four C."

"Four C? You live in four C?"

I nod.

He swipes his hand across his forehead. "How long?"

"We moved in today."

He looks up at the sky.

There's a long pause. I think he's done. I think he's going to go away. Why does so much have to happen in one day? I can't keep up with it all.

He looks at me. "I've seen you before."

A veiny patch of red covers the bridge of his nose, stretching out across his cheeks. His eyes widen. "The night of the murder. You were in the storage room."

I wonder where he keeps his gun. If I opened his jacket, would I find it there, strapped against his chest?

"We called Buddy's brother David. He said we could move into four C," I say.

"David is Buddy's son."

My heart pounds unevenly. "And Doug?"

"Doug, too," he says.

A cab drives by. Its tires throw out a spray of gutter water.

Air comes into my lungs in ragged breaths.

Buddy lied to me.

Why?

The detective's eyes grow soft. He's not a bad man. He's just doing his job. Buddy's lies aren't his fault.

"So Buddy's not thirty-four?"

"No. He's close to fifty."

I look over at Nicola's. "Is he Italian?"

"No. He's Jewish. Jacobson is a Jewish name."

I didn't know that.

A young girl walks by dragging a little chrysanthemum-faced black-and-white shih tzu. The dog lifts his leg on the agency stoop. The girl doesn't notice. The leash snaps against his collar. He almost falls over. He finds his feet and trots off behind her. The girl's ponytail swings back and forth.

The detective folds his hands in his lap. He taps his thumbs together. He clears his throat. "Have you heard the name Cheryl Corey?"

"The girl who fell from the balcony?"

He looks down at his thumbs for a second. "She lived in four C."

I stand up. I want to walk now. I want to take a nice long walk. I look at the detective and sit down.

Now I know why Donna was all blinky eyed.

I hope the apartment isn't jinxed. I look at my water glass. I want a new one now.

"What can you tell me about the day of the murder?"

"What?" I say.

"The day of the murder. What did you do?"

A ladybug crawls across the brick step. She lifts her wings and flies away. I didn't know Manhattan had ladybugs. Maybe she came in on somebody's car. From Long Island or something.

I turn my unfocused eyes on the detective. There's the detective, a band of light around him, and then darkness. I think I'm going to pass out. I'm sweating. I never sweat.

"Do?" I say. "Ummmm . . ."

My head rocks back like a newborn baby's. "I don't remember." I feel prickly and nauseous.

The detective takes me by the elbow and leads me to the elevator. He pushes the button. "I'll come back another time."

I turn my head in the direction of his voice. "Why can't I remember anything?" I say softly. My words echo in my head.

"You've had a shock. It's normal."

The elevator door opens. I get in. I stare at the floor buttons. I can't remember what floor I live on. The detective leans in and pushes four.

"I'll come back another time," he says.

"*Joey gave me a big thing* of salad if you want any," I say to Rayna as I walk into our apartment.

"You better hurry your butt up. Brant is meeting you out front in a half hour," she says.

I shake my head. "I can't believe I forgot to ask his name. How ridiculous is that?"

Rayna waves her hand at me. "Shoo," she says.

"Yes, ma'am."

I neaten up my hair, put a smear of pink blush on the apples of my cheeks, and roll some cherry-flavored gloss across my lips. I walk out into the living room.

Rayna looks at me. "No ponytail," she says. "You look like you're twelve years old."

I pull the rubber band off. My hair falls down around my shoulders.

Rayna frowns. "Go get me a brush and hair spray. Your hair looks like a cat's been sucking on it."

She brushes my hair in long, even strokes. My head feels all tingly. She turns me around.

"Spray," she says, like a surgeon to an operating room nurse. Rayna takes hair styling very seriously.

I hand her the can of hair spray. "Don't make it all poofy," I say.

"Close your eyes," she says.

I close my eyes.

She waves the bright pink can all around my head. A plane couldn't land in this kind of fog. I hold my breath. Aqua Net is the worst.

"Is there anything left in there?" I ask when she's finished.

"You need powder."

She takes her compact out of her purse, pops it open, and dabs the soft, powder-caked pad all over my face.

"Look up."

I look up at the ceiling while she works on the important under-eye area. "Rayna, there's gum stuck on the ceiling. It's pink. I think it's Bazooka."

"Uhhh-huh," she says. When Rayna's got makeup in her hand, there's no distracting her. She rubs my cheeks with her thumb. "You didn't blend your blush. We've talked about this."

"Promise me you're not going to lick your finger," I say.

"That's much better," she says. "You look pretty."

I'm all ready. It's time to go.

I sit down on the floor.

I don't want to go out with an attorney whose name I just learned a few minutes ago. I want to stay here with Rayna. She brushes my hair and blends my blush and tells me that I look pretty.

"How was work?" I say.

Rayna smiles. She knows I'm stalling. "Work was good," she says. "As a matter of fact, I made enough extra commission money to buy a trundle bed for us today. It's a floor sample. Michael gave me a great deal on it."

"We're going to have a real bed!" I clap my hands. "When?"

"Tonight. Mario's squeezing it in between his other deliveries."

"Rayna?"

"Yeah?"

"I don't make enough money to help pay for it. I feel bad."

She stares at me. Her green eyes widen. She's not looking at my makeup anymore. She's looking at me. The inside me. "I'm not keeping score. Are you?" she asks.

I shake my head and smile.

She goes into the bedroom and comes out with my cowboy boots. The ones with the tall heels that I can barely walk in. "Put these on. They'll make your legs look nice and long," she says.

I've learned not to argue. I put them on.

"Perfect," she says. She's so happy for me.

I think about what she said about not keeping score.

I don't know what it's like not to have a score. There's always been a score for me.

"I keep a roof over your head, now get your ass up. We're going to clear rocks from the top five acres. Don't look at me that way, I'll knock your fucking teeth down your throat." I can barely see. There's too much sand in my eyes. I'm five years old. I want to ask if I can change out of my pajamas, but I'm too afraid. My father might knock my teeth out. The sun hasn't come up yet. I get up and throw rocks onto the back of a flatbed truck in my pj's for the next six hours. We all do. Even my sister. My father likes to pretend that she can see. He doesn't believe in weakness.

"Have fun tonight. Don't do anything I wouldn't do," Rayna says.

My heart goes *thump*. I sit back down on the floor. "I'm scared," I say.

She takes my hands and pulls me to my feet. "I'll wait up for you."

I can tell she wants to hug me, but she doesn't. She knows I don't like to be touched. A flat-handed whack, a hard-knuckled backhand, a head-snapping shove, a bare-bottom beating, that's what touching means to me.

I look up and study the gum on the ceiling. I wonder how it got there. I wonder how we're going to get it down. I look at Rayna. I have to go. I know I do. I said I would and I always keep my word. "A man without his word is nothing." That's what my father always says. And he should know, he's a marine. At least, he said he was.

I go outside and wait for Brant to come get me. I see him walking down the sidewalk. He's wearing khaki pants and a light blue button-down shirt. With a jerk of his head he tosses back his silky blond hair and grins. A pencil-skirted woman trots by. She looks Brant up and down. She smiles at him. He doesn't notice. He's looking at me. I'm glad Rayna fixed my hair.

"Hi," he says. "Ready to go?"

I look up at him and nod. He's really tall.

"What are we seeing?" I ask. I hope he says *Grease*. Rayna saw it and said it's really good.

"*Animal House*," he says.

I don't know anything about it. I like the title, though. I wonder if it's about talking animals or something.

The ticket line is long. Two ladies stand in front of us. One whispers into her friend's ear. The friend turns and smiles at Brant. He turns around and faces me.

"Your hair looks pretty like that. You look really nice."

"Thanks." My face gets hot. I look down at my feet. I want to tell him that he looks nice too, but he might think I'm only saying it because he did. I'll try to fit it in later.

He's such a gentleman. He pays for everything. The tickets, the sodas, the Milk Duds, the big box of buttered popcorn. My arms are full of good things. I'm so happy.

We walk inside the theater and sit down. The lights dim. The movie starts. There's a long shot of a blue-blooded college campus. Regal-sounding music plays. I take a bite of popcorn. All of a sudden a mannequin's twisted torso crashes through a frat house window. A scruffy-looking guy urinates on the sidewalk. I swallow my bite of popcorn. Brant slaps his leg and laughs. Guys talk about porking girls. They break out ribbon-wrapped rubber penises. I wipe the butter off my fingers. Novel-writing professors get high on pot. A guy named Bluto punches his mashed-potato-filled face with his fists. Food sprays out of his mouth onto everybody. "I'm a zit. Get it?" he says. I want to go home. I look over at Brant. He's shaking. Tears are pouring down his face. I hold my buttery napkin like a blankie. Girls wearing rubber gloves sit in parked cars with their boyfriends, complaining about their tired arms. My neck hurts. A horse has a heart attack and dies. Brant can barely catch his breath. That's not funny. Men jump around like chimps. Chanting the words, "Toga, toga, toga."

I can't wait for it to be over.

The credits finally roll. Brant looks over at me for the first time since the movie started. "What'd you think? Funny, huh?"

"Yeah," I say.

He grins. He looks like a boy who just got his Slinky to go all the way down the stairs without falling over. "Ready to go?" he asks.

I nod. "Uh-huh."

We leave the theater and turn for home. Brant walks really fast. I have to hurry to keep up. A blister pops on the back of my heel. I pretend it doesn't hurt. Brant is so quiet. I wonder if I did something wrong.

He stops and looks at me. "Want to come up to my apartment?" he asks. "It's right here."

The doorman holds his polishing cloth behind his back and opens the door. Gray hair peeks out from under his stiff, address-embroidered cap. He squeezes the brim. "Evening, sir. Miss," he says.

"Evening, Milt. How are you?" Brant asks.

"Fine, sir. Just fine."

I stare at Milt's fancy gold buttons. They're engraved with his initials. I know because one of the letters is *M*. They're very nice. I bet they were a gift. That's the kind of thing a rich person gives to someone who has to wear a uniform for a living.

Milt's waiting for us now. If I don't go in, I'll embarrass Brant. He paid for the movie. He bought me soda and Milk Duds and that big thing of popcorn. He's been so nice. I don't want to hurt his feelings.

Brant takes my elbow and leads me in toward the elevator. His penny loafers squeak on the black marble floor. Round-faced cherubs dance in a swirl of pale pink ribbons across the lobby's high blue ceiling.

The elevator doors slide open. Brant pushes the tenth-floor button.

"Fourth door on the left," Brant says as we step off the elevator.

He unlocks his door. He flicks on the lights.

"Oh my gosh," I say. "What a view." The far wall of his living room is nothing but floor-to-ceiling windows. I'm afraid I'll get sucked out if I stand too close.

"I'll be right back," Brant says. He puts his keys down on a small silver tray. I sit down on the foyer floor and pull off my boots. I wiggle my toes. My socks are bloody where the blisters rubbed through. I lean my boots against the wall and walk across the living room's springy white carpet. A long row of perfectly plumped pillows line the back of a black leather couch. I sit down on the edge, making sure that I don't lean back. I don't want to mess it up. In front of me is a wide, black lacquer coffee table. On top of it *Esquire, GQ,* and *Sports Illustrated* magazines sit stacked like orderly stair steps.

A framed print of a naked girl hangs on the wall. Her hair is black. Her skin is white. Her bee-stung lips are red. She looks off to the side, holding her thin arms across her full breasts. A narrow black choker circles her neck. It reminds me of a collar.

"Nice, huh?" Brant walks out. He smells like patchouli. "I have another one in my bedroom. Come see it. I just got it." He holds his hand out for me to take.

I don't really care about the picture, but he wants me to see it, so I take his hand and follow him into his bedroom.

The quilt is folded back on his queen-size bed.

Donna Summer sings in the background. I look for the picture, but I don't see it.

"Where is . . ."

Wham. I'm on my back. I don't know how it happened. It takes me a second to realize that it's Brant. He's on top of me. I try to get out from under him, but I can't. He's too heavy.

I push at his shoulders. I think he's joking. "Brant, what are you doing?"

He leans down and kisses me. He pokes his tongue through my open teeth. My first French kiss. I knew I wouldn't like it.

I turn my face to the side. His shirt is damp. His body is hot. I did not leave home for this. "Brant, stop."

He holds my hands down with one hand and unbuttons my blouse with the other. He rocks back and forth against me. His sweat drips down on my bare skin. It rolls down my side and off onto the sheets. He shuts his eyes. "You're so fucking hot," he says.

He's lying. I'm not hot. Nothing about me is hot. He's crazy. And crazy men are like crazy horses. All you can do is try to get away from them before they hurt you.

He bites my earlobe. I look down at my open blouse and try not to cry. This is all my fault. I'm so stupid. He drags his teeth down my neck. He bites my breast. I bite my lip. I'm out of air. Think. Breathe. Think. Breathe. Air in. Air out. I get one hand free. I want to kill him. If I can't kill him, I'll blind him. He's gonna know he was in a fight. I poke my thumb into the corner of his eye socket. I'm too slow. He catches my wrist. He's mad now. If he knew what I was trying to do, he'd be madder. He grabs my hips and flips me over onto my stomach.

He can't do that. He can't do that. The words bang around in my brain.

If I'm on my stomach, I can't fight back. He hasn't pinned me down yet. I throw my head backward. My skull smashes into the bridge of his nose. He lets me go. I roll onto my side and jam both of my feet into his stomach. I have strong legs. I'm a horse girl. He doubles over. I jump off the bed. He grabs my hair. He pushes me down onto my knees. I look down at his shoes. Folded-hundred-dollar-bill eyes stare up at me from their penny loafer prisons.

He unzips his pants and shoves my face against him. Keeping an even pressure, I slowly lower my head.

"Now you're catching on," he says. "A little Woman 101 always does the trick."

Woman 101. I'll bite it off, bastard, I think to myself.

I take in a deep breath. And then, using the top of my head like a battering ram, I drive my skull up against him. He yelps like a tied-off dog.

He drops down onto the floor. His face is red. He holds his stomach, and pants through his slack, O-shaped mouth. His shirt is wet with sweat. He smells. He just got his ass kicked by a hundred-pound girl.

I don't know what I ever saw in him.

I step off the elevator. Rayna opens our door. "I heard the ding," she says. "How'd it go?"

I walk into the apartment. I roll my eyes. "I got myself a good one, all right," I say.

"What happened?" she asks.

I tell her.

She puts her hand up over her mouth. "Should I call the police?"

I shake my head. "No."

I look up at the pink, peanut-shaped gum on the ceiling. If we draw on a top hat and walking stick, we can leave it there and call it Mrs. Peanut.

"I need a drink," Rayna says. She pours herself a big glass of Coke. She moves the glass around in quick circles. The soda spins like a whirlpool.

"I'm going to get ready for bed," I say.

Rayna takes a sip of soda. She rubs her nose. "Woo, bubbles got me," she says.

She puts her drink down and follows me into the bedroom.

A softly glowing lamp sits on an overturned milk crate. Two twin beds, one slightly lower than the other, sit next to it.

"Oh my gosh, the bed! I completely forgot about it," I say.

Rainbow-colored butterflies float across bright yellow sheets. Matching curtains hang in the window. It's a little girl's dream. I don't say that, though. I don't think that was Rayna's goal.

We sit down. The mattress is thick and springy. I bounce up and down a little.

"Very comfy," I say.

Rayna looks at me. "I'm sorry about tonight," she says.

"It's okay." My bottom lip shakes.

"Every path has some puddles," she says.

I look at her. "I don't know what I'd do without you."

She wipes my wet eyes with the underside of her sleeve.

"I'm making my own puddles," I say.

"Hey," she says. "You're one of the strongest people I've ever met. You should be really proud of yourself."

I trace an indigo butterfly wing with my finger. Pride

is bad. It attracts attention and causes trouble. At least, it does where my father is concerned.

"You ride in the back of the van with the horses," my father says. He likes to put me in my place. He doesn't know I like riding with the horses.

I run up the steep ramp. I don't fall. I know how to do it now. My father slides the ramp up. I look at him with my best blank face.

"What are you staring at?"

If I don't look at him, it's disrespectful. If I look at him, it's disrespectful. There's a right thing to do. There must be. I just haven't figured it out yet.

I look down at my feet.

"Look at me when I'm talking to you." He hooks one of his thumbs over his belt.

"Yes, sir."

"You think you're hot shit, don't you?"

"No, sir."

"Excuse me?"

"No, sir."

He stares at me. It hurts to look at him. I blink.

"You little shit. I hope you lose. I hope you and your fucking little pony lose today. That would serve you right. Arrogant bitch."

He slams the van door.

I look at the closed door. I push my teeth together. I'm a good rider. Everybody says so. He can't take that away from me with his bad thoughts and bad wishes. I won't let him. I walk over to Cricket. His legs are spread wide. My father takes the turns too fast. I whisper in Cricket's ear, "Help me, Cricket." I scratch his neck. He leans into the rub. He's my best friend. I'd do anything for him.

The next day I come home from school and Cricket is gone. My father sold him. Bob says he got five thousand dollars for him. That's a lot of money for a little black pony named Cricket. He was a good pony. He was a good friend. I guess he's going to be somebody else's friend now.

I go out into the big field behind the barn. I run and I run. My muscles hurt. My heart pumps into my throat. My breath comes out in ragged gasps. By the time I get back home, I'm too tired to say what I want to. It's almost dark. It's suppertime. My mother's eyes are puffy and red. She won't look at me. My father lifts his chin and looks me straight in the eyes. I know he wants me to say something. Then he could throw things around and blame me for what he did.

You don't do that.

You don't sell someone's best friend.

I want to say, "I hate you. I'm going to knock your fucking teeth down your throat," but I'm too young to aim words at people the way my father does. If they came true, I might get in trouble for it. So I pick up a fried chicken leg and eat that instead.

• • •

Early the next morning there's a knock at the door. It's the detective who tried to interview me the other day. There's no place to sit, so we stand on opposite sides of the kitchen counter. He asks me questions about where I was the day of the murder. This time I remember the answers. I wonder why I couldn't before. It's like I have a brain curtain that opens and closes whenever it feels like it. Maybe I have lots of brain curtains, one for every bad thing that's ever happened to me. I wonder if other people have them too.

The detective undoes the metal clasp of a big manila envelope. One half of the clasp breaks off. He leaves it on the counter. I pick it up and throw it away. He shows me an eight-by-ten photo of a dirty-looking, dark-haired guy.

"Have you ever seen this man?"

I shake my head no. He shows me more photos of men I've never seen before. At least, I don't think I've ever seen them. I want to tell the detective about my brain curtains, but I don't think he'd understand.

"Last thing," the detective says.

He lays a clipped stack of papers down on the counter. He slides the packet over in front of me. I see the word "autopsy." I push it back at him with the back of my fingernail. A coroner with autopsy hands might have touched it.

"Do I have to?" I ask.

He looks at me. His eyes droop down in the corners. I think he knows he just stepped over some invisible interview line.

He picks his papers up and puts them back into the envelope. He fastens it closed with what's left of the clasp. "Thank you for your time," he says.

I walk him to the door. "Sorry I couldn't be more help," I say.

And I really mean it. Maybe if I recognized one of those men's faces, the charges would be dropped and Buddy would get out of jail.

Buddy would love me forever if I could do something like that.

I get up off the bed and look out the bedroom window. "We should hose the front sidewalk today," I say.

"I'll do it while you're at your meeting with William Schuller," Rayna says.

I plop back down on the bed. Rayna puts her romance novel down. "You're as wiggly as a worm in a bait bucket," she says.

"I'm so nervous. What if they don't like me?"

"They'll like you."

I pull my hair up into a ponytail.

Rayna picks her book back up. "Go do something," she says.

"Am I bugging you?"

"Yes."

I laugh. For some reason that's funny to me.

I put my sneakers on. William Schuller is a children's

talent agency. I don't have to pretend I'm tall anymore.

"I'll be back in a few hours."

"Good luck," Rayna says. "You're going to do great."

On the way out of the building I decide to hose the sidewalk down myself. I've got time. I grab the hose and give everything a good spray. A bright red leaf blows onto my clean area. The days are getting shorter. Fall is coming. Back home Muffet's coat will be getting fuzzy.

If she's still alive, that is.

I walk over to Fifth Avenue. Central Park is on my right. I've walked alongside it a bunch of times, but I've never walked through it. I don't feel like I belong there. I'm not a tourist. I don't get a lot of blisters anymore. But I'm not a native, either. Even though I follow all of Vince's rules, people can tell I'm not a real New Yorker. They look at me like, *You can try, but you'll never be one of us.*

A teenage boy slides his hand into his girlfriend's back pocket. She leans against him and laughs. They walk into the park. I take it as a sign and follow them in.

It's cool under the tall trees. I zip my jacket up. The metal zipper rubs my chin. Beams of light filter through the leafy canopy. The air smells like leather and fireplace wood.

I hope Muffet forgives me.

I stop in front of a big bronze sculpture of a young girl. It's Alice in Wonderland. She sits on top of a giant, lopsided mushroom. Her long, thin arms float out like ballerina arms over a tutu. The White Rabbit stands on her right. The Mad Hatter, on her left. A cookie-nibbling Dormouse sits below her. The Cheshire Cat is there too. He bugs me. I don't like how he comes and goes whenever he feels like it.

Parents sit nearby. Reading. Gossiping. Staring off into space. They don't seem to care that their kids are climbing all over the sculpture, scaling the White Rabbit's waistcoat, tugging the Dormouse's tail, sitting on top of the Cheshire Cat's head.

Yellow-, orange-, and red-leaved trees rustle in the wind. A young girl sits in Alice's lap reading a book. Using the Mad Hatter's oversized nose as a step, her little brother climbs up to her. He picks up a small yellow leaf and draws it across her chin. With her eyes still on the page, she swats him away. "Mom, he's touching me," she yells.

The boy climbs down onto the ground, puts his hands on his hips, and studies the Mad Hatter's face. He pulls his lips back with his palms and grins, perfectly mimicking the Hatter's loopy, mercury-addled expression.

I walk over and touch the Rabbit's shiny pocket watch. It's smooth and cool, like the afternoon air. Their imaginations on overdrive, the children climb around me.

I leave Alice and head toward a big oval pond. The shimmering, concrete-rimmed water reflects the bright midday sun. Model boats sail across the water's surface, their white sails tacking against the breeze. A miniature motorboat drifts against the water's edge. *Bump. Bump.* It rocks against the coping. A great willow leans over the water. Its long, whip-thin branches murmur and sway in the gently blowing breeze.

I sit down on a bench. Next to me is a boy. He's wearing thick, black-rimmed glasses that won't stay up on his nose. He holds a pair of binoculars in his lap.

Down by the water a little girl points at a bright red boat. She lifts up on her toes and claps her hands. "Boat, boat!" she squeals. Her father picks her up. She wraps her arms around his head and presses her rosy cheek against his. His eyes shine.

Five round-bellied birds totter around at my feet. One pecks my sneaker. When I snatch my foot away, he looks surprised. He turns and wobbles off. He looks unsteady. Come to think of it, so do his friends. I hope they're not sick.

"They're drunk," the boy says.

I look at him. "What?"

"They're drunk."

"Who would do that?"

"They eat fermenting berries and get drunk."

"Oh," I say.

He pushes his glasses back up with his index finger. "Don't worry. They'll sober up soon."

One of the birds falls over. He looks around like somebody just pushed him.

"How old are you?" the boy asks me.

"Sixteen. You?"

"Thirteen."

I realize that "How old are you?" is to kids what "What do you do?" is to grown-ups. It's a conversation starter.

The boy hands me his binoculars. "Look." He points at a low-hanging oak tree branch.

I look. A small royal blue bird with large black eyes peeks out from the leaves.

"Oh my gosh. It's so beautiful! Is that a—"

"It's an eastern bluebird."

"I've always wanted to see one! *The Blue Bird* is my favorite movie!" I say.

"Mine too," the boy says.

I look at him. "Really?!"

He smiles. "It's called *The Blue Bird*. I love birds," he says.

The bird flies away. "Bye, little bluebird," I say.

I hand the binoculars back to the boy. "Thanks."

I look down at my watch. "Oh no! I'm going to be late. I've got to go."

"Maybe I'll see you again. I come here all the time," the boy says.

"I hope so," I say. "Thanks again. Bye."

I can't be late. I can't be late, I say to myself.

I learned a long time ago what can happen if I am.

• • •

"We're leaving for the carnival at five sharp. Don't be late," my father says to me.

I wash up and change out of my barn clothes. I open the front door and walk outside. The station wagon sits in front of the house. I hurry over to it. Everybody is in the car. The engine is running. I reach for the door. My fingers curl around the handle. My father floors the engine. The car lurches forward, wheels spinning in the gravel. Pea-size rocks pelt my bare legs. I run after the car. "Dad, stop. I'm here." Bob looks at me from the car's backward-facing seat. He shakes his head. I stop running. It wasn't an accident. It was on purpose. I look down at my watch. It's five minutes after five. I was late. When my father says five, he means five.

An older black woman sits behind the agency's reception desk. Her phone buzzes. She picks it up. She smiles at me. "Kelle, Ron will see you now. Go right in."

I close my church-steeple fingers and take a deep breath.

"Good luck," she says. Her eyes are warm and encouraging.

I walk into Ron's office. He stands up and reaches out his hand.

"Hi, Kelle. I'm Ron."

I give his hand a nice firm shake. My hands are strong from riding horses.

"Have a seat," he says.

I hand him my little album of snapshots and sit down opposite him on an oversized leather chair. The back of it curves around my head like racehorse blinkers.

He hands the album back to me. "I'd like to talk to your mother, Kelle. Is she in the waiting room?"

I shake my head.

"Where is she?"

"Maryland."

He wrinkles up his forehead.

"But I live here in the city," I say.

"Oh. Parents not together?" he asks.

They sure as heck shouldn't be, I think. "Uh-huh," I say. I'll tell him the truth later. I don't want him to think I'm an unreliable runaway or something.

"The agency books print and television commercials. We're one of the top children's agencies in town. I like you, Kelle. You've got a very commercial look. I'd love to have you as a client. Would you like that?"

"I would love that!" I say a little bit too loudly. *Act professional,* I tell myself.

A little plastic chicken sits on Ron's desk. I push its bottom down. A bright green gumball drops out. It rolls across the desk. I look at Ron. He smiles.

"You can have it."

I put it in my pocket for later. I like that chicken. I want one.

"Iris will give you some paperwork for your father to sign. I'll be out in a minute," Ron says.

I walk out to Iris's desk.

She hands me a stack of official-looking papers. "Welcome to the agency," she says.

Ron comes out of his office. He hands me a slip of paper. "You'll need head shots right away. This photographer is really good. It'll cost a few hundred dollars. But he's worth it. Bring me the contact sheets before you order anything, though."

A few hundred dollars. My mouth goes dry. I swallow. Where am I going to get that kind of money?

"Okay," I say.

"An acting class would be a good idea too. The more prepared you are, the better."

I nod.

Iris looks at me. I think she can tell I'm making stuff up. She has that see-right-through-you mother's stare.

"In the meantime, a photographer just called about a print ad he's shooting. Are you ready for your first go-see?"

"Me? Yes!"

"Great," he says. "By the way, how old are you?"

"Sixteen."

He tilts his head to the side. "Really?"

I nod. I can't tell if that was good news or bad news.

"If the photographer asks how old you are, tell him thirteen." He shakes his head and smiles. "Sixteen, huh? You're going to be a very busy girl."

My first go-see is for a Kiss jacket ad. I wonder if Gene Simmons will be there. I hope so. I want to see his tongue.

I look down at my watch. I could use some perfume. Bloomingdale's is close. I have just enough time to stop and get some.

Black-white-and-gold Bloomingdale's reminds me of a great big layer cake. Behind its thick plate-glass windows vacant-eyed mannequins show off the latest fashions. I pretend I'm Marlo Thomas in *That Girl* and one of them is winking at me. I want to be That Girl. Except I don't want to do temp work and I don't want such a goofy boyfriend.

A long row of flags hang limp over the main-entrance awning. A group of tourists stand in the doorway taking pictures and pointing up at stuff.

"Excuse me, can I get by, please?" I say.

One of the tourists reaches out and touches my shoulder. "Oh, for goodness' sakes, of course, darlin'." She fans her hand at one of her friends. "Betty, move on over so this nice little girl can get herself in the store."

Betty moves over. I squeeze through.

As the door closes, I hear her say, "Where is that child's mother?"

The fragrance counter woman is tall, with sleek brown hair and wire-thin lips. She looks over her glasses at me. "May I help you?" she says.

"No thank you. I'm just looking."

She pinches up her mouth. If she saw what she looks like when she does that, she wouldn't do it anymore.

I look at the big tray of tester bottles. I pick up the red Opium bottle, hold it in front of my nose, and take a little sniff. It smells spicy. I think it's very womanly. The fragrance woman looks up from her sorting. She gives me a dirty look. She doesn't approve. I put the bottle back down on the tray and pick up the Anaïs Anaïs.

She waves a little sliver of paper at me. "Use this for testing, please," she says.

"Okay."

I spray it, swish it, and put it in my pocket. I can rub it on my wrists later. It'll make a nice little pick-me-up. The fragrance woman holds out her hand for the bottle. I pretend that I don't see her.

I pull my pant legs up as high as they'll go and spray my knee pits and ankles. After that I do my wrists, my throat, the crooks of my arms, and behind my ears. I don't want to miss any of my pulse points. Anaïs Anaïs doesn't last that long.

I put the bottle back down on the tray.

"Thank you," I say.

The fragrance woman pulls her nose up in a lopsided sneer.

I walk back outside smelling baby-powder sweet, wondering why anyone would ever actually buy perfume when there's such a thing as tester bottles.

I get to my go-see five minutes early. It's at a small brownstone advertising agency on the Upper East Side. As I'm walking in, a young girl with bouncy red hair walks out. She's got big green eyes and freckly cheeks.

A woman leans against a lamppost at the bottom of the agency steps.

"All done, Mom," the freckle-faced girl calls out.

"How'd it go?"

"Great. The photographer really liked my book. I think I'm going to book it. He said he'd let Ford know by the end of the day."

Of course. She's with Ford. I lean my head against the open door and sigh.

The mother smiles. "We better hurry or we'll be late for your Penney's shoot."

The girl takes her mother's hand and they walk away, swinging their arms back and forth, laughing.

I close my eyes. I wish I had a mother who waited

outside brownstones and held my hand between go-sees.

"Shut the door, please," a man says.

I turn around. "Sorry," I say.

He reaches out his hand. But when I go to shake it, he pulls it away.

"Your photos." He points at my little snapshot album. "Is your name Lloyd? Are you the photographer?"

"Uh-huh."

He quickly flips through my pictures and hands them back to me.

"Is that it?" I say.

He looks at me. "That's it."

He sticks his hands in his pockets and walks back down the hall.

I shake my head. I didn't even make it past the waiting room. I'm going to serve salads forever.

When I get home, Rayna is waiting for me. She jumps up off the floor.

"Kelle, did you call your service?"

"No. Why?"

"Your agency just called. You booked the job."

"What?"

"You booked the job!"

"Oh my gosh. Oh my gosh."

We jump up and down, laughing and squealing. The downstairs neighbor takes a broom handle to our floor. We freeze. Rayna puts her hand over her mouth and giggles.

I'm looking for 40 Fifth Avenue. Lloyd said it's between Tenth and Eleventh Streets, not far from Washington Square Park. It's late. It's dark. I'm all alone. My eyes shift back and forth between the bug-haloed streetlights and my building-number countdown.

When Lloyd told me he lived on Fifth Avenue, I was very impressed.

"Kelle," he said. "Why don't you come over tonight? I'll cook for you."

"Where do you live?" I asked.

"40 Fifth Avenue."

"45th, what avenue?"

"Fifth Avenue."

"45th, Fifth Avenue?"

Instead of "Who's on First?" it was "Who's on Fifth?" Lloyd shook his head.

"No, the street number is forty. The avenue is Fifth."

I laughed. "Sorry."

"Happens all the time," he said.

I look up at Lloyd's building. A streetlamp casts its shadowy light against the building's dull, cement-colored walls. Sooty black stains ooze down the building's sides like infected wounds. Its narrow windows are dark and gloomy. It's not the Fifth Avenue I expected. I expected fresh paint, hunter green awnings, and nicely dressed doormen who tip their hats and say "Good day" or "Good evening" when you walk by them.

Inside, a thick, padlocked chain stretches between the handles of the building's two front doors. Over in the corner of the small lobby an elderly black man sleeps in an old push-back chair. A fat yellow pencil dangles between his softly closed fingers. His chest slowly rises and falls, lifting his crumpled word search up and down, up and down.

He looks so peaceful. I don't want to wake him up. The elevator doors open and Lloyd walks out. He waves. I wave back.

Lloyd shakes the black man's shoulder.

"Leonard, wake up."

Leonard opens his eyes and looks around. He doesn't know where he is. He's stuck between his dream and Lloyd.

Lloyd claps his hands. "Leonard, unlock the door."

Leonard limps over and unlocks the big chain for me.

I walk in. "Thank you," I say.

"You're welcome"—he looks at Lloyd—"young lady."

Lloyd looks down at his feet.

We get into an old freight elevator. As Lloyd closes the elevator door, Leonard pulls the big chain back through the front-door handles.

We get off on the fourteenth floor.

"You live here?" I ask as we walk down a long, musty-smelling hallway.

"Yeah."

"Isn't this a commercial building?"

"Yeah."

"Does anybody else live here?"

"There's a couple on the eleventh floor."

"That's it?"

"That's it," he says like that's a good thing.

"Here we are," he says. The light above his door is burned out. The hallway is dark. It takes him a while to unlock all his dead bolts. He pushes the door open. "This is it, home sweet home."

Home sweet home is a sparsely furnished, high-ceilinged loft. Lloyd's photography equipment's on one end, and his couch, coffee table, and kitchenette are on the other. Tucked in the corner, a narrow spiral staircase leads up to a small sleeping area and shower. The walls are painted a cool gray.

I look around. "Where's your bathroom?" I ask.

"It's outside on your left."

"You don't have one in here?"

"No."

I walk out into the hallway. There's only one bathroom

and it's for men. It's pretty dark. Maybe I missed it. I go back to Lloyd.

"I can't find it. Did you say on the left?"

"Oh yeah. It says 'Men,' but that's okay. The ladies' room is way down the hall by the elevators. Don't go down there."

"Okay," I say. I want to ask why I can't go down there, but I guess if he wanted me to know, he'd tell me.

I open the bathroom door with my elbow and walk in. It smells like an outhouse. My foot slips in something wet. I look down. I'm standing on a splatter of something brown. I lift my foot and look at it. *Oh my gosh. Oh my gosh.* It's diarrhea. A long, wide trail of it leads into one of the stalls.

I run back to Lloyd.

"Lloyd, Lloyd, there's diarrhea all over the bathroom floor. It's awful."

"Oh. Sometimes the old tailor down the hall doesn't make it in time," he says calmly.

"I stepped in it. Look."

He looks down at my shoes. "Don't move," he says.

He puts some newspapers down by the door.

I kick my shoes off onto the paper and follow him over to the couch.

"Make yourself comfortable," he says.

He puts two glasses of red wine and a big bowl of popcorn down on the coffee table.

"Dinner is served," he says.

Okay, so it's not my idea of dinner. But the popcorn smells especially good and I'm hungry.

I eat it by the handful. It's covered in butter and salt. I love butter and salt. I lick my fingers. They taste almost as good as the popcorn. I wash it all down with my wine. The more I eat, the thirstier I get; the more I drink, the better the popcorn tastes. It's all so good. I can't stop myself. Lloyd is so thoughtful. As soon as I empty my glass, he refills it.

I've never enjoyed a bowl of popcorn more. "This is good," I say.

"I pop it in a pan with special oil," Lloyd says proudly.

I take a big gulp of wine; a little bit splashes onto my chin. There aren't any napkins around, so I wipe it off with my hand. Now my hand is messy. I hold it up in front of Lloyd's face.

"I've got wine on my fingers," I say. I start to giggle.

He takes one of my fingers and sucks it clean. I think about my brother's friend and the suckling calf. Lloyd closes his eyes and starts on another finger. He looks so funny. Sucking away at my pointer finger with his eyes rolled back in his head. I try not to laugh, but I can't help myself. My fingertip pops out of his mouth. He makes a loud sucking noise.

"Did you toot?" I say.

I'm too funny. I curl up on the couch and laugh till tears run down my cheeks. My stomach hurts. I gasp for air. I'm having so much fun. I want more of that wine.

Lloyd takes my glass into the kitchen.

"Hey, where ya goin' with that?" I yell.

"Eat some popcorn. You've had enough to drink."

He slides a tumbler of ice water in front of me.

I poke his stomach with my foot. "Party pooper," I say. "Pooper. Ha, pooper. I got poop on my shoe tonight. Did you hear me? I got poop on my shoe tonight," I squeal. I kick my feet and pound my fists, laughing hysterically. I'm a riot. I've never been funnier. This is the best night of my life.

"How old are you, big boy?" I say, my voice all low and throaty. All I need is a cigarette dangling off my lips and I'm Sandy at the end of *Grease*.

"I'm twenty-eight."

"Twenty-eight. Uh-uhhhh. You're older than that." I slap my hands over my mouth. I can't believe I said that.

Lloyd crosses his arms. "I grew up in Arizona. The sun ruined my skin. People always think I'm older than I really am." He presses his lips together.

"I'll be right back. I've got to pee," he says.

"Watch out for the poop piles," I say. I like the way the *p* sound pops out of my mouth. So I say it again. "Poop piles, poop piles, poop piles."

Lloyd walks up the spiral staircase. I hear a tinkling sound.

"Are you peeing in the shower?" I shout.

"Hey, quiet down there," he says. He turns the shower on so I can't hear him anymore.

I want my wine. That stuff's good. I stumble over to the kitchen.

I put the bottle of wine to my lips and drain what's left of it in one long swallow.

That's when I get a great idea.

"Lloyd, get down here."

He hurries downstairs.

"Is everything all right?" he asks.

"Lloyd," I say. "Let's do it."

He furrows up his forehead. I reach out and run my fingers along his wrinkles. He swats my hand away.

"Do what?" he asks.

"You know, do it," I say.

I try to wink at him, but my right eye won't pay attention to me. I guess it's got better things to do. Like keep the studio from spinning around me in circles.

"You mean have sex?" he asks.

I lean up against him and whisper in his ear, "Shhhh . . . don't tell anybody, it's my first time."

Lloyd smiles. "I won't tell a soul." He holds out his hand. "Follow me," he says.

"Saidthespidertothefly." I slur it all together into one long word. I'm so clever. I cackle and stomp my feet.

Lloyd ignores me. I don't think he gets it.

I climb up the steep spiral staircase, one hand and one knee at a time. I keep my eyes fixed on the carpeted steps.

Upstairs Lloyd turns the covers back and pats the bed. He's completely naked. I keep my eyes above his waist. I lie down, close my eyes, and wait for the magic to begin. My head starts to spin. I open my eyes. Oh dear. One naked Lloyd would be shocking enough. Now I've got two of them. I push my right palm over my right eye. I'm back to one Lloyd. That's better.

He pulls my pants off with a jerk.

He's got something in his hand.

"What's that?" I ask him.

"Vaseline," he says.

I don't want to know what he's going to do with that.

He smears a big glob of it between my legs.

I slam my eyes shut. Muffet's face floats in front of me. She looks at me with her big brown eyes. Her nostrils open and close, open and close. I feel her warm breath on my neck. My sweet Muffet.

"Muff Puff Cream Puff," I say.

"What?" Lloyd says.

Muffet goes away.

I open my eyes.

Lloyd's crouched over me. Rubbing himself, breathing hard into my neck. I stare at the wall.

All of a sudden he spreads my legs and pushes himself inside me. It hurts really bad. I move away from the pain. He takes my hips and holds me to him.

I bite my lip and start to cry.

"Don't cry," he says. "I'll lose my erection."

He shouldn't say that word to me. I don't like it. I don't want him to say it again.

I make myself stop crying.

He pulls out of me. I think it's over.

It's not. He rubs himself again, hunches over me, and stuffs his not-so-wild thing back inside me.

He moves it in and out really fast, like a horny Chihuahua. With his every thrust, the top of my head bangs against the wooden headboard.

Whump. Whump. Whump.

He groans, his mouth drops open, his eyes roll back in his head. I heard that men can die having sex. He better not die on me.

"Lloyd?" I say.

He rolls off of me.

Something wet runs down between my legs. I touch it with my finger. My finger comes back red.

Lloyd rubs my cheek. I stare up at the ceiling. I don't want him touching me. I know where those fingers have been.

He looks over at me. "You know, I was thinking. You'd probably work a lot if you lost some of that baby fat," he says.

Suddenly I don't feel so well. I tell myself it's the wine, but I'm not so sure. I jump out of the bed.

"I have to pee," I say.

"Use the shower," he says. "And clean yourself off while you're in there. I don't want you to stain my sheets."

I yank the shower door open, lean down over the open drain, and throw up. When I'm finally done, I rinse my mouth and walk back to the bed. Lloyd's lying there, eating a fistful of popcorn.

I don't say anything.

I walk downstairs, put my shoes on, and leave.

Down in the lobby Leonard is busy working on his word search. He puts it down and looks at me.

"Let me get that door," he says softly.

He pulls the big chain out one clattering link at a time. "Bye, little one," he says.

I look at him with big eyes. I always wanted someone to call me "little one." I always wanted someone to say it like that. Like I was something precious. Like I was something worth protecting. I want to throw my arms around his big, strong, prizefighter neck, bury my face in his shoulder, and cry and cry and cry. I want to tell him, "I don't know why I did it. I'm sorry. I'm so sorry. My father was right, I really am the bad word that starts with a *c*. I really am all the bad words he ever called me."

Leonard holds the door open. "You take care of yourself, now," he says.

I look up at him. I can't move. I can't breathe. My bottom lip quivers. I hold my arms out to him. He steps forward and softly folds his powerful arms around me like sheltering angel wings. With the folds of his shirt clenched between my fingers, I hold on to him tightly. I'm never letting go. Never. He pats my back and says, "There, there."

I love him for his "little one's" and his "there, there's."

I love him for not letting go first.

"You take care of yourself," he says.

He gives me a little kiss on the cheek.

It's the nicest kiss of my life.

My panties are wet with blood and something else I don't want to think about. I can't take a cab. I don't have enough money. I have to walk home. It's one o'clock in the morning. The streets are deserted. But I'm not scared. What would anybody want with me anyway? If a bad guy stops me, I'll pull my pockets inside out. He'll see that all I'm good for are a couple of fifty-cent subway tokens. Bad guys aren't interested in tokens. They don't use them. They just jump the turnstiles. If he wants something more than money, one look at my panties and he'll quickly change his mind.

Burgundy-colored dots and dribbles run down the front of my white cotton blouse. Red wine Morse code for "Send help, sinking fast."

Catholic-school Sister Mary would be so disappointed in me. Her rules for dating were simple. "Girls," she said in her most serious voice, "always carry enough money to get home if you have to, and never wear white. It reminds boys of bedsheets."

Moths spiral the streetlight like little twirly tops. I wonder how they ever get anywhere flying around in circles like that.

I count down the street numbers and think about moths, Morse codes, and men. I've got plenty of time. Home is over seventy blocks away. That's a lot of blocks. My thoughts go round and round. I've got moth brain.

Before I know it, I'm home. I tiptoe into the apartment. I don't want to wake Rayna up. A sliver of light slants out under our bedroom door. I open it. Rayna lays her romance novel down on the bed and looks at me. Her head is covered in spongy pink rollers. I don't know how she sleeps in those things.

"Thank goodness you're home. I was worried sick," she says. Her hair rollers rock back and forth in rhythm with her words like spongy pink exclamation points.

I open the dresser drawer and pull out my nightgown.

"I'm going to take a quick shower," I say.

Rayna's forehead crinkles up. "A shower? Now?"

I don't say anything. I turn toward the bathroom.

"Wait a minute." She jumps up off the bed. "What's that on your blouse? Is that wine?"

I nod.

"Wine? He gave you wine?" She paces back and forth in front of me.

She stops. Her eyes grow big. "Oh no, oh no, oh no."

She grabs my shoulders with both her hands and shakes me. "Tell me you didn't do it with him?"

I look down at the carpet. "I just want to take a shower."

"Did he force himself on you?" Her voice is sharp.

I shake my head really fast. "No. No. It was me. It was my fault. I seduced him."

"You seduced him! Please! You've barely even kissed a boy. That bastard."

I've never heard Rayna cuss before.

"Rayna, please, don't be mad at me."

"He took advantage of you. I hate him." She turns away.

"No, I wanted him to do it. I asked him to do it."

Her head whips around so hard I think her rollers might fly right off her head. "He's forty years old, you know."

"No, no, he's not. I asked him. He's twenty-eight," I say.

"Have you looked at him? He is not twenty-eight."

"He's from Arizona. The sun wrinkled him up."

"I promise you, he is not twenty-eight. And even if he was, that's still too old." She runs her hand along my forehead. "You're all clammy. Come sit down."

"No. I can't."

I lean my face against the brass bedpost. It feels cool against my cheek.

"You can't sit down?"

"No."

"Why not?"

I close my eyes. "Because I'm messy down there."

Her eyes grow huge. "No, no, no, no, no," she says. "Are you telling me he didn't wear a condom?"

"Condom?"

Rayna's eyes puddle up. "Oh, Kelle. Why? Why'd you do it with him? Why'd you do it at all?"

I put my hands up over my face. "I don't know."

She pulls a fluffy white towel out of a big canvas bag and hands it to me. "Here," she says.

I look down at the towel. "You went to the Laundromat tonight?"

She nods.

My eyes get watery. "I was supposed to go with you."

"I wish you had," she says softly.

I head into the bathroom, turn the shower on, and step in. The water is warm. I make it hot. I scrub my skin until it's pink and sore. The water pours over me, stinging my raw skin like thousands of tiny pinpricks. I'm glad it hurts.

Rayna knocks on the door. "Are you okay? You've been in there a long time."

"I'll be right out."

I turn the water off and dry my tender skin with Rayna's fluffy towel. I push my nose into it and take a deep breath. It smells like baby powder. I'm not a baby anymore. I swipe a circle of steam off the foggy mirror. I don't look any different.

I walk into the bedroom. Rayna has the trundle part

of the bed pulled up close to hers. My pillow is plumped and the covers are drawn back. She's got my little stuffed cougar, Brandon, sitting in the middle of the bed. His head is tilted to the side and his paws are splayed out. He looks cute.

I point at him and smile.

"Feel better?" she asks.

I climb into bed. "No."

I turn my face into the pillow.

She switches off the light and gets into her bed. She rests her hand on my back.

"We'll get through this," she says.

I close my eyes and fall asleep.

A noisy trash truck wakes me up. I look at the clock. It's 4 a.m. I roll over onto my back and stare at the ceiling. I'm thinking.

I shake Rayna's shoulder.

"Rayna, wake up."

She opens her eyes. "Is everything okay?"

"I figured it out," I whisper.

"Figured what out?"

"I figured out why I did it with Lloyd."

"Oh. Why?"

"Because I don't like him."

"Because you don't like him?"

"Yeah. If I don't like him, he can't hurt me. Right?"

She thinks for a minute. "Hmmmmm," she says.

"I'm so happy I figured it out," I say.

"Me too."

"Night, Reindeer."

"Night, Kelle."

I wake up. The morning sun is in my eyes. I rub them and blink. A dog barks. A baby cries. "Hush, hush," a woman says. I lie still and listen. I'm not ready to get up yet. Rayna pulls her sheet over her face and groans.

"Rayna, are you awake?"

"Yeah."

"Can you believe it's morning already?" I pause for a second. "I thought only Lloyd came that fast!"

Lloyd may have taken my virginity, but that's all he's getting. I can still laugh. Even if it's at him. Especially if it's at him. He deserves it.

Rayna giggles. "I can't believe you just said that."

"Me either!"

I kick my covers off and laugh.

The next-door neighbor bangs on the wall. I hit the crook of my arm with my fist and yell, "Pasta fagioli." Rayna flicks her chin and squeals, "Panini." We're off and running.

It's a brand-new day.

Rayna taps the kitchen calendar with her pointer finger. "What are all these little red *x*'s for?" she asks me.

I don't say anything. I walk into the bathroom, turn the water on, and stick my toothbrush in my mouth.

She comes in after me. She's got her hands on her hips.

"Kelle, why are there red *x*'s on the calendar?"

"Wha?" I say through my mouthful of toothpaste.

"Kelle, what's going on?" she says quietly.

I turn the water off and look at her.

She puts her hand up to her mouth.

"Oh, Kelle, no." She shakes her head from side to side.

I nod. "I'm late," I say softly.

"How many days?"

"Six."

She runs her hands through her hair. "Why didn't you tell me?"

I look down at my sneakers. "I didn't want to say it out loud."

She paces back and forth. "Okay," she says. "There's no need to panic." She pauses. "Yet."

The phone rings. Rayna picks it up.

"Hello?"

She puts her hand over the receiver. "It's Lloyd."

I run into the bedroom.

"Kelle just left. She's got a go-see. . . . Uh-huh. I'll give her the message. Bye."

She comes in and sits down on the bed. "Has he been calling you?"

I nod. "He's been leaving messages with my service."

"He wants you to call him," Rayna says.

"He can leave a million messages. I'm never talking to him again." I push my face into my pillow.

She rubs my shoulder. "Listen, I've got to go to work now. Why don't you meet me afterwards. We'll go to McDonald's."

"Okay."

"See ya later, alligator," she says.

She stands at the door and waits for me to say the words. I know she won't leave until I do.

"After while, crocodile," I say, even though I don't feel like it.

Rayna smiles. She pats the door with the palm of her hand. "Lock up," she says.

"I will."

She doesn't want me lying around all day moping. She thinks once I get up, I'll stay up. I guess she's onto something, because once I get up, I really do stay up. I snap a small plastic adapter into the center of my new favorite 45 and slide it over the turntable spindle. I turn the record player on. The spinning red and black label quickly becomes one color. I slowly lower the needle down toward the record. I have to let it go at just the right time, in just the right way, or it will bounce or slide sideways and scratch the record. Like an airplane meeting the tarmac, the needle touches down perfectly. Staticky popping sounds come through the little speaker holes. I like those sounds. The music starts. I turn the sound way up and look out the window. When the singer says, "And a rock feels no pain. And an island never cries," I feel like I swallowed a rock. The words are stuck in my chest. As soon as the song is over, I put it on again. I'm going to play it until the words don't make me want to cry.

I meet Rayna at six at Jennifer House Convertibles, where she sells couches that change into beds. She's one of their best salespeople. She gets all the men customers. When a man comes in, she opens up the bed, lies across it, pats the foam mattress, and says with her words all stretched out and Southern, "Try it out, sugar." Men eat it up. They call her a Georgia peach. I guess that's a compliment.

She says good night to her coworkers and we walk outside.

"Well?" she says to me.

I sigh. "Not yet."

She hands me a box. "I bought these for you."

I open the lid. Inside is a pair of rubbery-smelling New Balance running shoes.

I scrunch up my nose. "Running shoes?"

"If it turns out you are, you know . . ." She looks down at her feet. "Maybe it's not attached yet. Maybe you can shake it out."

I tuck the box under my arm.

Early the next morning I shake Rayna's shoulder. "Rayna, I think I have cramps."

"Go see," she says.

I sit on the toilet and wait for the water to turn red. Rayna stands outside the door.

"Anything?"

"No," I say.

She goes to work.

I put on the running shoes.

When Rayna comes home from work, I pull my shirt up. "Look at my belly. I'm getting fat."

She looks at my stomach. "That's from all those fried corn muffins."

I laugh. "I love those things."

The next day I get out the yellow pages and look for the nearest clinic. It's free. They offer counseling. I can walk out if I want to. And I'll know if it's the corn muffins or something else that's making my stomach grow. I take a quick shower and head out.

I look up at the office building where the clinic is located. The big modern windows are all shiny and clean. It looks like the kind of place where advertising executives and architects work. I walk into the wide, high-ceilinged lobby. My sneakers make little squeaking sounds on the granite floor. I stand in front of the elevator and push the up button. The doors open with a *whoosh*. I walk in. A man rushes in behind me. He presses six. I press eleven. When he gets out, I press eight.

Ding.

The doors open. I get out.

The clinic waiting room is painted a cheery robin's-egg blue. A long floral-print couch sits along one wall, and three oversized armchairs sit along the other.

A girl behind the counter hands me a clipboard. "Sign in, please. A doctor will see you soon."

I can barely hold the pen, my hand is shaking so hard. I press the point against the paper. Just as the ink starts to flow, I realize I shouldn't use my real name. What if my agency finds out? I turn my *K* into a sloppy-looking *L*.

While I wait for someone to come get me, I tidy up the magazines. I line them up alphabetically in a straight line. When I'm done, I look around the room. It feels like a dental office. I pretend that it is.

A flinty-eyed, lab-coated doctor walks out. "Linda?" she says.

At first I don't realize she's talking to me.

"Linda?" she says again.

"Oh, sorry." I stand up.

I follow her into an examination room. She hands me a little plastic cup. "I need a urine sample. The bathroom is down the hall on your right."

I look at the cup. I'm not sure how much a "sample" is. I don't want to fill it up too much. I hope a quarter cup will do.

Back in the exam room she hands me a big sheet of rough paper. "Take your clothes off."

"Everything?"

"Yes."

"Even my socks?"

"You can keep your socks on if you want," she says. I think she's getting tired of all my stupid questions. She leaves.

I fold my clothes into a neat stack and sit down on the edge of the metal table. I swing my feet back and forth, back and forth. My paper cover-up makes little crinkling sounds. I'm cold. I start to shiver. I wonder what those metal things are for at the end of the table. They look like big stirrups.

I wish Rayna were with me.

The doctor rushes in. "Lie down on the table," she says. I do.

She puts my feet in the stirrups. "Slide your bottom down to the edge."

I do.

She sticks something cold in me. "Relax," she says.

I can't.

She throws her rubber gloves away.

Her lips pull down at the corners.

"Get dressed and come to my office."

I dress, go to her office, and sit down across from her.

My heart pounds in my chest. I'm cold from the inside out. I start to shake.

She looks at me. "You're not pregnant," she says.

"I'm not?"

I cover my face with my hands. While my hands are there, I wipe the corners of my eyes so that she won't know some tears snuck out.

She tears a small piece of paper off a pad and hands it to me.

"This is a prescription for the pill. You need to fill it and start taking it right away. I don't want to see you back here again, Linda."

She says Linda louder than the rest of the words. She knows Linda's not my name. I can tell.

I push the prescription across her desk. I shake my head. "I don't need it," I say. "I'm never having sex again. Ever."

She pushes it back in front of me. "Take it anyway. Just in case you change your mind."

I put it in my pocket. Just in case.

Rayna and I celebrate my good news at McDonald's.

I buy a small container of milk for my Gillie's granola, and Rayna gets a burger, fries, and a Coke.

"I'm going to keep running," I say. "I kind of like it."

When we get home, the phone is ringing. Rayna answers. "Oh, hi, Lloyd." She raises her eyebrows at me.

I take the phone. "Hi, Lloyd," I say.

Lloyd told me I had to buy a messenger bag to carry my go-see things in. He said that's what all the top models use. Lloyd knows about stuff like that, so I believe him.

I got a blue one. Lloyd thought it was too bright, that I should have gone for something more sophisticated, but I like it. It reminds me of blue ribbons.

It's so weird. I'm not sure what I'm doing with him. Maybe I just like having somebody around telling me what to do. I hope that's not it. But something tells me that it is. We're not dating. He's just helping me out. I think he feels guilty about the whole virginity thing.

I walk down the street, looking at myself in all the ground-floor windows. I do it from the corner of my eye, though, so people won't know. In the country you can't watch yourself moving around in the world like you can in the city. That's probably a good thing.

I stop in front of a small dress shop. Inside the window is the prettiest dress I've ever seen in my whole life. With its delicately trimmed sleeves, fitted bodice, and yards of gauzy white cotton skirting, it looks like something Tess of the d'Urbervilles would wear during the good parts of the book. I want that dress. That dress would make me something special. In it, anything would be possible.

Someone taps my shoulder. I turn around. It's a police officer.

He tilts his head back. "I'm stoppin' you for trooncy," he says.

"Trooncy?"

He nods.

A woman walks around us into the dress shop. The door makes a soft *shush* sound as it slowly closes behind her. I hope she's not after my dress.

It takes me a second to figure out what "trooncy" is. "Oh," I say. "I'm out of school. I graduated."

The policeman crosses his arms. He doesn't believe me.

I want to say, "I did too graduate. I got really good grades and everything." But I don't want to sound like I'm bragging.

He stares at me.

"I don't have my diploma on me, if that's what you're waiting for," I say instead.

A horn beeps. The cop looks over. A bum squirts

water on a car's windshield and "cleans" it with a dirty scrap of paper. The driver turns his wipers on.

I flip open my messenger bag. I show the officer the head shots Lloyd took of me the week before. If this doesn't convince him, I can introduce him to some detective "friends" of mine.

"Wha'd these things cost you?" he asks.

I'd say "My virginity," but I don't think he'd think that was very funny.

So instead I say, "A couple hundred dollars." Wow. That's depressing.

"I got a daughter wants to model."

He turns my head shot over and looks at my résumé, which lists my measurements and credits. My credits amount to my Kiss job and a bunch of plays I've never heard of.

He cocks his head to the side. "You don't look five foot six to me."

I pull the photo out of his hand. "Can I go now?"

He nods. "Yeah."

He walks over to the window-washing bum. Five cars wait for the light to change. All have their wipers on.

I turn back to the dress shop window. My dress is gone. The mannequin is naked. It doesn't matter. I couldn't have bought it anyway. I may as well go home.

I turn the corner onto Eighty-fourth Street. Someone is hosing the sidewalk in front of my building. That's my job. It can't be Rayna; she's at work. I squint my eyes. It kind of looks like David, but I can't be sure. I walk a little faster. No. David doesn't roll his shoulders forward like that. He doesn't push his hand in his pocket like that. I start to run.

"Buddy," I yell.

He looks up.

It's Buddy!

Buddy's home!

I push my sneakered toes into the concrete. I'm pretty fast. I'm a runner now. I hurl myself into his arms. He nearly falls over backward. I press my wet cheek against his. His eyes shine.

I feel all filled up. Like I don't have any empty spots.

Now I know how the little girl at the boat pond felt.

I hear a series of soft clicks. I turn toward the sound. A flash of light hits my eyes. It's a photographer.

Without talking or even looking at each other, Buddy and I put our heads down and walk into the building. Buddy pushes the elevator button. It's like he never left. His clothes are wrinkled. He needs a shave. He's not wearing any socks. Gosh, it's good to have him back.

The elevator door opens.

"Wait. The hose!" I say.

I pull the hose back inside the lobby. A reporter tries to come in with it. I slam the door in his face. "Go away," I say.

He does.

Buddy grins.

We step into the elevator. Buddy pushes four and seven.

"This is the best day ever, ever, ever," I say. "I'm so happy you're free! Did they catch who did it?"

Buddy stops smiling. "I'm not free. I'm out on bail."

I feel like I just got punched in the stomach. "Oh," I say.

The elevator stops at my floor. Buddy holds the open button. "Babe?"

"Yeah?"

"How would you like to work for me?"

I lift up on my toes and smile. "I would love to work for you."

"You can start tomorrow if you want."

"I'd like that." I give him a little wave. "Bye, Buddy."

He grins. "Yep, see ya, babe."

Babe. I love it when he calls me that.

"Hey," he says as I start to walk away.

I turn around.

"That thing with the reporter earlier." He shakes his head. "You're one tough cookie," he says. He sounds surprised.

People always are. . . .

"I want to do it too," I say to my brother.

"No. You'll tell. I'll get in trouble."

"Please, please, please. I promise I won't tell."

My brother looks at me. He knows I keep my promises.

"All right. But don't whine about it later."

"Guys," he calls out to his friends. "Kelle wants to try."

"She's a little girl," one of the friends says.

"She's tough. It'll be good for her," Bob says.

The boys line up at our electric fence. I go to the last one and reach for his hand.

"No," my brother says. "You have to be first. You have to be the one who grabs the wire."

My eyes get big. I don't want to do it now, but my brother said I was tough. I don't want him to look like a liar.

He leans down and whispers in my ear. "The last person gets it the worst," he says.

I walk to the front of the line. I look over at the fence. I'm afraid to touch it, but I know I have to. I reach out my hand. My fingers hover over the humming wire. My hand shakes. My brother takes my other hand.

"Ready?" he says, more like a command than a question.

I look down the long chain of tightly clenched kid fists.

I nod, take a deep breath, and grab the wire.

A sudden surge of electricity rushes through my body. My hand flies off the wire. The guy on the end pops straight up into the air. He lands on the ground with a thud. We hold our arms and laugh. A fast, nervous laugh. A *We're happy to have survived that* laugh. The boys pat me on the back and tell me I'm something else. Bob is really proud of me. I can tell by his sparkling eyes.

Early the next morning I head up to Buddy's apartment.

The elevator door opens. I've never been on the top floor before. It looks just like all the other floors. Buddy is working in the hallway.

"Morning," I say. I point at his door, 7D. "Should I go in?"

He motions over his shoulder. "My apartment's over there," he says. "I changed the letters."

"Oh," I say.

If Buddy's apartment is behind me, then that means the one I'm pointing at is Tupper's.

I look from door to door. What was Melanie thinking? Moving right across the hall from Buddy. Rubbing his nose in it.

Melanie met Tupper right here in this hallway. He

asked her to go jogging with him. She said yes. Less than three weeks later he was dead.

"Go on in. The door's open," Buddy says.

I go on in.

Inside there's an old couch, a television, a couple of brown crinkly-leaved plants, and an exercise bike. If my brother had an apartment, this is exactly what it would look like. All function. No form. Definitely not "luxurious." If those crazy reporters can be wrong about that, then they can be wrong about anything.

I'm feeling really good about my crazy-reporter theory until I look up and see a row of small, round portholes. Portholes that look directly into a rooftop swimming pool. Okay, so a pool is luxurious. But the way I see it, the plain apartment cancels out the nice pool. The morning sun shines down through the sparkling clean water. Glances of light move across the pool's bright blue floor and walls. Rayna didn't tell me Buddy had a pool. It was nighttime, though. Maybe she thought they were just windows.

Buddy walks in.

"You have a pool. That's so neat. I like pools," I say.

"Swim in it, then," he says.

I decide that I have to at least once, just so I can say I did.

"Can I go look at it?"

Buddy nods.

I climb up a steep spiral staircase into a small room with a mattress on the floor. That's all there is. Just a mattress with a navy blue sheet pulled across the top of it. I don't even see a pillow anywhere. I'm pretty sure this is Buddy's bedroom. Not quite what I expected.

I go out on the roof. The pool is cute. It's way too shallow for diving, but you wouldn't want to anyway with those living-room portholes. Somebody might see your bottoms come down.

I climb back down the staircase. Buddy is on the exercise bike, watching television. The picture is sharp and clear. He's lucky. He's got cable. Back home we used rabbit ears. They didn't work very well, though. The only way to really make them work was for someone to stand next to the set holding on to one of the ends. Everybody always went on about how I made the clearest picture. That I was gifted and how my gift shouldn't be wasted. I felt so special.

I used to be really gullible.

Buddy sees me looking at the television. "You can watch while you work, but it has to be educational."

I haven't watched a television show in so long I'd watch *Sesame Street* if I had to.

I chew on my lip. "Buddy?"

"Yep."

"If I get any auditions, can I go on them?"

"Yep," he says.

Well, that was easy.

The phone rings. I pick up the receiver and hand it to Buddy. The phone's long cord swings back and forth between the kitchen counter and the exercise bike. Buddy talks and pedals, talks and pedals. When he's finished, he holds out the phone. I hang it up.

"Go to the deli and get me half a pound of thin-sliced turkey," he says. He opens his wallet, pulls out a hundred-dollar bill, and hands it to me. "And make sure the guy cuts it by hand."

"Okay," I say.

As I walk out of the building, a reporter tries to catch the door. I push it closed with my heel. He looks over at the directory and rings Buddy. Or he thinks he's ringing Buddy. He's actually ringing Tupper's empty apartment. Buddy changed the directory letters around too. He's so smart.

A man leans back against the open deli door. He's got a meatball-stuffed hero in one hand and a lit cigarette in the other. As I squeeze past him, he blows a big puff of smoke in my face.

"Heads up," a long-haired boy says. He's really cute. I think he's Italian.

When I smile at him, he smiles back. His teeth are really white against his soft pink lips. I wonder if he's too old for me.

He pushes a big broom toward my feet. I step around it.

"Thanks, darlin'," he says with a wink.

My face flushes.

I look down at the floor. He missed a crumpled napkin, two curly-topped toothpicks, and a Bazooka bubble gum wrapper. But I don't think he cares, because when I look back up, he's gone.

I walk up to the deli counter. The meat man ignores me. When he stoops down to get something out of his meat case, I tap the cold glass with my fingertips.

He looks at me.

"Excuse me," I say. "I'd like a half pound of turkey, please."

He scowls, pulls the turkey out, and slaps it onto the meat cutter.

"Excuse me. Can you please—"

"Thick or thin?" he interrupts.

I cross my arms in front of my chest. If he knew that this was for Buddy, he'd listen to me.

"Thin, and cut by hand," I say. My voice is flat. I give him a hard stare.

He looks down over the counter. His lips pull up at the corners. "By hand. Of course, young lady," he says.

I watch him cut the meat. Every few slices he looks at me. I stare right back at him.

When he's done, he wraps the turkey in white paper and hands it to me. "Is this for Mr. Jacobson?" he asks.

I look at him blankly. "No," I say.

When I get back to Buddy's, I give him the turkey and his change. "Buddy? Why does the meat have to be sliced by hand?"

I don't want to irritate him with stupid questions, but I really want to know.

"Those machines, they never clean 'em. The bottoms are filled with rotting meat."

I make a face.

I'm going to learn a lot at this job.

Next Buddy snaps a rubber band around a thick bundle of cash and hands it to me. "Here," he says. "Take this to Chemical Bank and open a CD for twenty thousand dollars. Ask for Lancing. He's got the paperwork."

I don't know what a CD is. I'm glad Lancing's got the paperwork. I take a paper bag out from under the kitchen sink and slip the money inside.

"Bye, Buddy," I say.

He doesn't say anything back, so I close the door and head out to the elevator.

As I leave the building, I tighten my fingers around the paper bag. The bank is a couple blocks away. I look up. Buddy is standing out on his balcony watching me. I don't wave. I don't want anybody to know I'm with him. They might figure out I'm carrying his money. I just look in the direction of the bank and keep walking.

"I'll give you girls a hundred dollars if you'll clean out Tupper's apartment," Buddy says.

"Each?" Rayna asks. She sells couches for a living. She's the deal closer.

"Each," Buddy says.

Rayna and I look at each other. I don't really want to, but the hundred dollars is hard to resist.

"We'll do it," Rayna says.

Buddy hands each of us a crisp hundred-dollar bill. It's my first ever. I'd draw a little heart on it, but I think that's against the law.

Buddy gives us some cleaning supplies and unlocks Tupper's door. I hope there's no blood anywhere. I think about my hundred-dollar bill. I wonder what the going rate for crime scene cleanup is.

"See ya later," Buddy says. "I gotta go see some bum about a building."

Buddy always calls people bums.

We walk in. Not a drop of blood in sight. Just an empty apartment with old paper cups, take-out containers, and a million dust bunnies. Rayna sweeps while I scrub coffee stains off the kitchen counter.

"I was scared there might be blood in here," I say.

Rayna tips a pile of floaty dust bunnies into a big black garbage bag. "It didn't happen in here. It happened in Buddy's apartment."

I move my head from side to side. "Uh-uh," I say.

She nods her head up and down. "Uh-huh. I read it in the *Post*."

I scrub the counter a little harder. Coffee stains are hard to get rid of.

"They say a big drug dealer lived in the building too."

I look at her with wide eyes. "Lived?"

"He's gone. Nobody knows where he is now."

I can only imagine.

"But guess what?" Rayna continues. "They're saying Cheryl Corey's death was an accident. Buddy had nothing to do with it."

I think she's trying to cheer me up now.

When I don't say anything, she changes the subject.

"How much is Buddy paying you to work for him, anyway?"

"I don't know," I say.

"You don't know?"

I shake my head. "I didn't ask."

"Do you want me to ask for you?"

"I'll do it," I say. *When hell freezes over*, I think. I don't like asking for things. It shouldn't be such a big deal, but it is. My father taught me to keep my mouth shut. If I didn't, he'd shut it for me.

"Lloyd wants to take me out on a real date tomorrow night. There's some Chinese restaurant he really likes. It's a dive, but the food is fantastic, he says. He's going to pay and everything."

Rayna looks like she just bit into a sour grape. "What'd you say?"

"I said okay."

She rolls her eyes. "Why?"

"I'm sticking with my 'I don't like him, he can't hurt me' idea."

"I'm not so sure about that," Rayna says.

"Anyway. He doesn't do drugs. He barely drinks. He's very righteous."

"He just sleeps with girls who pass for thirteen," Rayna says under her breath.

"What?"

"Nothing."

I pretend I didn't hear her.

We toss Tupper's porno collection into a big cardboard box, then drag it and our bloated trash bags out into the hallway. We're all done.

I rub my hands on my pants. Cleaning up after a murdered man wasn't as bad as I thought it was going to be.

Probably because I never met him.

"Time to go shopping," I say.

"Have fun," Rayna says.

I'm hoping that little dress shop still has my Tess dress. I run the whole way there, jumping the sidewalk cracks just for fun. I look at the window display and catch my breath. The mannequin's dressed in a button-down shirt, necktie, vest, and tweed trousers. Very tomboy meets hunt club.

I open the shop door and walk inside.

"Excuse me," I say. The saleslady looks at me over her glasses. "Remember the white dress you had in the window? Do you still have it?"

She looks back down at her paperwork. "Sale rack," she says.

I find the rack at the back of the store. There it is— my dress! I try it on. It's perfect. And it's half price.

I lay the dress down on the counter in front of the saleslady. "I'd like to buy this, please."

As soon as I get home, I put it on and show it to Rayna. Her hands fly up to her mouth. She backs away. "You can't wear that!" she says.

I shake my head. I don't understand. "Why can't I?" I ask.

She throws her hands up in disgust. "For heaven's sake, Kelle. What is wrong with you? Everybody knows that you can't wear white after Labor Day!"

*B*uddy *drops a stack of bills* and a fat blue binder down in front of me.

"Pay these," he says.

"Okay," I say.

I don't tell him I've never written a check before. That I get by with cash and money orders. He doesn't like to hear about things like that. He doesn't like excuses.

"And make sure you pay yourself while you're at it," he says.

He shoves his hands in his pockets, looks down at his toes, and walks out the door.

I open the bills with a paring knife. Most are past due. I open the binder and study the old carbons. It looks easy.

It is.

The last check is the only hard one. It's my check. Buddy didn't tell me how much to write it for. He wants me to decide. I'm not used to measuring my own worth. I'm used to people doing that for me. I get three dollars an hour at Healthworks. I decide to give myself a raise. Five dollars an hour. I'm worth it.

Buddy bursts through the door. His entrances used to scare me, but I'm used to them now. His nose is red. He rubs his arms.

"Brrr-rabbity out there, huh?" I say.

He smiles. I like it when he's happy. He flops down on the couch.

"Buddy, do you want to sign these now?"

He springs up off the couch and comes over to where I've been working.

The checks are lined up in horizontal rows of ten on the kitchen counter. The matching bills lie vertically by their sides. I hand Buddy a pen. He signs one after the other without stopping. He's getting close to my check. What if he doesn't sign it? What if he doesn't think I'm worth it? I should have made it $3.50 an hour. Why didn't I make it $3.50 an hour? It's my check's turn. I hold my breath. He doesn't read it. He just signs it, drops the pen down on the counter, and goes back to the couch.

There's a knock at the door. A soft knock. A girl knock. Guys don't announce themselves that way. I look over at Buddy.

"That's a model I'm interviewing. I'm opening a new agency."

Buddy doesn't believe in wasting time.

I open the door. A willowy girl with brown hair and large brown eyes looks over my shoulder into the apartment.

"Oh. Sorry," she says. "I was looking for Polly Models."

Polly Models? That's goofy.

"Come on in," I say. Her eyes dart from side to side. She's trying to look around the apartment without moving her head. It's a bad technique.

Buddy jumps up off the couch. He points at her portfolio. "Can I see that?"

"Sure," she says. Her voice is soft and sweet.

"What's your name?" he asks.

"Audrey."

"Have a seat, Audrey," Buddy says. "Tell me about yourself."

She pulls a small cross back and forth along its thin gold chain.

"Well," she says. "Right now I model garments for buyers on Seventh Avenue."

"So you're a clotheshorse," Buddy says.

She nods.

So that's what "clotheshorse" means. I thought it was just a saying. I didn't know it was a title.

"Buddy's a famous racehorse trainer," I say.

I can't believe I just said that.

Audrey lets go of her cross. "You are?" she says. She sounds impressed, but maybe she's just buttering him up.

Buddy smiles. I think he likes her. She smiles back. I

wonder if she knows who he is. Something tells me she doesn't.

I look at Buddy and tap my watch. He nods. I have a go-see. This one's for Constant Comment tea. It's my first commercial audition, not counting the pretend ones I did with Rayna and Sharon.

As I step out onto the sidewalk, a gust of wind blows hard against me. Dry leaves and bits of paper roil and tumble forward, at the mercy of nature's invisible push broom. For a few seconds all I hear is the wind swooshing through my brain. Sweeping it clean. The skirt of my dress lifts and swirls around my bare legs. People stare at me. If Rayna were here, she'd say it's because I'm wearing white after Labor Day.

My audition didn't take long at all. I told Lloyd I'd meet him as soon as I was done. I walk toward his place smiling. Thanks to Rayna and Sharon, I knew exactly what to expect. The casting director said I'm good at doing what I'm told. I guess I can thank my father for that.

My father stands next to an old shed with a crowbar in his hand. The whole family stands behind him. He likes an audience when he's working around the farm. Bob and Rick wait to see what he wants them to do. He won't say, "Do this, do that." He gives them little clues. A glance. A point. Other than that, they have to guess it from his mind.

He wants to take the old metal siding off and put new stuff up. He's always coming up with projects that have to be done. Today it's metal siding. Who knows what it'll be tomorrow. He doesn't like to see us sitting around doing nothing when he's got better things for us to do.

He takes off his shirt. My mother lays it over the fence railing. He slides the claw end of the crowbar under one of the siding nails and pops it out with a yank. He throws the nail on the ground. I run over and pick it up. By the time he's done, I've got a pocket full of rusty nails. Better my pocket than Misty's foot.

"Sons," my father says. He grabs a corner of the sharp-edged siding. My brothers rush over and take the other side. They pull and tug. They're having a hard time getting it loose. I step closer so I can see why.

"Get out of the way," my father barks.

Bob stops and wipes his forehead with the back of his arm.

"You lazy fuck," my father says to him. "Put some muscle into it. Nobody ever drowned in sweat."

Bob puts some muscle into it. Rick pulls it as hard as he can. The siding rips loose. They stumble backward. I'm too close. I can't get out of the way. The edge of the siding slices down across my forehead. Blood pours down my face. It lands on the dirt like raindrops.

"Fucking bitch," my father screams. "Stay the fuck out of the way."

My lip shakes. A slick of water covers my eyes.

My father points his finger in my face. "Don't you fucking cry. Don't you fucking cry."

I open my eyes as big as they go so the wetness

doesn't puddle up. I bite my lip and nod. "Yes, sir," I say.

He looks over at my mother. "She up on her tetanus shots?"

My mother nods.

My father turns around and starts on the next sheet of siding.

My mother motions at the house with her chin. "Go clean yourself up," she says. She can't go with me. She has to stay with my father.

I look at my watch. My audition went so fast I'm going to get to Lloyd's place early. That's okay. I can do that now. We're an item. Well, kind of. He won't let me hold his hand in public or anything. But that's not his fault. Too many people give him dirty looks. With that dried-up Arizona skin of his, he looks pretty old.

Even his friends have a problem with our being together. They shake their heads. "What are ya doing, man?" they ask, like he's a pedophile or something.

A subway train rumbles under my feet. I cross my arms. I'm cold. I can take the train downtown. Lloyd taught me how.

Lloyd doesn't mind that I'm early. He says he's hungry. I can start dinner now. He's flexible that way.

It's getting dark. I look out his big window at the building across the street. A bright light burns in the apartment directly across from me. A girl runs around in front of her window. A guy chases her. They're naked.

He catches her arm. She throws her head back and laughs. He squirts whipped cream onto her breasts. I wonder what it's like to have fun like that.

"They want you to watch," Lloyd says over my shoulder.

He picks up a pair of binoculars. "Want a closer look?" he asks.

I shake my head.

I put two small pieces of thawed whitefish into the broiler, broccoli into a pot, and brown rice into the rice maker. Every night it's the same thing. I miss my mother's fried chicken. She's such a good cook.

"Lloyd?"

"Yeah?"

"Can we go out to dinner again sometime?"

We haven't gone out since our Chinese restaurant date.

"If you want to pay, we can," he says.

I check the fish. It's almost done.

He stands behind me with his arms around my waist. He only does that when he wants to "do it." That's his idea of foreplay.

"You need to lose weight anyway," he says.

That's no way to get lucky, I think to myself. I move away from him.

"I only say that because I care. You want to work, don't you?"

"Yes."

He puts his arms back around me. I let him. "Want to spend the night?" he whispers in my ear.

I nod. "If you don't mind," I say. "Rayna's got that new boyfriend. She really likes him. I don't want to get in her way."

He pats my butt. "I've got some filing for you to do anyway," he says.

"What if I don't feel like filing?" I say.

He laughs. He thinks I'm kidding.

He tells me what to do, how to dress, what to eat. He'd fix my words before they came out of my mouth if he could. But he can't.

Not yet, anyway.

I shouldn't complain. He doesn't scream at me or hit me. I can put up with bossiness. It shows he cares.

The door to Lloyd's studio is latched open. I walk in. The smell of darkroom chemicals drifts out into the hallway. Lloyd's darkroom is like his Batcave. He's very secretive about what goes on in there.

"Lloyd?" I say. I poke my head inside. He's gone. He must be down the hall in the bathroom. The darkroom glows red. Black-and-white photos float in chemical-filled trays. That means he's going to be right back.

A wooden clothespin holds a contact sheet up on a long string. I touch it. It's dry. I look at the rows of tiny pictures. At first I can't make out what it is I'm looking at. I lean forward and take a closer look. They're pictures of a girl's butt. Figures. Hey, wait a minute—that's *my* butt! I'm looking at a contact sheet of my naked butt.

I hear Lloyd shuffling down the hallway. When he walks, he doesn't pick his feet up all the way. His mother never taught him how to walk properly. It's annoying. I hurry out to the living room. I don't want him to know that I know what he's done.

He walks into the studio. "Oh, hey," he says to me. "I'll be out in a bit. I've got some work to finish up."

Yeah, I bet you do. I wonder what other surprises he has in there.

He slides the darkroom door closed.

An hour later he's out, grinning, waltzing along on the balls of his slidy little feet. He's Sylvester the Cat. I'm Tweety.

I want to know how he got those photos.

He unlocks his elephant-sized floor safe. He slides a thick manila envelope between a stack of other thick manila envelopes. I watch him over the top of the magazine I'm pretending to read.

There's a knock on the door. He pushes the safe door closed. He doesn't spin the cylinder. He always spins the cylinder. My body tenses. Lloyd has the paranoid mind of a perpetually guilty man. I'm surprised he doesn't keep a hungry Doberman tied to that safe. He's obsessed with people stealing from him. This may be my only chance. He walks around the corner to see who's at the door.

It's the elderly tailor down the hall. I can tell by his accent. He's complaining about the models that come to Lloyd's door. He doesn't like the way they dress. He wants them to cover up.

"Go away, you old coot," Lloyd says.

The old man wraps his cane on Lloyd's door and starts to rant, "I call police on you. You have young girlfriend. Too young." He shakes his cane at Lloyd.

With one eye on Lloyd's back, I rush over to the safe. I pull the door. My breath catches in my throat. The safe opens. Hallelujah.

"If you don't like it, don't look," I hear Lloyd say.

The man yells at Lloyd in Yiddish. I don't have to understand what he's saying to know it's really bad.

I quickly flip through the stack of envelopes. They're labeled, of course. I knew they would be. Lloyd's a very thorough man. My heart beats. *Thump. Thump. Thump.* "Lauren Hutton/Italian *Vogue*." "Cover/Depeche Mode." "Ad/Pietrovanni." "Dimple/Black &White."

That's me! I'm "Dimple/Black & White." I've got a dimple on one side of my butt. Lloyd says it's very unique. I grab the envelope, shove it under a couch cushion, and lie down on top of it.

Lloyd stomps over.

"Problem?" I ask.

"Asshole. Threatening me." He runs his fingers through his kinky mousy-brown hair.

I shake my head and look concerned. "He's just mad. You weren't very nice to him."

Lloyd frowns. "I'm headed over to *American Girl* now."

"I have to go anyway," I say. "I told Buddy I'd be there by noon."

Lloyd's head pops up. His eyes get big. I can almost see the lightbulb go on over his head. He walks over to the safe, spins the cylinder, and gives the door a good tug.

"You look flushed," he says.

"I do?"

"You feel okay?"

I nod. "I think so. Rayna had a little cold last week."

"Take vitamin C," he says. "I've got a big week. I don't want to get sick."

He goes back into the models' dressing room to get his jacket. While he's out of sight, I put mine on too. Before I button it, I stick the envelope under my arm.

"Ready?" Lloyd asks.

"Yep," I say.

The envelope makes little crinkly sounds. To cover up, I babble about the weather and his *American Girl* appointment until we're safely outside.

I look down at my watch. "Gotta hurry," I say.

The second I'm home, I rip the envelope open. No need to be tidy. I won't be saving this one.

There it is. My dimpled horse-girl butt in all its black-and-white glory. The light slants softly through the window. The skirt of my ruffly white dress is casually flipped up over my back. My panties are pulled in toward the center. Like the elastic was stretched loose. It looks like it just happened. But I know it didn't.

I guess as butt photos go, they're not so bad.

I know how he did it now. He took them while I was sleeping.

It was a couple days ago. It was cold outside. The afternoon sun came in warm through his living-room window. The sun made me tired. I stretched out on the couch and fell asleep.

I fell asleep and Lloyd got busy.

Snap. Snap. Snap.

If I hadn't stumbled into that darkroom, I never would have known.

What is it with this guy?

What is it with me?

Why do I stay with him?

My hand closes into a fist.

I don't know.

I really and truly don't know.

I stare at the stack of photos.

There's a contact sheet, eight-by-tens, and the negatives. I hope that's everything. I don't want my butt ending up in some French ad. It would be just like Lloyd to do something like that.

There's something really creepy about a person photographing your butt in your sleep.

I wonder what else he does while I'm asleep.

I drop the negatives, the photos, and a lit match into

our metal trash can. It catches fire right away. In less than a minute all that's left of "Dimple/Black & White" is a floaty pile of ashes.

Poor Lloyd.

All that work for nothing.

I flush what's left of it down the toilet.

The phone rings. It's my agency.

"Congratulations, Kelle. First commercial audition. First booking!"

"What?!" I say.

"You booked the Constant Comment commercial."

I hang up the phone. I jump up and down. I wish Rayna were here to jump with me. It's not as fun jumping around by myself.

I run up the stairs to Buddy's. He and Audrey are sitting at the counter eating Rueben sandwiches. I can smell the corned beef and sauerkraut from the door. Buddy loves them. I think they're disgusting.

Audrey holds out her sandwich. "Want half?" she asks me. She's polite that way.

I wave my hand in front of my nose. "No thanks."

She leans against Buddy's shoulder. Their knees touch. Bump, bump, bump. She asks him where his socks are. They laugh.

Lloyd and I never laugh.

Buddy looks at me. "What's going on with Lloyd?" he asks.

It's like he can read my mind.

I shrug. I want to tell him about the butt photos, but I don't want to stir anything up.

"Has he taken you out to dinner?"

"Once."

"A show?"

"No."

He looks at me like I should know better. "He's a bum," he says. He hops off the bar stool and gets on the exercise bike.

"Guess what?" I say.

"What?" Buddy asks.

"I booked my first commercial!"

Audrey claps her hands. "Oh, Kelle, that's fantastic."

Buddy nods. "You're such a snap," he says.

I don't know what a snap is, but I can tell by the way he says it that it's something really good.

He stops pedaling. "I'm proud of you," he says.

I smile.

I've waited all my life to hear those words.

It was worth the wait.

Buddy sits on his exercise bike pedaling away like a hamster on a wheel. The television is on. He's watching the news. Audrey's sitting on the couch writing a letter. I've just come from Lloyd's. I have an audition in an hour.

"You're here early," Buddy says. "I thought you had an audition this morning."

There're a couple of dishes over in the sink. I walk into the kitchen and start to wash them. I don't have to. But I always do it anyway. My back's to Buddy.

"Babe?"

I pick up a dish towel and start to dry the plate I've been working on. "Yeah?"

"I thought you had an audition this morning."

I look down at my frothy sink of dishwater and nod. A small bubble floats up and over my shoulder. "I thought I'd come by and see if you needed anything done before I went."

"Let me see you," he says.

I turn around. The floaty bubble pops against my cheek.

"What's wrong?"

"Nothing," I say.

He presses his lips together and tilts his head. "Your eyes are all red."

"I got soap in them."

He turns off the TV.

I take in a big gulp of air. Sometimes I forget to breathe.

"When I was getting ready this morning, putting on my makeup, Lloyd said I needed to learn how to do it better because I look fat."

Buddy crosses his arms. "You're not fat."

"That's ridiculous," Audrey says.

"He said my face is fat." I hold the dish towel up like I'm inspecting it for stains or something. I don't want Buddy to look at my fat face. I want him to think I'm pretty. Why doesn't Lloyd think I'm pretty? Why does he always have to tell me all the things I'm *not*?

"He said I should lose weight and get my back molars pulled. That might help. But he's not sure."

I don't want to go to my audition. I have a fat face. I don't want a record of it.

Thump. Thump. Thump.

My heart is talking to me. It does that. Especially when I'm upset. I'm not sure if it's saying *Keep going* or *Give up,* though.

Buddy stands in front of me. He takes the dish towel and lays it on the counter. He holds my face in his hands and looks at me. His calloused palms warm my baby cheeks. "You are beautiful," he says.

Nobody's ever said that to me before. Not unless they wanted something.

Buddy grins. He slides his thumb and pointer finger over the tip of my nose. He shows me his thumb peeking out between his fingers. "Got your nose," he says.

I laugh.

He gives it back.

Buddy spins me around and pushes me toward the door. "Now, go book that job," he says.

And I do.

Rayna and I walk down the sidewalk toward Lloyd's studio. Every block or two we stop and study a different window display so that she can tell me what's good or bad about this season's clothes. She likes to talk about stuff like that, so I let her. It's freezing out. We stand in front of a window, puffing steam.

She points at a thick, down-stuffed coat in the window. "Hideous," she says.

"Warm," I say.

She blows out a long stream of air. She's surrounded in breath clouds. "It's colder than a frosted frog," she says.

"Thanks for coming with me," I say. "I need a second opinion."

"Yeah, well, if you think it's bad—it's got to be. Your man standard isn't very high."

I don't say anything. I know she's right. Whenever I'm around Lloyd, I feel bad. Like I've done something wrong.

I knock on Lloyd's door. He doesn't know Rayna's with me. He opens the door, sees her, and frowns. Rayna walks past him into the studio. I follow. She's got her hackles up.

"Hello, Rayna," he says stiffly.

"Hello, Lloyd," she says.

She doesn't like him. She knows too much about him.

He doesn't like her. He knows she knows too much about him.

"Me and Rayna are going to a movie. Want to come?"

"Rayna and I," he says.

I guess I got my answer.

Rayna sits down on the couch. I sit down next to her. Lloyd ignores us. He walks over and opens his safe. Rayna raises her eyebrows. She knows about the butt photos. He flips through the stack of manila envelopes, steps back, and puts his hands on his hips. I bump Rayna with my knee. We pretend to look at the *Vogue* magazine Lloyd has on the coffee table.

"Oh, look at that," Rayna says. I see a grin behind those green eyes of hers. She's pretending she's talking about the magazine, but we both know she's talking about Lloyd.

Lloyd searches the stack again.

"That's funny," Rayna says.

Lloyd rubs his chin.

She taps her index finger on the open page. "I wonder where . . ." Her voice trails off.

I give Rayna a look.

Lloyd goes into his darkroom. We hear him shuffling things around. He comes back out. He runs his hands through his hair. "I had a big envelope. Did you see one lying around anywhere?"

Rayna's shoulders shake. I move away from her. I can't afford to get the giggles right now.

I widen my eyes. "I saw one on your desk yesterday."

"No. I said a big one. That wasn't big."

My inside ears hear the words "you idiot" attached to the end of his sentence.

Rayna softly clears her throat. She doesn't like the tone of his voice.

"Lloyd. Guess what! I booked a national Almond Joy commercial today."

He looks me up and down. He smiles. "I don't know why you work so much. It must be your personality," he says. He shakes his head.

Rayna clears her throat again. She's keeping score. "Kelle's quitting Healthworks today."

"Rayna's coming with me for moral support."

Lloyd's head whips around. "Why?"

"I've never quit a job before. I'm nervous."

"No. I mean why are you quitting?"

"I don't think I need to work there anymore."

"You shouldn't quit. It's a steady paycheck."

"I've got Buddy. That's a steady paycheck."

"He's a murderer. You need to get away from him."

Rayna slams the magazine she was holding down on the glass-topped coffee table. "We're going to be late for the movie. Ready?"

I nod.

"Kelle. He's awful," she says as soon as we get outside.

I stand next to her shivering. It's not the weather. It's Lloyd. He freezes me up from the inside out.

"Put your coat on."

"I don't want to."

Rayna takes my coat and gives it a shake. I stick my arms in the holes.

"You know what's weird?" I say. "When people see Lloyd and me together, they think he's my sugar daddy. Sugar mommy's more like it. He saves his money and spends mine."

"'Tick tock goes the clock,'" Rayna says. "It's time to cut bait."

"I can only quit one thing at a time," I say.

When I get back to Lloyd's, it's dark out. He's taking photos of a girl.

A nude girl.

He's got partitions set up. She doesn't know I'm there. A space heater runs next to him. The studio is cold. The poor girl must be freezing. She is. One look at her nipples and I know it's true. I wouldn't be surprised if he kept the place cold on purpose.

He fingers his camera lens. "Tilt your chin back. Beautiful," he says.

"All Revved Up with No Place to Go" blares through the stereo speakers.

How ironic.

I look at the girl's feet. Band-Aids cover her blistered heels. Big red nerve splotches cover her neck and chest.

I remember when I was new like that. Wide eyed. Innocent. I feel sorry for her. She doesn't know about the Lloyds and Perrys of the world.

She will soon.

I think I know why she doesn't just stand up for herself and say no. She's afraid Lloyd'll throw her out, or tell her agency that she's a lousy model, or not hire her, or even worse, he might tell all his friends that she's difficult and that they shouldn't hire her either.

Sometimes when you do the right thing, people aren't going to be happy about it. But you have to do it anyway.

I learned that a long time ago. . . .

I push back against the wall and try to stay out of the way. My father swings a metal chair at Bob like a baseball bat. It catches Bob's leg. He falls to the floor. My father stands over him. Legs spread wide. His dark eyes flashing fire. He pulls his foot back to kick him.

"No," I say. "No."

I step between them. I push my face up at my father. "Stop," I say quietly. My eyes are cool. He can do what he wants to me, but I'm not going to stand by and watch him abuse one more person.

He stops. He's surprised. He doesn't know what he's supposed to do now.

Nobody's ever stopped him with words before.

He looks down at me.

"You're a little man. I despise you," I say.

The glint goes out of his eyes. His face sags. His shoulders slump forward. "I'm going to go kill myself," he says.

He picks up his keys and leaves. His tires scatter stones as his car whips past the house and out onto the street.

I turn to face my family.

My mother looks at me. "Why would you say that?"

"If he kills himself, it'll be all your fault," my sister yells.

Rick shakes his head.

Bob gets up off the floor, goes to his room, and slams the door.

I look at Lloyd. I look at the girl.

This is one of those have-to-do-it-anyway moments.

I walk in front of Lloyd's camera. The girl holds her blouse up in front of her breasts.

"I think you're done here," I say to him.

Lloyd clenches his jaw. He's mad.

I don't care.

The girl gathers up her things and leaves.

If I get the chance, I'll burn her negatives too.

A commotion in the apartment across the street catches my eye. A couple is arguing. She's yelling. He's flailing his arms around. This isn't the first time for them. He storms out onto the balcony and slams the door. She walks over and locks it. He's in his underwear. He sits down on a chair, rests his chin on the palms of his hands, and sighs. It starts to snow. An hour later he's still out there.

THE LETTER

A stream of letters spills through the studio's small brass mail slot. I sit down at Lloyd's desk and sort them into piles. Lloyd is working on location today. He won't be back for a couple of hours. The last bit is some sort of card. It says "Hallmark" on the back. Lloyd never gets cards like that. Normally, I would just add it to his stack of personal mail, but there's something about it that makes me suspicious. If he's up to no good, I want to know.

I flip it over and look at the rows of curvy, round letters. It's definitely from a girl. A light box is built into the top of Lloyd's desk. He designed it himself. He's very proud of it. I press the envelope against the lit surface. I can't see anything.

I go into the kitchen, put a pan of water on the stove top, and turn up the flame. Steam rises off the rapidly boiling water. I wave the envelope through it. I've never done this before. The envelope flap pops open. That's the good news. The bad news is that all the envelope flaps pop open.

They make it look so easy in the movies.

Dear Lloyd,

Thanks for calling me on my birthday. Happy fortieth birthday to you, too! I want you to know that I meant it when I said I'm over the problems that led to our divorce. I'm happy now. It turns out it was for the best.

Love,
D

Forty! Divorced! My hands shake. Rayna was right. I'm sleeping with an old man!

The phone rings. I pick it up. It's Lloyd. He finished early. He's on his way home.

I look down at the envelope. Lloyd has glue. I can glue it back together. I smear a dab across the seams with my fingertip and press it all back together. The flaps pop open. I sit a big book on it. When I take the book off, the flaps stay put. The hot steam made the envelope all wavy, though. I get out Lloyd's iron, lay a dish towel over the envelope, and iron it. I peel back the towel. I sigh. Still wavy.

Maybe I should just throw it away. It wouldn't be the first time a letter got lost in the mail.

I know! I gather up all the mail and set it on the coffee table right next to the fern plant. I water the fern. Water leaks out over the catch rim and onto the table. The Lloyd's-forty-and-divorced card soaks up the dirty water.

When Lloyd sees what I've done, he'll be mad.

But he won't know.

I don't want to be there when he shows up. I don't have the best poker face in the world. I'm going to go see if Buddy wants me to do anything for him. Audrey helps him so much now he doesn't need me like he used to. He'd pay me just to sit there. But I don't have to. I'm doing a lot of print work, and my commercials are running a lot. Every once in a while someone will ask, "Aren't you the girl in that Camay commercial?" Some people have the best memory.

On the way up to Buddy's I stop by the apartment. Rayna is getting ready to leave. I tell her about Lloyd. She rolls her eyes.

"Rayna," I say. "He wants me to move in with him."

She puts her hairbrush down.

"He says I'm there so much anyway, I might as well move in and split the rent."

"Split the rent? You're kidding, right?"

"He says that even if I don't move in, I should split the rent anyway. It's only fair."

"That guy's nuttier than a squirrel turd."

"Yeah," I say. "It got me thinking, though. I think maybe I should get my own place now. I can afford it. You can afford it. That way you can decorate however you want. Not worry about having people over late at night. What do you think?"

For some reason I'm not afraid to say things like that to Rayna.

"It'll be so weird not having you here," she says.

"It won't be that much different. We'll still see each other all the time."

She nods. "Will you let me help you find a place?"

"I was hoping you'd say that."

I walk into Buddy's apartment. He waves the latest issue of *Time* magazine at me. "Here," he says.

That means I'm supposed to read it. The whole thing. Not just the good parts. "The brain is like a muscle," he always says. "Keep it in shape."

"Buddy?" I say.

"Yep?"

"Do you think I'm smart?"

He looks at me like I've lost my mind. "You? You're one of the smartest cookies I know."

Maybe my father was wrong about me.

Buddy springs up off the couch. "Listen. I have to be somewhere. I need you to do something for me."

"Sure," I say.

A small chest of drawers sits against the wall. He

moves it aside. Behind it is a safe. It's built right into the wall. I didn't know Buddy had a safe. He tells me the combination.

"Don't tell anybody. Not David, Audrey. Nobody," he says.

He doesn't have to worry. Secret keeping is my specialty.

When Buddy's sure I know how to work the lock, he leaves.

An hour later he calls. "A bum is coming over soon. Go to that thing and give him ten."

"Okay," I say.

I sit down on the couch and worry. Ten what? Ten dollars? Ten hundreds? Ten thousand?

What if I'm wrong?

I open the safe up and pull out a stack of hundred-dollar bills. There's a bunch of them in there. I've never held that much money before. I'm going with a thousand dollars. I count out ten hundred-dollar bills, lock the safe, slide the chest of drawers back . . . and wait.

There's a knock at the door.

I open it.

It's a man in a suit. He's not scary looking or anything. I didn't know what to expect.

"Are you Kelle?" he asks.

"Yes."

"Buddy sent me to pick up an envelope."

An envelope! I run over to the counter, grab an

envelope, and put the money inside. I should have known that. People don't just hand out cash willy-nilly. It has to be contained.

I give him the envelope.

He smiles. "Thank you," he says.

"You're welcome."

I shut the door. I hear the elevator ding and voices. I open the door and peek out. It's Buddy and Audrey. Buddy's talking to the guy I just gave the money to. I think he's from his attorney's office. They're talking about Buddy's case. I quietly close the door. I don't believe in eavesdropping. Sometimes you hear things you wish you hadn't.

Buddy and Audrey come in, drop their coats on the couch, and ask me if I want to eat with them. I say sure. Audrey spreads cream cheese on slices of date bread and hands them around.

"Buddy," I say. "You know who you remind me of? Albert Einstein. I saw some pictures of him in a book at Rizzoli's."

"I love that bookstore," Audrey says. She's quiet for a minute, then she laughs. "It was the hair, wasn't it?"

"The hair, the mustache, the eyes. Everything," I say. I grin. "What was with that guy's hair, anyway?"

Audrey points to Buddy's head. "What's with this guy's hair?"

We all laugh.

I like eating date bread and laughing with Audrey

and Buddy. As simple as it is, it's better than any meal I ever ate at my father's table. It's not the food. It's the company.

"God is great. God is good. Let us thank him for our food. By his hands we all are fed. Give us, Lord, our daily bread. Amen," we say together. Even though we say it really fast, every word works its way into my heart. The "God is great" prayer is my favorite. The other one, the "If I die before I wake" one, scares me. I don't like that one.

My father always serves himself first. We wait with our heads down and our hands in our laps until he's done. Then the "please pass the's" start. We say them quietly. My father doesn't like a lot of talking at the supper table.

I put my elbows up on my place mat. My mother looks over at me. She shakes her head slightly. Elbows aren't allowed on the table. When I go to lift them off, I knock my glass of milk over. It pours all over the table and drips down through the extension cracks onto the floor.

"Can't a man eat in peace?" my father says. He puffs up. He's mad.

I jump up to get a rag. "Yes. I'm sorry, Daddy."

He grabs my arm as I run by. I swing back around.

"Yes what?" he says in my face. His air smells. He hasn't had time to wash his cigarette breath down his throat yet.

"Yes, sir," I say. My arm hurts. I say the word "sir" louder than the "yes" so he knows I'm serious.

He twists my arm. "Are you fucking mocking me?"

"Richard. Let her go. She's not mocking you," my mother says.

"What the fuck," he yells. "You're defending her?"

He lets go of my arm. I don't move. He doesn't like it when you run. He stands up, grabs the big plate of fried chicken, and smashes it down on the table. The plate explodes. China shrapnel flies everywhere, getting into everything. The string bean bowl. The mashed potato bowl. The chicken gravy bowl. The plates. The glasses. My father is good at breaking dishes. He's had a lot of practice.

Nobody moves.

He storms out of the room.

No one says a word. We just stand up and start to clear the table. I get the vacuum. We don't stop until everything is all cleaned up. When we're done, my mother gives us each a ham and butter sandwich.

I feel bad.

I really wanted some of that gravy.

Rayna calls me at work.

"Kelle, I found the perfect place for you. There's a studio apartment available for three twenty-five a month in a newly remodeled apartment building near Gramercy Park. You're not going to beat that price anywhere. I think you should go check it out right away."

"I'm leaving now," I say.

"*Stand still,*" Rayna says. She draws a pencil across the top of my head. "There."

I step away from the wall and look back at the little black mark she just made. It's two inches higher than the last mark.

"I told you!" I say.

"You slumped the last time."

"I did not," I say. "Think how tall you'd be by now if you hadn't drunk all that Coke."

She waves her hand at me. "I don't want to be a model anymore anyway. I want to be a singer."

"A singer?"

"I'm going to take lessons and everything."

"You'll be a good singer," I say.

Rayna tapes down the lids on my moving boxes. They're actually used grocery store boxes. Rayna got them for me. I told her that as long as they never had food in them, they would be fine. So one toilet paper and one paper towel box later, and I'm packed. The only other thing I have is a tall physician's scale that my mother sent me. She got it at an estate sale.

We take it all down to the sidewalk. I stand back with my boxes and scale while Rayna flags down a cab. Cabdrivers don't like to double for moving vans. One stops. Rayna jumps in. When the driver sees my boxes, he tries to throw her out. She won't budge. She's Southern; he doesn't know what he's dealing with. He opens the trunk, I load it up, and off we go.

"There it is," I say, "304 East Twentieth Street." I couldn't wipe the smile off my face if I tried. My own apartment. I never dreamed this day would come.

We prop the building's front door open with my scale and carry the boxes back around the corner to the elevator. It takes about thirty seconds. When I get back to the front door, the scale is gone. How is that possible! I expect someone to pop around the corner and say, "surprise!" I walk out onto the sidewalk and look around. Not a scale to be found.

This would never happen at Buddy's building.

That's one of the perks of living across the street from a famous Italian restaurant and having a suspected murderer for a landlord. Nobody steals things off your front stoop. You're safe there.

I go back inside. "Rayna, you're not going to believe this—somebody just stole my scale."

"Hope they have a big bathroom," she says.

Rayna never liked that scale. She called it a space hog.

I never liked it either. I just kept it because my mom gave it to me.

We get in the elevator. I push LL.

"What's LL?" Rayna asks.

"Lower level."

"The basement?"

"Uh-huh."

"You mean like Laverne and Shirley?"

"Uh-huh."

When I showed Rayna the floor plan, I didn't tell her about the basement part. I was afraid she'd try to talk me out of it.

"It's so convenient. I can use the stairs. I never have to wait for the elevator unless I want to."

We push the boxes with our knees around the corner and down a narrow hall. The carpet is new. The smell makes my nose itch.

"I don't have any neighbors next to me, below me, or above me. I can play my music as loud as I want."

"That's nice," Rayna says. She always tries to be supportive.

I unlock the door. It's pitch dark inside.

"Kelle, I can't see anything."

I reach around and turn on the light.

"Isn't the kitchen cute?" I say. "Everything is brand-new. I even have a dishwasher. I'm going to keep my papers and stuff in it."

Rayna looks around. "Separate kitchen. Nice bathroom. Good-size living space. I really like the hardwood floors. The builders did a great job. If they'd included a window, it'd be perfect."

"There's a window."

I point up at a tiny recessed window. It sits a couple of feet back from the living-room wall in a deep alcove.

"You'd need a ladder to see out of that," she says.

"It looks out on a stairwell anyway," I say.

"Isn't it going to bother you to be in the dark all the time?"

"No."

There's a loud crashing sound behind the kitchen wall.

Rayna jumps. "What was that?"

"Oh. That's the building's trash chute. It backs up to my apartment. It's so convenient."

"Hmmmm," Rayna says.

"The furniture got here in good shape," I say.

My convertible couch and love seat are covered in a periwinkle blue print from Laura Ashley. They're so cheery looking. Rayna helped me pick them out.

We move them around until we're happy with their placement.

"You need some nice lamps, a little table for the kitchen, an end table, and maybe a bookshelf."

"I'm going to get a TV," I say.

"I'll pay for half of it," Rayna says. "That'll be your housewarming gift."

"Beats a tear gas gun," I say.

Rayna points at an alcove on the other side of the living room. "A bed would fit perfectly there. You could put some pretty fabric up in front of it. You should do that."

I shake my head.

"A real bed is more important than a TV," she says.

Just then my door buzzer goes off.

"Who could that be?" Rayna asks.

I shrug.

I know who it is. I just don't want to tell her. She's going to go crazy.

I push the intercom button. "Yes?"

"Delivery. Baldwin Pianos."

I push the button that unlocks the building's front door.

"Piano! What?" Rayna's mouth hangs open.

With all the things we've been through together, I've never seen her look so shocked. I've never seen anybody look so shocked.

"Umm . . ."

"I didn't even know you played."

"I don't."

"What!"

"Lloyd talked me into it."

"I'm going to wring his neck," Rayna says. "How can you afford a piano?"

"Payments."

Rayna looks at me.

"Lloyd said it was good. I should start to get a credit rating. It's never too early, he said."

There's a knock at the door. The movers haul my thirty-year-old, ivory-keyed baby grand in on its side. Rayna falls back onto the couch. I always wondered what it meant for a woman to swoon. Now I know.

I point at the alcove. "It goes there," I say to the movers.

Rayna stands up. "Call me after you get settled."

The piano has legs now. The men flip it upright and slide it into place. It's really big. Rayna refuses to look over there. I don't think she can take much more.

She gives me a little hug. She likes to do that. I'm starting to get used to it.

"Thanks," I say. "I don't know what I'd do without you."

Her eyes puddle up. "It's not going to ever be the same, is it?"

I rest my hand on her forearm. "No," I say. "It's going to be even better."

Rayna musters up a smile. "Promise me I'm going to see you the second you're settled."

I look at my two boxes of stuff. "I'll see you in about an hour, then."

She laughs.

"Hey," I say. "Tell me the truth. Did you pay someone to take that scale?"

"No. You just got lucky," she says with a grin.

As she walks away, she throws a "See you later, alligator" over her shoulder.

"After while, crocodile," I say.

I close the door and open up the paper towel box. Right on top is my silver-framed photo of Muffet. It's not the expensive kind of silver. It's the kind that rubs off if you polish it too much. Muffet and I are at a horse show. She's reaching out to me with her soft, sweet nose. I'm looking back at her, smiling.

This is one of my favorite pictures. If it weren't for Bob, I wouldn't have it. He sent it to me. My father had thrown it away. Every once in a while my father goes throwaway crazy. When that happens, he goes from room to room throwing everything he doesn't like out the window. When he's done, he piles it all up in the back of his truck, drives it out to a back-field ditch, and dumps it. After that he pushes dirt over it with his tractor plow. Bob saved my picture right before the plow stage.

I place it on top of the piano's shiny black lid. It looks so nice there. Like something out of a magazine.

If nothing else, my vintage baby grand makes a really good five-thousand-dollar end table.

Just what every girl needs.

Next I hang my clothes up according to type and color, spacing each hanger so that nothing gets wrinkled. It looks so nice and tidy.

When it's time for bed, I stack the couch cushions on the love seat and pull out the sofa bed. I tuck a flat sheet around the foam mattress and spread my blanket out on top of it. The last thing I do before I climb in is tuck my tear gas gun under the love seat cushion. Rayna didn't want it.

I lie in bed staring out into the darkness. No Rayna. No Lloyd. No family. Nobody to come along and put their thoughts in my head. Just me.

I slip off into an easy sleep.

Someone is tickling my hand with a feather. "Stop it," I say.

I open my eyes. It's not a feather. It's something else. I run over to the wall switch and turn on the light.

A million roaches run for cover. The biggest roaches I've ever seen in my life. I think they could take me in a fight.

I run to the sink and wash my hands in the hottest water I can stand. There's no crumbs on the counter. Everything is sparkling clean. Why are they here?

The trash chute.

Oh no. I signed a year's lease. What have I done? I feel all creepy-crawly.

I force myself to stop, take a deep breath, and think things through.

Okay, so I have a few hundred unexpected guests to contend with, but seriously—what did I expect for $325 a month? If the place were perfect, I wouldn't be able to afford it. Nothing a little Raid can't handle.

No need to panic.

These are good problems.

THE LIGHT OF DAY

My alarm clock rings. I get up off the couch and head into the bathroom. I don't bother with the bed part anymore. The wires poke up through the foam mattress. It's really uncomfortable.

I've got lamps now. Good lighting is important when you live in a cave.

The phone rings.

It's Lloyd.

"It's been a month now, how about I come over tonight and see your new place?" he says.

"I'll come to yours," I say. "I don't want you to see it until it's all finished. I want it to be perfect."

That's what I always say to him. I don't want him here. Right now it's filled with good feelings; he'll bring his stinky attitude in and ruin it all. This is my place. Not his. I'm not going to let him do that.

I have a big audition today. For Coke. It's the talk of

the teenage-actress town. Everybody wants the lead part. I'll take any part. As long as they pay me for my time.

I walk outside. The bright winter sun reflects off the sidewalk and dirty white snow piles. My eyes sting. I've gotten used to that now. There's a transition between the darkness and the light. It actually hurts. I hold my eyes halfway closed until my big black pupils shrink back to size.

I walk into the casting-office waiting room and sit down. I know all the faces. They're the best of the best. The ones who book everything they go out on. At least, they make it seem that way. With their mothers by their side for courage, they stare and talk behind their hands.

I grew up in the show ring. I eat competitive little girls like them for breakfast. I read my sides and ignore them. The mothers are even worse. The way they look me up and down makes me want to laugh. I read my sides and ignore them, too.

The casting director calls four of us to go in together. I like one of the girls. Stephanie. Her mother knits and minds her own business. The four of us line up in front of the camera. We each take turns being prom organizer Bobbie. That's the lead role. The other girls are so much better than me. They're good with their lines. They don't even have to look at the cue card.

I do.

The more important something is to me, the more I forget what I'm supposed to remember. That goes for bad things too, which I suppose is a good thing.

"I've got an hour between auditions," Stephanie says to me as we walk out. "Want to have a slice of pizza with me and my mom?"

"Want to come see my new apartment instead?" I say. I'm excited to show it off. "I live close to here."

"Mom?"

Her mother nods. "Let's go," she says.

"Nice building," Stephanie's mother says as we walk up to the front door.

I decide we should take the elevator, not the stairs. It presents better. I think it throws Stephanie and her mom when it goes down instead of up, though. Maybe I should have warned them.

I open my door and turn on the light.

"Can I use your bathroom?" Stephanie asks.

"Sure." I point straight ahead. "Right there."

She walks in, closes the door, and lets out a blood-curdling scream.

Her mother whips the door open just in time to see five cockroaches dive down the sink drain. Stephanie runs out into the kitchen. She hops from foot to foot, squealing like a stuck pig. Surely they have cockroaches in Long Island.

Every room has a can of Raid tucked into some corner or cabinet. My living room has four. I want my little friends to know I'm armed and dangerous. I squirt some Raid down the drain and close it. I don't know if that works, but it always makes me feel better.

"Want some tea?" I ask.

"That would be nice," the mother says. Stephanie isn't talking.

Teacups in hand, they sit down on the couch.

"I love your antique oak. You have such nice pieces."

"I just got them. I'm looking for a bookcase, too, but it has to be just right."

She doesn't say anything about the piano. Rayna calls it the elephant in the room.

They put their cups down in the sink. Luckily, the cockroaches are gone. They usually only come out in the dark.

"Thanks for coming by," I say.

"Thanks for having us. Your place is lovely," the mother says.

As soon as they leave, my agent calls. I have a callback on the Coke commercial tomorrow.

I get there early. Tucked in a tiny nook next to the waiting room is a mirror. You have to be a regular to know about it. I stand in front of the mirror rolling on lip gloss and pinching my cheeks. I recognize Stephanie's voice. She's telling a story to some of the other girls. They're all laughing. It's a mean laugh. They're making fun of somebody. I peek around the corner.

"Roaches?!" Tammy squeals.

"A sinkful," Stephanie says. "It was hideous."

Stephanie's mother knits and minds her business.

I lean my head back against the mirror. I didn't need to pinch my cheeks.

"Kelle?" the casting director calls out. "Is Kelle here?"

"Right here," I say.

I level my eyes at Stephanie. She looks down at her knees. I've got a name for girls like her: Slap Face. She's the kind of girl you want to slap some good manners into. Somebody should. Maybe her mother needs to stop minding her own business and do something about the brat she's raising. When I'm really upset, I let the anger out in my brain. I stop it before it gets to my mouth.

The casting director leads us all into the room. I stand next to Stephanie. I want her to know I'm there. A bunch of official-looking advertising types sit at a table behind the camera.

Game on, girl, I think.

The casting director points the camera at me. "Slate your name," she says.

I tilt my chin down slightly. I know I look better that way.

I laugh like someone just said something funny. "Hi! I'm Kelle," I say.

"I like her," I hear one of the advertising types say.

Before I go home, I stop at the small asphalt park next to my building and watch the children play. That always makes me feel better. The kids are bundled up from head to toe. Jets of steam pour from their mouths as they call back and forth to one another. Two young girls hold a long jump rope between them. *Swish. Swish.* They swing it through the air. A third girl jumps in. "Teddy Bear, Teddy Bear, turn around," they say. The girl turns around. The rope smacks her ankle. She wants another try. They say okay.

A little boy stoops at the top of a small slide. He grips the handrail. His mother is at the bottom, wiggling her fingers. "Come on," she says. He shakes his head. "You can do it." He presses his lips together and sits down. He slowly slides down to his mother. It's a baby slide. It's not the slick banana-peel kind where you're lucky not to fall back and whack your head on the way down. The little boy laughs. With his tummy leading the way, he marches around with his hands on his hips, picking his knees up high like a bowlegged cowboy. He's very proud of himself. "Gan, gan," he says.

Sitting on the metal bench makes my butt cold. I go inside and make a big mug of hot chocolate. My answering machine light is on. I have a message. I push the play button.

"Hi, this message is for Kelle. This is Susan. I need to get your sizes for the Coke commercial. Call me as soon as you get this message."

The Coke commercial! I booked the Coke commercial! I put my hands on my hips and walk around the apartment like the little slide boy just to see what it feels like. I'm so ridiculous.

I dial the phone. "Hi, Susan. This is Kelle."

"Oh, hi, Kelle."

I give her my sizes.

"We'll see you Thursday," she says.

"Susan?"

"Yeah?"

"Do you know which part I got?"

"Oh," she says. She sounds surprised. "You got the lead. You're Bobbie!"

$\mathcal{I}$ have my second acting class tonight. After the first class a girl asked me if I wanted to do a scene with her. I'm supposed to meet her in an hour. I'm glad she wants to rehearse at her place. She's really sophisticated. She wears a fluffy fur coat and diamond earrings. And that's just to acting class. I don't know how she'd react if one of my roaches sauntered by her on his way into my kitchen.

Before I leave, I get out one of my big cans of Raid and spray it all around my couch and love seat. I don't want my six-legged friends getting too comfortable while I'm away. They're like bad roommates. When I'm not home, they leave their crap all over the place. Literally. At least the spray keeps them off the furniture.

My new scene partner lives in a very nice building just off of Fifth Avenue. I knock on her door. Nothing. I knock again. Still nothing.

I look down at my watch. I'm a little bit early. Maybe she's not home yet. I sit down across from her door and wait.

After a few minutes I hear voices coming from inside her apartment. I stand up. The door opens. My scene partner and a cashmere-coated gray-haired man look out at me. The man opens his lips to say something but then doesn't. As he walks past me, he smiles.

My scene partner gestures for me to come in. "He likes you," she says.

I think that's a weird thing to say. "Was that your father?"

She laughs. "Have a seat," she says. She pats the couch.

"Bebe," she calls out softly.

I think she's calling her French maid to bring us drinks or something. That's how nice her apartment is.

A little white dog jumps up into her lap. Her collar sparkles in the lamplight.

"Real diamonds," she says. "A gift."

"Bebe or the collar?"

"Both."

"It's getting late. We should probably get started," I say.

She stares at me. "That gentleman you just saw. He's a very wealthy, powerful man. He likes you. Do you like him?"

I shrug. "I don't know him."

I think I know what she's getting at. I pretend I don't.

"I make a lot of money entertaining men like him. They buy me nice things. Take me nice places. Would you like to have nice things and go to nice places?"

I stare at her. She makes it sound so easy.

"Kelle. A lot of men would pay a lot of money to spend time with someone like you."

Okay, now it's getting creepy.

"Want to rehearse?" I ask.

She looks over at a big, black-rimmed school clock hanging in the kitchen. I guess when you're not in school anymore, that's cool.

She shakes her head. "I have a guest coming soon. Last-minute thing. I can't come to class tonight. Do you mind if we do it another time?"

"No. That's okay," I say.

She opens the front door. "Think about what I said."

Oh, I'll be thinking about it, all right. She's like the gold-toothed man at Port Authority. She just makes more money.

I sit in class watching everybody do their scenes. I want to do a scene too. Sitting next to me is a beautiful blond boy. He's got blue eyes and a Danish accent. His name is Viggo.

He makes my hips want to move.

I've never felt like that before.

I think about my scene partner. I'm not going back to her. I don't know how she lives like that. Sleeping with old men she barely knows. Men who don't make her hips want to move. I couldn't do that.

Suddenly I go cold.

I am doing that.

With Lloyd.

I unlock the dead bolts on Lloyd's studio door. There're three of them. I count off the clacks—one, two, three—push the door open, and walk inside. I hear a girl's voice. Lloyd told me not to come until seven. He must still be shooting. I put the food I bought for dinner down on the floor and relock the door. In the background Bob Dylan sings about someone having a lot of nerve.

Lloyd walks around the corner. His shoulders slope forward even more than usual. He's got his hands in his pockets and he's walking flat on his feet. More shuffle than walk. Something is wrong.

His photography equipment is neatly stacked against the far wall. He's really fussy about tidiness. I walk over and touch one of the lights. It's cool. I look over at Lloyd. He looks down at his toes and shrugs.

My brain fires up. This can only mean one thing.

"Lloyd?" I say.

The spiral staircase creaks. I turn around. A petite, brown-haired girl sashays down the steps. She's a lot older than me. Her hair is cut in a pixie. She weighs about ten pounds.

She bats her long, false-lashed eyes at Lloyd. "*Au revoir,*" she says in a singsong voice. She winks at me. She probably thinks I'm his daughter. But you never know with the French.

Lloyd walks her to the door. Before she leaves, he whispers some stupid French words in her ear. She giggles. I don't know what she has to giggle about. I may not know much, but one thing I'm absolutely certain of is that sex is not Lloyd's forte. How good can anything be that, on a good night, barely lasts a minute? Lloyd shuts the door.

I stare at him with blank eyes. I don't cry. I don't yell. I'm completely empty. Numb.

He goes boyish on me. He's playing the naughty-boy card. He drags his toe across the hardwood floor. "That was Sophie. I met her while I was shooting French *Vogue* last month. She's a stylist. I told her to stop by if she ever came to the States."

Stop by? Does he think I'm an idiot?

The States. Does he know how stupid he sounds when he talks like that? He's not from Europe. He's a wrinkly old man from Arizona who can't keep it up, with a crazy-ass mother who told him good girls are virgins, bad girls are whores. So like any zealot, he bounces between the two. I know because his whore just left the building.

I slowly climb the staircase steps. It takes everything in me not to drop down on my knees and crawl up them like I did the first time I was here.

The bed I made this morning is a mess. The top sheet lies off to the side in a twist. A tube of lubricant lies on the pillow. Streaks of blood cover the gray and white pin-striped sheets. That girl was no virgin. She left behind another kind of blood.

I bought those sheets.

I put my hand up over my mouth.

"You might want to change those," Lloyd says over my shoulder like he's doing me a favor or something.

He rests his hand on my shoulder. My brain screams, *Get away from me,* but my mouth stays quiet. I stuff the top sheet into one of the pillowcases.

"She doesn't mean anything to me," Lloyd says. "You're young. If you were older, you'd understand."

A furnace-hot heat surges through my body. My heart thumps. Like my veins are too narrow for my blood, they throb in rhythm with my quickening pulse. My fingers curl into fists around my pillowcase laundry bag.

I want to elbow his belly, wrap my arm around his neck, flip him over onto his back, slam my heel down on his ankle, and turn it from side to side like it's a cigarette that needs rubbing out. I want to kick him with my steel-toed cowboy boots. I want to kick him and kick him and kick him. When he's broken and bloody and sobbing at my feet, that's when I'll finally stop.

I look down at my fists. I'd do it, but he's not worth a jail sentence.

He's not worth my spit.

Instead I slowly turn to face him. I hand him his dirty sheets. "Good-bye, Lloyd," I say. My voice is flat.

He drops the sheets. He's shocked. He's forgotten that I have something really important now. Something I've never had before.

I have a place to go.

I walk down the staircase and out the door. He chases me down the hallway. "Please come back. Don't leave like this. I'll make it up to you."

It's tough to see a good servant go.

The elevator doors open. I step in. As the doors close, I look him straight in the eyes. My face is quiet. My eyes aren't. Like lasers, they bore into him. Erasing the parts of me he holds inside his jet-black heart. I'm not his anymore. He knows it. He backs up a step. I hope it hurts.

I walk into the lobby. Leonard is sleeping. I need him to unlock the big chain.

I softly touch his shoulder. "Leonard," I say.

He opens his eyes. "You okay?" he asks.

He knows.

He let Sophie out before me.

I kneel down by his side. I lay my head on his shoulder.

He strokes my hair. "You remind me of my grand-daughter," he says. "She's a good girl too."

"I don't feel very good," I say.

A tear rolls down my cheek and onto my neck. I wipe it away with my open hand.

"Shush, shush," he says.

He gets up and pulls the chain out of the door. It wasn't locked. I could have gotten out all along.

"Bye, Leonard." My lip quivers. "Don't forget about me."

Little puddles form in the rims of his eyes. "I won't forget about you."

He opens the door and out I walk.

I'm going home.

I don't lock my apartment door.
I don't care.

I sit down on my sofa and stare at my baby grand piano. It's half the size of my studio. Because of it, I sleep on the couch. There's no room for a bed. Stupid Lloyd. He talked me into buying it. I don't even play the piano.

I curl up into a ball and start to cry. Stupid Lloyd. He's the worst person in the world. Stupid me. Why can't anybody love me? Why aren't I good enough? I try so hard. I must be doing it wrong. I'm not enough. I'm all wrong. The cushion under my face soaks up my tears like a sponge. I slam my fist into the armrest. "I hate you, I hate you, I hate you," I say. I'm not sure who I hate. My father, Ken, Brant, Perry, Lloyd.

Me.

I roll over onto my back. The room is as dark as my thoughts. I'll never be right. Babies raised without love never learn to love. We learned that in school. They have a hole that can't be patched up. I think I have a hole too. I've had just enough love to know what it is, but not how to find it. My stomach twists like a tightly wrung dishcloth. I clench my teeth. It hurts so bad. I'm being punished for all my bad decisions.

My mother would say, "It serves you right. That's what you get."

I think about Muffet. How she had a really bad bellyache one night. She wanted to lie down, but I wouldn't let her. I knew if she did, she would thrash around, twist her gut, and die. That's what happens to colicking horses that lie down. I walked her back and forth, back and forth. All of a sudden she stopped. She wouldn't take another step. Her legs folded under her and down she went. She wouldn't get up. I pulled at her halter.

"Muffet, get up," I screamed. "Please, Muffet. I can't do this without you."

She rolled over onto her back. Her legs paddled the air. Ducking her flying hooves, I pushed her back onto her side. She lay there panting. Her eyes rolled back into her head. Drool puddled under her soft, sweet nose. She groaned.

"Muffet. No! Get up. I love you. Don't leave me."

She was giving up. She was in too much pain.

I couldn't live without her. I would do anything to save her.

I closed my eyes. "Dear God, forgive me," I said. And

then I kicked her as hard as I could in her soft, round belly. She looked back at me. She couldn't understand why I would hurt her like that. I kicked her again.

"Muffet, get up!" I screamed. "Muffet, get up!"

I kicked her again and again and again. She raised her head, pushed up with her front legs, and with a loud groan got back on her feet. Her head hung low. Her sides heaved in and out. But she was standing. I threw my arms around her. I kissed her a million times.

She got back up. She got back up for me.

We walked for the rest of the night. We watched the sun come up.

Later that day she ran around the pasture and played in our stream. She was so happy. It was like it never happened.

If Muffet survived that, I can survive this.

I get up off the couch and change into my favorite nightgown. The one that makes me feel like a princess. I light the little lavender candle I keep in my bathroom. The flickering light multiplies in the mirror. I look at my face. My brown eyes look back. I'm so far away from the girl in the mirror. A tear falls from my eye. I follow it with my finger.

This isn't good enough. Avoiding pain isn't good enough. If it worked, I'd keep doing it. But it doesn't work. No matter how hard I try, it still finds me. I was wrong about Lloyd. He took advantage of me. He used me.

I let him.

I thought it was safe. Serving him. Making his life better. Mistaking criticism for love.

There is something better for me out there. I hold my hand over my heart. "There's something better for me in here," I say out loud. "And I'm going to find it."

I've always been good at finding lost things.

There's a soft knocking at my door. I splash some water on my face and open it. It's Rayna. I knew it. She looks at me.

"It's time for you to come out and play," she says. "It's been a week already. Why are you ignoring my calls?"

I shrug my shoulders.

She opens up my closet and pulls out a pair of jeans, a silk blouse, and my cowboy boots. "Here," she says. "Get dressed. We're going out."

I've learned not to argue. I take the clothes into the bathroom and start to change.

"Kelle. What are all those books on your kitchen table?" Rayna asks through the bathroom door.

"Sex books."

"I can see that. What are you doing with them?"

I open the door.

"You look nice," she says.

"Studying," I say.

"Studying?"

"I don't think I'm ever going to do it again. But just in case, I want to be prepared."

Rayna looks over at the big stack of books. "Is that a highlighter?"

I walk over to my answering machine. "Listen," I say. I push the play button.

"Hi, Kelle. I'm calling from the Ford Modeling Agency. We'd love to represent you if you're interested . . ."

I turn the sound down. "It's that lady I met when I first got here. I can tell by her voice. A casting director told her about me."

"Oh my gosh. That is too funny! Are you going to meet with her?"

"Let me think. Ummm . . . noooo."

Rayna laughs. "Let's go," she says.

"Where are we going?"

"A bar."

"A bar!"

"It'll be fun."

We go outside. "Taxi," I say. I stick my hand out. It's so exciting to see the light on top of the cab lit up. Especially when it's cold out and you're wearing high-heeled boots. When it pulls over, you feel like you just caught a big fish or something. It's very rewarding.

"The White Horse Tavern, 567 Hudson, please," Rayna says.

The driver flicks the meter on, and off we go.

It doesn't take long to get there. We stand under the tavern's buzzing neon sign. Rayna freshens her lipstick.

I pull at my earlobe. "Doesn't that buzzing tickle your ears?" I say.

"What buzzing?" Rayna asks.

She can't hear it.

We go in and sit down at a little table just off the long bar.

"This place is famous," Rayna says. "Dylan Thomas drank himself to death here."

"Can someone really do that?" I ask.

"If they drink eighteen shots of whiskey, they can," she says.

"What can I get you?" the waitress asks us.

I'd say "Eighteen shots of whiskey," but you can't say that kind of stuff to strangers. They might think you're serious.

"Two glasses of white wine and an order of onion rings," Rayna says.

The waitress leaves.

"Onion rings! Yum. I haven't eaten fried food since I met Lloyd." Saying the word "Lloyd" takes my excitement away. I look at Rayna. "Do you think I liked him more than I thought I did?"

"No," Rayna says. "You're just scared. You don't want to hurt anymore."

A few minutes later the waitress puts our drinks and onion rings down on the table.

"You're going to feel better soon."

"Pinkie swear?"

She links her little finger in mine.

"Pinkie swear."

I take a bite of onion ring. The oniony goodness explodes in my mouth. "No fried food? What was I thinking?" I wash it down with some wine.

Two guys sit at the bar behind us. They're knocking back beers. Laughing. Slapping each other's shoulders.

"Shit," one of the guys yells. "My old lady is going to be pissed. I was supposed to be home an hour ago." He smacks his eye with the palm of his hand.

Rayna and I spin around in our seats.

The guy looks down at his palm and smiles. He swings his legs around and slides off the bar stool. His arms teeter-totter. He points at the eye he just smacked.

"Punch me," he says to his friend.

"Wha?"

He pulls his friend off his stool. They lean together like drunks do when their brains get into a spin.

"Punch me. I'll tell my old lady I was mugged." He pokes at his eye some more. "Make it good."

"I don't know, man."

He knocks his friend's shoulder. "Do iiit," he says.

"Right here?"

"Yeah. We don't want to lose our seats."

The friend makes a fist and pulls his arm back behind him. His balance is thrown off, he stumbles into Rayna's chair. She doesn't say anything. That's the price of admission.

The guy runs at his friend with his arm cocked back and his fist pointed at his eye. He's taking the battering-ram approach. He plows into his friend. His friend yelps and drops to the floor. Rayna and I gasp.

The guy's shoulders start shaking. He rolls over onto his back. He's giggling like a little girl. "Help me up, man."

His friend holds on to the bar with one hand and pulls him up with the other. The two of them lean over the bar. "Bartender. Another round," they yell. The punched guy's eye is already swelling shut.

Rayna and I go back to our onion rings and drinks.

"Asshole," I say.

Rayna knows I'm talking about Lloyd.

I wonder how it happened. How Lloyd happened. And then I realize: This has nothing to do with Lloyd. It has everything to do with me. I don't have to figure out how Lloyd happened. I have to figure out how I happened.

"You know what?" I say to Rayna.

"What?"

"I say, 'Thank you, ten-pound French girl. He's all yours. You can have him.'"

And I mean it.

Rayna taps my glass with hers. "That's the Kelle I love," she says.

"Did I tell you about the blond boy in my acting class?"

Rayna shakes her head. "Tell me about the blond boy in your acting class. . . ."

I run up my stairwell steps and out the lobby door. A brisk breeze blows against me. The cool air feels good on my face. If I were headed to an audition now, I wouldn't need to put on any blush, not when I've got the chilly fall wind blowing around, coloring my cheeks. But I'm not headed to an audition. I'm headed to a gym I just joined. It's really close to my apartment.

As I walk under a scrawny-trunked tree, a bright orange leaf flutters down in front of my face. I catch it, hold it up to my nose, and breathe it in.

I look up at the sky and smile.

It's hard to believe that two whole seasons have passed since my breakup with Lloyd. At first I thought I'd never get over it. I was sure I'd never be happy again. And now here I am, happier than I've ever been.

For the first time in my life, I'm seeing myself through my own eyes.

As I push open the Apple Health Club's Red Delicious–decaled door, a woman hurries out past me. Our shoulders touch. She smells like soap. Black pumps in hand, she wears a business suit, opaque panty hose, and running shoes. It's two o'clock. I think she's late for work. Behind the front counter the manager looks down at a chart. Her chin rests in her palm and she's chewing on the eraser part of her pencil.

"Hi, Laura. How are you today?"

She sighs. "Trying to figure out everybody's schedule."

She waves me through without looking at my ID. That's a first. I have my own apartment, I'm booking, and I don't have to show my ID to Laura at the Apple Health Club. I'm a real New Yorker now.

I step up onto a treadmill. A woman gets on the one next to me. Shallow wrinkles frame her hazel eyes and soft pink mouth. She slides a pair of headphones over her ponytailed head. The foamy pads sit on top of her ears like great big earmuffs. She pushes her Walkman's play button. The music and words leak out into the quiet room.

"Is this the real life?
Is this just fantasy?"

The a cappella words slide out like a sacred chant. The little hairs on my arms stand up.

I look over at the woman. She's not moving. Her

shoulders slump forward. Strands of hair hang over her pale, down-turned face.

"Bohemian Rhapsody." I know this song really well. I studied it in Ms. Wood's tenth-grade English class. An actress-turned-teacher, she was the first Ms. I ever met. She was small and thin, with a tiny, heart-shaped face and high, round cheekbones. She reminded me of an elf.

"Open your eyes
Look up to the skies and see."

Freddie Mercury stretches the last word out, high and long. The note goes in my ears and up to the top of my head.

The woman closes her eyes.

"I'm just a poor boy
I need no sympathy."

The harmonic sounds slip sideways. Strange and wonderful, the notes swirl and whisper through my ears like a loved one's breath.

The woman turns the treadmill on and starts walking. She's got a faraway look in her eyes. I think her mind-screen matinee is playing a movie that I can't see.

"Mama, life had just begun
But now I've gone and thrown it all away."

I think about how sad it is to throw it all away.

The woman leans her head back and closes her eyes. When she brings her face back down, her cheeks are wet. Her chest goes up and down. She wipes her face with the back of her sleeve like she's drying off sweat.

"If I'm not back again this time tomorrow
Carry on, carry on,
As if nothing really matters."

She touches the backs of her fingers to her lips. A muffled sob goes down her throat. I wonder what's wrong. I want to help her, but I don't think I'm supposed to do that. I'm a New Yorker now.

I wonder if she has a son who's in trouble. Maybe he's done something really bad, and now she's trying to carry on at the Apple Health Club as if nothing really matters.

She hits the treadmill stop button. Shallow puffs of air pass through her open mouth. Her eyes are wide. Her body's rigid. She's frozen.

I wonder if she's lost someone.

"Thunderbolt and lightning
Very, very frightening me."

The music builds. The drums pound like hailstones. The woman punches the speed button and starts to run really fast. I want to say, "Stop. You can't outrun the bad thoughts in your brain. Nobody's that fast. It won't work. I know. I've tried before. Lots of times."

Her jaw is set. She grinds her teeth. She grabs hold of the side bars. She clenches them tightly. I look at the thin blue veins in her arms. They remind me of lightning strikes. Her lips move with the music in her head. She slams her feet down on the treadmill.

"I'm just a poor boy and nobody loves me."

Her arms swing back and forth.

"Will not let you go
Let me go!"

"No, no, no, no, no, no, no," she says along with the song, her voice defiant and sharp.

Maybe her husband beats her. I don't see any bruises but that doesn't mean anything.

"So you think you can stone me and spit in my eye?
So you think you can love me and leave me to die?"

She sings the words out loud. Like she doesn't care who hears her.

Maybe her husband left her for a younger woman.

The music turns soft. The piano weeps as its felt-clad hammers softly strike its strings.

She slows the machine and looks down at her feet. Splashy little wet spots spin round and round the treadmill floor.

"Nothing really matters to me."

Softly closing cymbals end the song. *Shuussshh*, they say.

The woman lifts her head. Her eyes are red and blurry. I give her a small, gentle smile. I know that's what I would want someone to do. She turns off her Walkman.

I match my treadmill speed to hers, rest my hand on the side bar across from her hand, and we walk together like that until her eyes grow dry. I wonder if she knows I'm walking with her. After a long time she turns her treadmill off. She picks up a Hula-hoop and spins it around her waist. I figure she must feel better because Hula-hooping and crying don't go together.

I turn my Walkman on and start to run. I sing along with Stevie Nicks about thunder only happening when it's raining. Which I know isn't true. I feel a light tap on my arm. It's the treadmill woman.

She mouths the words "Thank you," and walks away.

Sometimes it's good to have someone to walk with.

"*Smile*," *the photographer* shouts over the loud music.

It's a big day for me. I've never worked for *Seventeen* magazine before. I'm not nervous, though. The photographer's keeping me too busy to think about anything other than catching my next breath. I've been jumping up and down in front his camera for an hour. Every time I think we're going to stop, he asks me to do it some more.

Arms crossed, a serious-looking group of men and women study all of my "happiest-girl-in-the-world" hops and expressions. Apparently, having fun is no joke.

Every shot comes with a blink-inducing burst of light.

"Eyes wide," the photographer says. "And jump a little higher, too."

I jump a little higher. At the highest point I tilt my head to the side and kick my bum with my heels.

He puts down his camera. "Okay, got it," he says.

I go back to the dressing room and change out of the jazzed-up jogger the stylist dressed me in. Glued to it is a big felt hand and a bouquet of bright pink and yellow felt balloons. The copy will tell the reader to "go bananas with add-ons." It's completely ridiculous. You couldn't pay me to wear this. Then I realize someone just did.

I laugh.

"What's so funny?" the hair person asks.

"Nothing," I say.

Sometimes I crack myself up.

My hair is braided through with different-colored ribbons. The hair person takes them out, sprays water on my now kinky hair, and blows it back to its usual wavy self.

"Thank you," I say as I walk out the door.

I bundle up in the white angora hat and scarf that Rayna made for me. Everywhere I go, people stop and ask me where I got them. She did a really good job. I didn't even know she knew how to knit. That's the thing about Rayna. She's full of surprises.

I'm headed to Buddy's forty-ninth birthday party. It's a surprise. Audrey's throwing it for him at a restaurant called Claret's. It'll be a nice break after all the court hearings he's had to sit through lately.

I can't believe I've only known Buddy for a year and a half—it feels like I've known him forever.

It's dark out. I walk from shadow to light as I pass under the sidewalk's evenly spaced streetlamps. I stop in front of a fishmonger's shop. Starry-eyed fish look up at me from their bed of ice. People walk in and out. *Jingle, jingle,* go the bells on the door. "Monger" is a funny word.

I see the restaurant up ahead. Itchy-fingered photographers stand around out front. They're waiting for Buddy. They must know it's his birthday, because anybody carrying a gift gets their picture taken. I tuck mine under my coat. My gift is thin. My coat is thick. They'll never know.

The *maître d'* leads me behind a big screen to a long table that's set for eighteen. Rayna pats the seat next to her. "Kelle. Come sit," she says.

I slide Buddy's gift under my chair.

"Have you heard anything?" I ask.

She knows I'm talking about Buddy's case.

The trial is set to start in a few weeks. Rayna's been hanging on every detail. I'm pretending it's not happening. When something really bothers me, that's what I do. I put up a brain curtain.

Rayna takes a big sip of Coke. That means she's got a lot to say. She doesn't want her mouth to go dry in the middle of it all.

"Well," she says. "I just found out that on the day of the murder two of Buddy's tenants heard gunshots coming from an apartment near theirs." Her eyes get big. "Remember that apartment I cleaned for Buddy? The one that drug dealer lived in?" She touches my arm. "Kelle, I'm sure that's the apartment they're talking about!"

"What! Why?"

"It had red stains on the carpet and a hole in the window." She leans forward. "That drug dealer guy disappeared right after the murder, you know. Think about it. Why would he do that if he wasn't guilty of something?"

She shouldn't say the word "murder." Not here. Not tonight. I bump her knee with mine and glance down at my finger. I'm pointing it at a man that's sitting across the table from us. I know him. He's a writer. Buddy trusts him, but I don't. I mouth the words, "He's listening," to Rayna.

She shrugs. "I don't care," she says. "I want him to hear. I want everybody to hear."

The waiter runs back to our table. "Mr. Jacobson is out front," he whispers. I peek around the screen. Buddy's in the middle of a flashbulb lightning storm. Diners whisper and point. "That's him," they say.

Audrey takes Buddy by the arm and leads him behind the screen.

"Surprise!" we yell.

Buddy holds his palm over his forehead and looks at Audrey. "No kidding," he says, like he's surprised. I think he's faking it, though.

They've just come from court. Buddy is still wearing his suit. No socks, though. His bare feet comfort me.

After dinner the waiter brings in a big yellow cake. "Happy Birthday, Buddy," it says in loopy chocolate letters.

Buddy blows out his candle. Audrey only had one put on. Buddy's still touchy about his age. He'd need a fire extinguisher to put out that many, anyway. As far as I'm concerned, the fewer candles the better. Less spit per slice.

It's gift time. Everybody gives him some sort of alcohol. I guess they think he's going to need it. I'm embarrassed to give him mine.

"Give Buddy your gift," Rayna says.

"I don't know. It's stupid. Do you think I should?"

"It's from you. He'll like it."

She takes it out of my hands. "One more," she says. "This one's from Kelle."

Buddy looks over. She hands it to him. He tears the paper off and laughs. "This is the best gift of all," he says.

Someone yells out, "What is it?"

Buddy holds up the coloring book and crayons he just unwrapped. *Sesame Street*'s Big Bird is on the cover, surrounded by all his friends. Buddy opens the card I gave him. His lips move as he quietly reads it to himself.

Dear Buddy,

This coloring book is called *The All-Together Coloring Book*, and that's exactly how we're going to stay . . . all together.

I love you, Buddy.

Kelle

Buddy looks at me. His eyes are misty.

That's all I could think to get a man who can buy anything he wants.

Anything except the one thing he values most.

His freedom.

"*Hello?*"

"Hey. How ya doin'?" Bob says.

I get up off the couch, untangle my stretched-out phone cord, and walk into the kitchen. When I turn the lights on, the morning cockroach crew dives for cover.

"Good," I say. "How are you?"

Something's up. He never calls this early.

"I'm moving out," he says.

It takes a few seconds for his words to hit my brain. "How?"

"I've been saving up since you left. Workin' jobs on the side and shit."

"Wow," I say. "That's great, Bob."

My brother is one of the hardest workers I've ever met. When he sets his mind to something, he always gets it done. "Where are you going?"

I hope not far. He's always wanted to be a songwriter.

Maybe he's going to Nashville or something.

"I bought some land down the road from here. Once I saw the stream, I had to have it."

"I love streams," I say.

I guess Nashville'll have to wait. Bob's really practical that way.

"I'm leaving today. They don't know yet." He laughs nervously. "They're gonna pee their pants."

That's the thing about my family. Where most kids get praised for their accomplishments, we get punished.

"Is there a house?" I ask.

"No."

"Are you going to live in a tent or something?"

Only in our world would that be a serious question.

"No. I bought an old trailer. I'm going to live in it while I build my own house. I'm going to do it all myself, and when I'm done, I'm not going to owe anybody anything."

"If anyone can, it's you," I say.

And I mean it.

"Bob," I say. "This is good. You're doing the right thing. Someday you'll look back and wonder how you stayed as long as you did."

"Yeah," he says.

"Bye, Bob," I say. I want to tell him that I love him, but we don't say that kind of stuff. So I say it in my mind instead. He may not hear it in his ears, but he'll hear it in his heart.

"Okay, then. See ya," he says.

As soon as I hang up the phone, I get out my checkbook and write a check to Bob for three hundred dollars. I've been waiting for the right moment.

This is it.

There's something I'm really good at.

I'm really good at pretending nothing's wrong.

I'm so good at it that if it goes on long enough, I actually convince myself that it's true. It's funny. I'm not a liar. Anybody who knows me knows that. But in a way I am. I'm the worst kind.

I lie to myself.

Even worse.

I believe it.

January 30, 1980.

Judge Kapelman raises his gavel. "We will now proceed with the trial." His slams the gavel down. A gunshotlike sound echoes through the quiet courtroom. Audrey flinches.

At least, that's what she tells me. I'm not allowed to be there. I'm on the witness list. I'm glad I'm not allowed. One little detail and I might not be able to pretend anymore.

It seems like everybody involved in the case is a celebrity. And with all the press the trial is getting, if they aren't now, by the time it's over, they will be. I guess Andy Warhol was right. I wonder if I'm going to be one of those people too. I always wanted to be known for something, but for something good, not for something like this. And I want more than fifteen minutes. That's for sure.

Even Judge Kapelman is famous. He worked the Son of Sam case. I'm sure he's done more, but that's the only one I know about.

Buddy hired Dr. Thomas Noguchi to testify as an expert witness in his defense. Marilyn Monroe, Robert Kennedy, Sharon Tate, Janis Joplin. Dr. Noguchi met them all. The problem is, he didn't meet them until they were dead. He's called the coroner to the stars. When I think about Marilyn Monroe, I see her standing over a subway grate with her skirt swirling up over her knees. He sees her lying dead in a tangle of white sheets. I'm glad I'm not a coroner. Especially to the stars.

The prosecution's expert is Dr. Michael Baden. He's New York's chief medical examiner. I don't know much about him except that he told the world why Sid Vicious died.

My job is to stay at Buddy's as much as possible. There's nothing much to do. Everybody knows where Buddy's spending his time these days. But it makes him feel better knowing I'm there taking care of things while he's away. So I do it.

Right now Buddy's out working on a building he's converting into a co-op. He's not going to let something like a murder trial slow him down.

Audrey looks down at her watch. "He's late," she says.

The door flies open. Buddy rushes in. Audrey hands him his suit. He races off to change.

Audrey pulls at her bangs. She's so pale. Faint purple shadows under her eyes, the only color on her alabaster face. I'm worried about her.

"How're you holding up?" I ask.

"Lots of drama," she says. "The prosecutor is accusing Buddy of doing things I know he hasn't done. We're together all the time. It's not possible." She pauses. I wait. "The assistant DA's sister just got murdered. He blamed Buddy and quit the case. Now the new guy says Buddy's threatening his witnesses. It's so bad, there's so many rumors and different things being said, that the judge got mad and issued a gag order." Her voice starts to shake.

I take her hand. "That's crazy," I say. "Buddy wouldn't do those things. No way."

Her bottom lip pouts out. Her chin quivers. "No way," she echoes. Her own thoughts aren't coming, so she uses mine.

"Ready, babe?" Buddy asks.

Audrey puts on her coat. "Uh-huh," she says.

He holds the door for her. She stops to pick a little blob of plaster out of his hair.

"Bye, guys," I say.

Poor Audrey. She grew up in such a nice family. I feel sorry for her. She's like a little lamb running around a field full of buttercups, not knowing what next week's menu is. She didn't know what she was getting herself into. And now it's too late. She's in love.

The flower man always gives me free flowers. To thank him, I make him homemade pies. He gets very excited about it. I'm a pretty good cook. When I passed by his shop today, he gave me three stems of a flower he calls freesia. I stick my nose in one of the white, funnel-shaped blooms and inhale. If heaven has a smell, it smells like this. I push the vase to the middle of my table and set four place settings around it.

Rayna, Buddy, and Audrey are coming over for dinner tonight. Everybody needs a break. The trial has taken over our brains. It's all we think about. It's getting to be too much. Tonight is the night we pretend we're normal people, ones whose lives don't revolve around the subject of murder.

I've never had anybody over for dinner before. After the whole audition-friend roach fiasco, I avoid having guests over. Rayna, Buddy, and Audrey aren't guests, though. They're family.

I'm making barbecued spareribs, candied sweet potatoes, fresh steamed string beans, bran muffins, and Buddy's favorite dessert, key lime pie. I block the door open with my sausage-dog boot scraper.

"Knock, knock," Rayna says.

"Come on in," I say.

I take her coat and hang it on my shower-curtain rod.

"Need any help?" she asks.

I hand her a bottle of wine and a corkscrew.

"Rayna, did you know that you're never supposed to fake it with a guy? No matter what, don't do it."

She lays the corkscrew down and looks at me. "Okay. I'll bite," she says. "Why?"

"Because if you ever do it with him again, you'd have to say, 'Oh, that thing you're doing right now? You only think that works. It doesn't. I faked it the last time.' You can't say something like that to a guy. He'd never trust you again. You'd have to keep the lie up. And then, heaven forbid, what if you wind up marrying him? You're doomed to misery for the rest of your life."

Rayna laughs.

"Don't laugh. I'm serious!"

I hear voices out in the hallway.

"They're here," I say. "No more sex talk." I wag my finger at her.

"Me!?" Rayna squeals.

Buddy and Audrey round the corner.

"Come in. Come in," I say.

Audrey's nose is bright red. "It's freezing out there," she says.

"It's warm in here," I say.

She hands me two fat, basket-bottomed bottles and a cheesecake.

I look at the bottles. "What's this?" I ask. I know she won't hold it against me.

"Chianti," Audrey says.

"Chianti?"

"Red wine," she says.

"Ohhhh," I say.

Rayna opens the Chianti, pours it into four *Flintstones* jelly glasses, and hands them around.

Buddy looks tired. His pants are loose. His wrinkles, deep.

He looks around. "You've done a good job, babe."

"Thanks," I say. I feel like I just won a blue ribbon.

I pat a chair. "Sit down, everybody. I hope you're hungry."

"It smells so good," Audrey says.

Buddy rubs his stomach. "I can't remember the last time I had a home-cooked meal."

I know Audrey doesn't mind it when he talks like that. It's not her fault they're in court all day and she doesn't have time to cook.

Rayna helps me fit everything onto the table.

We sit down. We stare at the food. Nobody wants to go first. "Audrey, go ahead," I say.

She dishes up a big plate of food. For a skinny girl, she sure does eat a lot. She hands the plate to Buddy.

Buddy takes one of his shoes off, walks over to the sink, and slams the shoe down on the counter. He wipes the area down and comes back to the table.

"Pass the beans," Rayna says.

"Pass the ribs," I say.

We talk about the cold weather. We talk about Rayna's singing lessons. We talk about my auditions and jobs.

Like my baby grand, Buddy's trial is the elephant in the room.

I'm not the only one who's good at pretending nothing's wrong.

Audrey pushes back from the table. "That was delicious," she says.

"Wow," is all Buddy says.

I look over at the full plate of bran muffins.

I shake my head. "Bran muffins?" I say.

Everybody laughs.

I raise my *Flintstones* jelly glass. This is my first toast ever. I concentrate on Pebbles' little topknot and the Chianti that turns her skin red. Everybody's hand goes up.

I look at Rayna.

I look at Audrey.

I look at Buddy.

The out-loud words won't come.

Instead the words *Please, God, don't take these people away from me* whisper and swirl through my brain.

Our glasses meet.

Ping.

We drain our glasses to my wordless toast.

We drain our glasses to the elephant in the room.

Buddy's attorney, Jack Evseroff, looks intimidating. And he is. A tall, thin Brooklyn boy with a skin-wrapped skull for a face, he dresses to impress. He asked Buddy and me to meet him at a fancy restaurant across town. I look at him across the table. Buddy sits next to him. Alert. Listening.

I'm not here for the food. I'm set to testify soon. Mr. Evseroff wants to be sure I'm worth his minutes.

"I like your suit," I say.

He pulls one of his shirt cuffs out from under his pinstriped sleeve a fraction of an inch. His big, gold pinkie ring catches the candlelight. "Thank you. It's bespoke."

"Bespoke?"

Buddy straightens up in his chair. "Made from scratch," he says. I can tell by his voice, he doesn't want to talk about suits. He doesn't like distractions.

Outside the window, car headlights glint like animal

eyes. I pretend the cars are wolves. They've come to claim the city. A long, low rumble, sounding more growl than thunder, rattles the windowpane. The wolf is at the window. Raindrops fall. Fat veins of clear water roll down the glass.

"Kelle?"

I turn to face Mr. Evseroff. "I'm sorry?" I say.

"I'd like to ask you a few questions about the days leading up to August sixth."

He says "August sixth."

Not "the murder."

I like his style.

He asks me one question after another. Where was I that day? When was the last time I saw Buddy? Did he act strangely? How was Melanie when she came in with the detectives?

I think carefully before I answer each question. It's been a while. I put my finger on my chin and look up at the ceiling. I don't want to make any mistakes.

"Now that your memory is refreshed, I'm going to ask you the same questions again," he says.

"Where were you the night of August sixth, 1978?" His hands move through the air. Rhythmic and flowing, they give shape to his words.

"I was in the back storage room of My Fair Lady."

His hands move slightly. Directing me with his motions. Pausing when I should pause. I can't take my eyes off of him. He reminds me of a conductor. Except he's got case notes for score sheets and I'm his orchestra.

"Why were you there?"

"Buddy was letting Rayna and me live there."

His hands go palms up.

"Why?"

"We were homeless."

"Were you and Buddy romantic?"

That's a new question. I lean back in my chair. My hand goes to my heart. "Of course not!" I say.

He closes his palms and smiles.

"Perfect," he says.

As the subway train rocks and roars toward its next stop, Rayna and I make our way toward the door. The train comes out of its underground tunnel up onto an elevated track at 161st Street Station/Yankee Stadium, the Bronx. The brakes squeal, the doors open, and out we step.

I look back at the train. It's strange to see it in the open air. Down in the tunnels it's a furtive, gut-dwelling tapeworm. Slithering through the bowels of the city. Feeding at station stops.

Out here it's just a dirty old train.

Rayna points. "That's Yankee Stadium," she says.

"Wow," I say.

Even though I don't care about baseball, it's still exciting.

The sky is a hazy gray. A fine mist dampens my skin. It's March.

The Bronx County Courthouse isn't that far away. It just feels like it is. Around us tall, hollow-eyed buildings look down on the final resting places of unwanted things. We walk a jagged trail along the slimy, spit-decorated sidewalk around the broken glass, crumpled brown paper bags, and squashed gum. Up ahead a sunken-cheeked black man leans against a plywood-covered storefront wall. His rabid eyes turn toward us. He grabs his crotch.

"I've got something for youuuuu, baby," he says.

We put our heads down and walk faster. The sound of footsteps follows us.

We walk faster.

"Where you headed?" comes a voice.

Rayna and I look over our shoulders. It's a guy. He's wearing a red beret. Another guy walks next to him. He's wearing a red beret too.

We stop.

"The courthouse," Rayna says.

"We'll take you. Follow us," he says.

I look at Rayna.

Rayna nods. "They're Guardian Angels. You can tell by the hats," she says. "We should go with them."

"What if they're not Guardian Angels? What if they're just pretending they are?"

"You're so suspicious," she says.

We follow our red-bereted friends past building after brightly spray-painted building. Even though I can't make out what the fat, smushed letters say, I like looking at them. It's better than peeling paint.

"There you go," one of the guys says. He points up at a huge granite building. Rows of ribbon-thin windows run up and down its sides.

"Thank you," we say at the same time.

I bump Rayna's arm. "Owe me a Coke," I say.

Rayna whispers in my ear. "The tall one was so cute," she says. "I don't care what Mayor Koch says. I like them."

We walk into the courthouse's high-ceilinged, marble-floored lobby. It's one of those lobbies where everybody's sounds echo and blend into a kind of cafeteria drone.

We get off the elevator at the ninth floor. We're supposed to wait in a special holding room until we're called to testify. I sit down on one of the hard benches. Rayna sits next to me and takes out a romance novel. Before she decided to be a singer, she was on the cover of a big romance magazine. It was a dream come true for her.

I look around the room. A young guy sits on the bench opposite mine. He's dark and dangerous with a hurt smile that makes me want to bring him home.

Perfect.

Out of the frying pan, into the fire.

I look away.

A uniformed man comes into the room and calls out a woman's name. When no one answers, he leaves.

My stomach twists. I thought he was here for me. I rub my clammy hands across my skirt. What am I doing here? What if the prosecutor asks me something and I go blank? He doesn't know about my brain curtains. The bench I'm sitting on is covered in paper-clip carvings. Running my fingers along the word-scarred wood makes me think about all the people who've been here before me. They got through it; so can I.

A little boy runs across the floor. Hands waving. Squealing. His father scoops him up and swings him over his shoulder. The boy hangs down his strong back. His hair sways back and forth with every exaggerated stomp his father takes. He laughs and laughs. Everybody looks up and laughs along with him. Belly laughs have a way of spreading. Even in courthouse holding rooms.

"I want a man like that," I say.

Rayna sighs. "I want a man who'll support me," she says.

Southern girls talk like that. They can't help themselves. They inherit it from their mothers.

"I want a man who'll love me so much he'll never leave me," I say.

"Love is overrated," Rayna says.

Funny words for the world's most devoted romance novel reader.

I pinch her. "Take it back," I say.

"I take it back." Rayna laughs.

"Kelle?" a man calls out.

My head snaps around. "Yes."

"Come with me."

I follow him down the hallway into a big oak-paneled courtroom. Every seat has a person. I stand in front of the witness stand. All I can think about is the strange way my heart is fluttering. I look over at Buddy. His big suit gets bigger every day. He smiles at me with his eyes. I send an eye smile back to him. Nobody knows what we're doing. It's our little secret.

"Raise your hand."

I raise my hand.

"Do you solemnly swear to tell the truth, the whole truth, and nothing but the truth, so help you God?"

I feel like I just swallowed a marshmallow. It's hard to talk.

I nod.

"Answer for the court reporter, please."

By now I've forgotten the question.

"Yes," I say.

I sit down. The prosecutor stares at me like I just broke a classroom window with a rock.

He asks me the same questions Mr. Evseroff asked me at our practice dinner.

Except for the last one.

He looks concerned.

"Are you an actress, Kelle?" he asks.

I know what he's getting at. I look down at my fingers. "I do commercials," I say.

"So you're an actress?"

"Yes," I say.

"Louder, please. The court reporter didn't hear you."

"Yes," I say louder.

He looks at the jury. His hands fly up in the air. Touchdown.

I want to tell them that I'm not a faker, but I'm not allowed to speak unless spoken to. It's a rule.

As I walk out, Rayna walks in. We're not supposed to even look at each other until after her testimony. Our hands brush. She sticks her chin up. You can say a lot with a hand brush.

I wait for her out in the hallway. She's in there a long time. Finally the door opens. She walks out. A parade of reporters trails behind her. That's where red-stain and bullet-hole talk will get you. Photographers take pictures of us. I turn toward the wall. Rayna doesn't. I hope they don't follow us.

When the elevator door opens, they leave.

Outside we wait for a bus to pass before crossing the street. We don't wait for the light, though. We take our chances dodging traffic. We'd rather be moving targets than sitting ducks. Toes balanced on the bus's back bumper, a kid holds on like a baby monkey. No matter how badly I needed to get somewhere, I would never be brave enough to do that.

Outside the train station a huge ghetto blaster beats like thunder. Two cans of spray paint sit on each end. A boy spins around on his head. A flattened cardboard box the only thing between his skull and the concrete.

A crowd of people watch him. When he jumps out of the circle, another boy jumps in. Holding himself up on one hand, he swings his leg around and under, finishing in the flattest split I've ever seen. Boy number three handsprings in. Each boy tries to outdo the next. They won't have the energy to fight after this. They'll go to bed tired. That's how it was with my brothers back on the farm.

Rayna and I get on the train. It takes off with a jerk. I've learned to relax when that happens. If you tense up and fight the motion, it only makes it worse. We ride along, shoulders swaying in rhythm with the rough, rolling motion of the car. All of a sudden the car goes black. It's always a scary moment when the car lights go off. It's especially scary when you just left the Bronx and you're wearing your I-testified-in-court-today clothes. It's hard to look tough in a Peter Pan collar.

The lights come back on. Everybody's eyes dart around, checking to see if anything's changed. Nothing has. Nobody's been murdered or mugged. Not in our car, anyway.

Across from me are two young kids. A girl and a boy. Not quite teenagers. Almost. One black. One white. The girl whispers something in the boy's ear. He rolls his eyes. They're friends.

I remember when I was twelve. I rode the bus with a boy named Curly. I still see him so clearly. His slow-to-spread grin. His big front teeth that crossed over in the middle. His shortly clipped afro. His light, frizzy eyelashes.

Every morning when I get on the bus, I save a seat for my best bus friend, Curly. His older brother's name is Harry. He rides the bus too. Harry is Bob's best friend. We're all in the same school. It goes from seventh to twelfth grade. Sometimes a fight breaks out in the back of the bus. Knives get pulled. It's good to have a best bus friend. You feel like somebody's got your back.

Curly and Harry are black. There's no accounting for some parents' taste in names. They don't have a father. He ran off a long time ago. They don't like to talk about it.

I always sit up near the front. The closer you are to the driver and the door, the better off you are. At least I think so. Curly walks up the steps. I slap the seat.

"Good morning!" I say.

"Morning," he says quietly. Curly's very shy. Like a cold engine, he takes a few minutes to warm up in the morning.

Harry nods at me as he makes his way to my brother at the back of the bus.

"Show me your homework," I say to Curly.

He pulls a wad of folded papers out of his pocket. He writes really big. He needs a lot of paper. I get my Eeyore-topped pencil out of my pencil pouch. As I read his essay, I circle the things I think he needs to change.

Looking down at the paper makes me bus-sick. Every minute or so I stop and hang my head out the window. Curly likes it when I help him with his homework. He really wants to get out of special ed. He doesn't have anybody to help him at home. His mother works as a housekeeper at a big house in Monkton. She dropped out of school right after the sixth grade. Even if she knew how to help him, she'd be too tired to after a long day of cleaning up after a bunch of rich people.

I hand him back his essay and my pencil. "You're so creative, Curly. Much more than me."

He grins and hands me Eeyore. He doesn't want to use him up. He erases and writes and asks me why this and why that. By the time we get to school, he's happy and I feel like throwing up. It's worth it, though. He's one of my best friends.

The next day the bus pulls up to Curly's stop. Curly and Harry aren't there. Their house, which isn't much bigger than a chicken coop, is down a long dirt road. The driver waits. Curly and Harry are easy to like. If they're late, the driver always waits for them. Even if he sees kids running full bore down their driveways, arms waving, yelling, if he doesn't like them, he breezes right on by. Technically, they have to be at the stop, ready to board, when the bus comes by.

Harry is standing halfway down the dirt road. He signals to my brother. My brother walks to the front of the bus.

"Open the door," he says to the driver.

"Once you're on, you're on," the driver says. He's not being mean. That's the law.

Bob looks at him. "Want me to open it for you?" Bob's not being mean. That's the way around the law.

The driver opens the door. Bob heads down the dirt road to Harry. The bus pulls away.

When I get back home from school, Bob is waiting for me.

"What's wrong?" I ask him.

"Sit down," he says.

I sit down.

"Curly is dead."

I shake my head. "What?" I say.

"Harry was cleaning his gun. He didn't know it was loaded. It went off. Curly got his brains blown out."

I bury my head in my hands. My shoulders shake.

"Kelle," my brother says. "Come with me. I'm going to teach you how to handle a gun."

My wet eyes swirl Bob around like a fun-house mirror. "I don't want to," I say.

"You have to," he says. "Now."

I spend the next hour learning how to not blow somebody's brains out.

I spend the night at Rayna's. After our day in court neither one of us wants to be alone. I get up early the next morning, go to our coffee shop, and gather up all the morning newspapers. Why buy them when I can get someone's castoffs for free? When I get back to the apartment, Rayna is up, drinking her Coke.

I lay the paper down in front of her. "I guess it's your turn," I say.

Rayna looks down at the paper. Her mouth hangs open.

She's front-page news.

I tap softly on Buddy's door. Audrey slowly opens it. Her eyes are puffy. Her tissue-stuffed pockets bulge like hamster cheeks.

I look into the apartment. "Where's Buddy?" I ask.

Audrey's chin shakes. "As soon as the closing statements were over, the court officers took him away in handcuffs!"

"What? Why?" I ask.

She jerks her cross back and forth on its chain. "The district attorney says he's a flight risk. They're going to keep him in jail until the jury comes back with their verdict."

She starts to tremble.

"Let's sit," I say.

We sit on the couch. We stare down at our feet.

"They wheeled the box they found Tupper in, into the courtroom," she says.

I want to say, "It's almost over. Buddy'll be home soon." But I'm not so sure. Tupper's box. That's pretty bad. I search my brain for the words that will make Audrey feel better.

I can't find any.

All I can do is lean against her shoulder so she knows she's not alone.

All I can do is lean against her shoulder so I know I'm not alone.

"Audrey, I have a go-see," I say after a while.

She nods. "I'll be okay."

She walks me to the elevator.

I step inside. The door closes. The lights flicker. Off. On. The elevator seems so small today. Like a box. Like Tupper's courtroom box. Suddenly I can't breathe right. I broke some ribs once—the doctor mummied me up in swirls of white, gauzy wrapping. I couldn't catch my breath, so I took it off. That's how I feel now. Like my gauze is on too tight. Just a few seconds more, I tell myself, and I'll be out of this four-walled air stealer.

The door finally opens. I hurry out to the sidewalk.

I check my watch.

I'm running late.

The late Jack Tupper.

I look down the street at the oncoming traffic. If I hurry, I can make it across before the next car comes. When I step down off the curb, ten people follow me. That's good. There's strength in numbers.

Something in the gutter catches my eye. It's red. I stop. I put my hand up over my chest. A man knocks into me.

"What the fuck," he says like I've ruined his day or something.

I don't care. I want to see what's in the gutter. I turn around and look. It's a red scarf.

I thought it was blood.

Oh, Buddy.

I thought it was blood.

I don't believe them, Buddy. They don't know you.

They always want to talk about it. They ask me questions. When I tell them you didn't do it, they tell me I'm crazy. They tell me things they've read. Things I don't want to know.

And now it's in my brain. Now I have to think about it. It's the red scarf's fault.

That's the trouble with brain curtains. You can't control them. They're only good for so long. They're only good until something like a red scarf comes along and yanks them open.

The North Bronx. A vacant lot–turned–inner-city dump. Dull gray tenement buildings rise up out of the concrete, casting long shadows across the gloomy landscape like half-buried headstones. A heavy rain falls. The air is hot and thick. Beer cans, soda bottles, and rusting oil drums cover the garbage-strewn ground. A mud-splattered mattress soaks up the slanting raindrops. Lidless paint cans fill and spill over onto the ground. Blues, greens, yellows. The colors pool and mix together. Thinning more and more with every plinking raindrop. Nearby a waterlogged box buckles and slumps. In it, a stack of sodden cards and letters clump together. Reducing some scorned lover's memories to one thing. A teddy bear lies off to the side. Watching. Raindrops roll down its face like tears. A refrigerator with its door chained shut lies on its back. Mosquito larvae swim back and forth in their rubber-tire catch basins.

In the middle of it all a large wooden box smolders.

The police are called. It's a "nothing" fire. They almost don't even go. The rain will put it out.

They decide to go just in case.

By the time they get there, the fire is out. A man's legs poke out of the gasoline-soaked box. The officers open the lid. They see the matted hair. The clotted blood. The bullet holes. They lean in. Black, white, Puerto Rican? They can't tell. The victim's charred skin looks like a blackened marshmallow.

The medical examiner arrives.

"Partially naked black male, facedown in burned large wooden case. Wearing partially burned pants and underpants."

He's not black. He's Irish.

I turn away from the gutter-stained red scarf that makes me think about Tupper's blood-clotted, swooped-over hair. I don't want to think about it anymore, so I count the sidewalk cracks instead.

One, two, three, four, five, six, seven gunshot wounds.

His right ear. His chest. His back. His torso. His left buttock. The left-buttock one bothers me the most. Was he running away? Crawling?

"*Please don't kill me.*" I hear his imagined voice in my ears.

The images jump around inside my head.

"It was a mob hit." That's what Buddy tells Rayna. He never tells me his theories. We don't talk about it. Ever. I've heard enough already.

Rayna talks about it, though. I pretend to listen. Some of it slips in even though I don't want it to.

"The *Post* says Tupper was involved in a two-hundred-dred-million-dollar drug-smuggling ring. He and some other guys trafficked cocaine, hashish, and marijuana." She counts them off on her fingers. "The All Ireland was a front. It must be true. I read it in the *Post*. They have fact-checkers," Rayna says.

I don't know what hashish is.

"His head was busted up in two places. They think with a hammer."

I hold my hands up over my ears. "Rayna, stop," I say.

I look up from the sidewalk cracks. I don't care if I step on them right now. I feel light-headed. The city's buildings tower over me like sheer canyon walls. They press in on me. I need air.

I see him. I see Tupper. I think of him only by his last name. If he has a first name, it's scarier. Just "Tupper" makes it less real. I know it's stupid, but it works.

Drying clots of blood paste his thin brown hair to his skull. Knocked loose from their sockets, his dangling eyeballs rest on the floor of a charred wooden crate. The white part stands out against his blackened skin. Black and white. He's staring at me.

When I was young, a man set his old horse loose in the field next to ours. I guess he didn't want him anymore. He wanted him to die. But I liked the horse. I wanted him to live. So I fed him, gave him buckets of warm water, and named him Clancy. It was so cold out. It was freezing. To keep warm, he huddled up in the dark corner of an old lean-to that backed up to our property. One morning I called him and he didn't come. I pressed my face to the frozen ground and looked under the thin metal siding. He was lying down. His big eyes were pushed up close to mine. They were frozen open. He was dead.

That's what I think Tupper's eyes looked like.

I look back down at the sidewalk. *Eleven, twelve, thirteen, fourteen, fifteen stab wounds.*

Fifteen stab wounds on the left side of his round baby-boy face. A hand holding a ragged-edged knife jabs at Tupper's face. Did he duck? His hands didn't have any defensive wounds. Was someone holding them?

Did he close his eyes? I hope he did.

Stab, stab, stab, stab, stab. The tip of the blade slides under his skin. Stab, stab, stab, stab, stab. Blood runs into his eyes. The last thing he sees is the color red. Stab, stab, stab, stab, stab. I wonder if the killer counted. I wonder if Tupper counted.

My eyes sting. Tupper counted. His life counted.

The killer was right-handed.

I make a fist.

Buddy is left-handed. He couldn't have done it.

I open the door. The casting director is waiting for me. I'm her last appointment. I take a quick look at the sides, smooth my hair down with my hands, and stand on the *X* in front of the camera.

She pushes the record button.

I smile at the camera. "Welcome to Burger King," I say. "May I take your order?"

Four long days go by. Audrey tells me, "The jury is 'hopelessly' deadlocked."

"I think that's good news, don't you?" I say.

Outside a dog barks. "Heel," a man says. The rasp of a metal choke chain closing around the dog's throat floats in through the open window.

"Mr. Evseroff thinks so." Audrey looks up through her bangs at me. "Oh, Kelle. I miss him so much."

• • •

The next day Audrey calls me from the courthouse. "Kelle. There was a loud bang in the deliberation room. Everybody heard it. Mr. Evseroff thinks one of the jurors threw a chair against the wall or something. The court officer had to go in. A juror left the room sobbing."

One and a half hours later . . .

The jury has reached a verdict.

In the next few minutes the longest, most expensive trial in the history of the Bronx will be over. All it took was eleven weeks of testimony, seventy-nine witnesses, and 1.5 million dollars.

The courtroom is pin-drop silent.

Audrey holds Buddy's suit in one hand and her cross in the other.

Buddy looks straight ahead.

The foreman clears his throat. "We, the jury, find Howard 'Buddy' Jacobson . . . guilty of murder in the second degree."

Audrey gasps. Buddy turns to her. His face is strong. He wants her to know he isn't afraid. The court officers don't care about broken hearts and sad good-byes. Their job is to clear the courtroom. They take Buddy away.

And just like that . . .

It's over.

I have a go-see. I stand on the subway platform waiting for the next train to come. It's humid. I flap the skirt of my dress to dry my sweaty legs.

I can't complain. At least I'm free. Buddy's not.

They've got him holed up at the Brooklyn House of Detention. He has to stay there until his sentencing on June 3. That's in three days. Poor Audrey. She's a wreck. She never saw it coming. Neither did I. Not really. I guess the saying "Love is blind" applies to murder trial verdicts too.

Every time I look into Audrey's big, wet eyes, I want to cry. But I don't. If I do, my eyes will puff up too, and then I won't book any more commercials. Then where will I be? Back out on the streets, crying over myself instead of Buddy.

I still can't believe it's happened. My Buddy is in jail. It's like one of those dark-hour campfire stories has sprung to life in my head and I don't know how to stop it. My stomach hurts. My back aches. My father would say, "Buck up. Pain is weakness leaving the body."

I see the train lights deep in the tunnel. I step back. I still haven't shaken my somebody-might-push-me-in-front-of-the-train fear. All I have to do is look over my shoulder to find a crazy person. They're everywhere. Flailing their hands around. Yelling at imaginary enemies. Pulling at their hair. I don't like to think about them. I wonder if somebody, somewhere, loves them. I put up another brain curtain and walk on past.

The city is making me hard. Maybe that's not such a bad thing.

The train stops. I get on. There's a free seat midway down the aisle. I hurry over to it and sit down. I look at my watch. It's four thirty. I've got plenty of time.

"Kelle? Is that you?"

I look to my left. My mouth hangs open. Oh my gosh. It can't be. "Melanie!" I say.

For an instant I'm the girl with newspapers for Band-Aids again, hoping she'll say I'm good enough to be a model and she wants me to sign up with her agency. The sight of her sweet face completely wipes the murder from my memory.

"How are you doing?" she asks.

"I'm with a children's agency. They send me out a lot. So that's good."

"Was that you in the Coke commercial?"

I nod.

"What a great spot! I'm so happy for you. I knew you were going to work. I remember telling . . ." Her voice trails off.

"How are you?" I ask.

I really want to know.

"Pretty good. I'm dating a nice guy."

"How'd you meet?"

"He was selling Christmas trees."

"Really?"

She smiles. "Yeah."

"That's great, Melanie. Oh, this is my stop," I say. "Bye, Melanie. It was really nice seeing you."

"Bye," she says. "Congratulations on the Coke commercial."

"Thanks." I wave at her through the closing doors.

The train pulls away. We both pretended nothing bad ever happened. We did it so well it's almost like it's true.

I can't believe I ran into her like that. What were the chances? It was good, though. I really like her. I hope she marries that Christmas-tree guy and lives happily ever after. That would be so cool.

I wake up late the next morning, which is an easy thing to do in a basement apartment. I kick my sheets back and smile. I'm going to go get myself a croissant.

The bakery around the corner sells the best ones ever. Rayna says I might as well be eating a stick of butter.

Sounds good to me. I love butter. Thinking about the croissants makes me think about the French, which makes me think about Lloyd's little home wrecker, Sophie. I heard she was seeing a couple of other guys while she was seeing Lloyd. Shocking. When he found out, he broke it off. Lloyd is a single child. He doesn't share well with others.

I pull on my sundress and sandals, and run up the stairs and out into the lobby. A crowd is gathered right outside the front door. I don't pay them much attention. Once you're headed out to buy a big, buttery croissant, it's hard to think about much else. I can't really see yet anyway. My pupils are still too big.

I open the door. Voices shout at me. "Kelle, over here." "Kelle look this way." "Kelle" this, "Kelle" that. I don't know what's going on. Who are these people and why are they taking my picture?

"Kelle, did you drive the getaway car or just rent it?"

"Getaway car? What?" I say.

I back up into the lobby and close the door. I run around the corner. The super's apartment is right next to the elevator. I hear his buzzer going off. It's the reporters. They want in. The super's a stoner, he gets a lot of "deliveries"; he lets everybody in. The only time he doesn't is when he's overdone it and his mellowness morphs into a hazy paranoia. The front door buzzes. He's let them in. I push the elevator up button, reach around, and press PH. I hear the pitter-patter of little reporter footsteps. I hurry into the stairwell. As I pull the door closed behind me, I hear one of them say, "Look. The elevator's stopping at the penthouse level."

I run down the steps and into my apartment. My heart is pounding. I pick up the phone.

"Rayna. It's me," I say.

"I just left a message on your machine," she says.

"What's going on?"

"Buddy escaped from jail last night."

"What!" I yell. "That's great," I say.

Before this moment, if you told me that there would come a time when I would be happy to hear that a convicted murderer had just escaped from prison, I would have told you that you were off your rocker. And yet here I am. Feeling like I just won the Best Child Rider trophy at the Maryland Pony Show.

Leave it to Buddy. He pulled the get-out-of-jail-free card. And he doesn't even like board games.

"How did he do it?" I ask.

"Nobody got hurt," Rayna says right away. She wants to put my mind at ease.

It's funny. It never occurred to me that somebody might have gotten hurt.

"It says in the paper that Buddy had a two-hour meeting with his attorney, Michael Schwartz, in the jail's visiting room yesterday—"

"Buddy doesn't have an attorney named Schwartz," I say.

"Let me finish," Rayna says. "At the end of the visit Mr. Schwartz signed himself out, walked through three checkpoints, and left. Only thing is, Mr. Schwartz was actually a bartender who owed Buddy money whose real name is Tony DeRosa. And it wasn't him that walked out . . . it was Buddy!"

"But what about Buddy's prison clothes? Why didn't the guards recognize him?"

"Buddy cut his hair, shaved his mustache off, and swapped clothes with DeRosa. He left in a gray tweed suit and a dark-colored tie."

"Nobody saw all this?"

"You can thank attorney-client privacy laws for that."

I try to imagine Buddy without his mustache and crazy hair. I wonder if he still looks like Einstein.

"I feel like I'm in a movie," I say. "Buddy's so smart."

"There's something else. Are you sitting down?"

"Yes," I say. Even though I'm not.

"They say you rented the getaway car."

"What kind?" I don't know why I asked that. I think my brain is trying to distract me.

"A blue Dodge Aspen."

Leave it to Buddy to get out of Dodge in a Dodge.

"So that's why the reporters are here," I say.

"Listen. I want to read you what the *Times* says. 'The car had been rented to a Kelle K., who is believed to be a girlfriend of one of Mr. Jacobson's two sons.'"

"Girlfriend!" I shriek.

And then it hits me.

I sit down.

"Oh no. My name's in the paper. Nobody's going to want to hire me now."

"Papers," Rayna says.

"Papers?"

"Papers. You're not in one. You're in all of them. And Kelle . . ." She pauses. "One of them mentions your address."

"Oh no! What am I going to do?"

"Don't go anywhere. If you need anything, I can bring it for you after work. This should all blow over pretty fast."

I sit down on my couch. I'm so angry. By the time Rayna gets off work, all the croissants will be gone.

I was afraid no one would hire me after my name was in the papers.

I was wrong.

Suddenly I'm my agency's hottest talent. Everybody wants to know if I'm who they think I am.

I stick my headphones over my ears and walk outside. A handful of reporters wait for me on the sidewalk. I fiddle with my cassette player, frown, and act like I can't get it to work properly. When they try to talk to me, I pretend that I can't hear them.

The Doobie Brothers sing in my ears. When they tell me that "What a fool believes he sees, / No wise man has the power to reason away," I wonder if it's good or bad that I know exactly what they mean. I wonder if it's good or bad that I don't know if I'm the wise man or the fool.

A few days before Buddy's escape, Audrey told me something. She told me that each time she visited him in jail, he would shove soppy little notes into her mouth when they kissed. I didn't think much about it at the time. I couldn't get past the spit part. I just assumed they were love notes. But they weren't. They were escape notes.

A car pulls up alongside me. I'm not sure, but I think it's following me. I move closer to the buildings and pretend I'm looking for a particular address. The car stops. Two men get out and walk toward me.

"Kelle," they say.

They know my name. They reach into their jackets.

"Relax. We're detectives." They laugh. They show me their badges.

They point at the car. "Get in," they say.

"Why?"

"We're taking you to the Bronx. The DA has some questions he wants to ask you."

"Are you bringing me home after? 'Cause that's the only way I'm going." Every once in a while I put my foot down.

They smile. They think I'm funny. "Yeah. We'll bring you back."

They double-park in front of a Chock full o'Nuts coffee shop. Detectives get to do neat stuff like that. They come out with three coffees and a box full of doughnuts. They give me a bear claw and a cup of coffee. Black. Yuck. We drive to the Bronx, eat doughnuts, and talk about the nice weather. If they weren't taking me to the courthouse, I'd actually be enjoying myself.

They take me up to the DA's office.

He looks at me with suspicious eyes. "You've done a very serious thing, Kelle. You could spend a long time in prison for this," he says.

The detectives nod like it's true. Ten minutes ago we were eating doughnuts and talking like old pals. Now it's like we've never met.

"For what?" I ask.

"After you picked Buddy up, where did you take him?"

"I didn't pick Buddy up!"

"You rented the getaway car."

"I did not!" I say.

He softly pats the desk. "Just tell me, Kelle. You don't want to go to prison over this. Prison is no place for a girl like you."

I give him an icy stare. "I did not rent or drive the getaway car."

"Can you prove that? Where were you at four thirty p.m. the day of the escape?"

My brain curtains snap shut. "I . . . I . . . don't remember."

He pounds his fist down on the desk. His fountain pen pops out of its marble-slab stand. I flinch.

"Ummmm . . ."

I look down at my hands. Think. Think. Where was I? *Swish.* A curtain opens. I had a Fotomat audition. *Swish.* I wore my royal blue dress because that's the Fotomat smock color. *Swish.* I got on the train. *Swish.* I found an empty seat. *Swish.*

I slowly look up. I level my eyes at the DA.

"I was with Melanie," I say.

The detectives lean back.

The DA leans forward. "Melanie? Melanie who?"

I tilt my chin slightly to the side. "Melanie Cain."

He pushes his chair away from the desk and crosses his arms.

"I saw her on the train. I sat with her," I say matter-of-factly.

"You're telling me that at the very minute Buddy Jacobson was escaping, you were sitting on a train with Melanie Cain?"

You're a poet and you don't know it, I think to myself.

He shakes his head. "You expect me to believe that?" His voice is loud.

"Ask her," I say.

He storms out of the room.

I look at the detectives. Their eyes are smiling. They like me again.

The door opens. The DA stomps back in. He looks at me. "You're free to go. Melanie cleared you."

It takes everything in me not to stick my tongue out at him. The Tongue is the ultimate weapon. Men don't know how to respond to it, and when men don't know how to respond to something, they feel powerless.

Would serve him right.

Trying to scare me like that.

Jerk.

There's a long black limo parked in front of my apartment building. The car's dark-suited, leather-gloved driver stands next to it. When he sees me, he opens the back door. A nicely dressed man steps out.

"Excuse me, is your name Kelle?" he asks.

I stick my key in the lock. "Why?"

"My client would very much like to meet you. He is a Saudi prince."

It's official. Now I've heard it all.

"And you are . . . ?"

"I am his attorney." He smiles. "He will make it worth your time. Say yes, get in this car, and we will take the prince's jet to Miami, where he is waiting for you."

I laugh. I think he's kidding. If this had happened the day I came to New York, I might have believed him. But I'm not like that anymore. At least, I don't think I am.

"My boss is a very generous man," he says. His dark eyes glint in the lamplight.

"You're not serious," I say.

"I'm most serious."

"Well, tell your boss thanks but no thanks. I'm not for sale."

I wonder if this prince guy goes after every girl he reads about in the newspaper.

He hands me his business card. "In case you change your mind," he says.

I stick it in my pocket and walk inside.

I'm keeping this one.

I might want to look back at it someday and remember the time a Saudi prince tried to buy me.

It's the middle of the night. The telephone rings.
I pick the receiver up and rest it against my ear.

"Hello?"

"Hi, babe."

I sit up.

"Buddy?" I turn the light on so I can hear him better.
"Are you okay?"

"I'm great," he says.

"You shouldn't be calling me. I mean, I'm glad you
did. I'm just worried. What if my phone is tapped? The
cops are going crazy. They picked me up off the street
and asked me a bunch of questions."

I hear Audrey in the background. I didn't even know
she was with him. I'm so glad he's not alone.

"Hi, Audrey," I yell. "Buddy, guess what the detectives
fed me?"

"What?"

"Doughnuts!"

Buddy laughs. I like that I made him laugh.

"Listen," he says. "This is important. I need your help. If I send you some letters, do you think you could forward them for me?"

I don't know what to say. I don't think it's a good idea to secretly mail things for a convicted murderer. Especially a famous one who's on the run. What if the police are watching me? They'll throw me in jail. Then it'll be my picture on the front page of the *Post* and the *Daily News*. That's not what I had in mind when I asked to be a cover girl.

I bite at my knuckles. I want to help, but I'm nervous. I don't want to get in trouble. If the detectives find out, they'll get mad. They'll take me to the Bronx and scare me with their talk of prison-time punishments.

Planned punishments are much worse than random ones. You know they're coming. You have to be brave about it. And afterward you never forget them.

My father loved a good planned punishment. But he didn't just talk during them, he used his belt, too.

"Behind the lilac bushes at three," my father says, tapping his watch.

An hour later I'm there, waiting.

He strolls up. "Pants down," he says.

I undo my buttons. My blue jeans fall down around my ankles.

"Underwear, too."

I pull my panties down. I lean forward. I grab my knees and point my toes out. That way I won't lose my balance. It makes him mad if you fall during a punishment.

He unhooks his belt and yanks the leather strap through each of the loops. *Twwwiiippp. Twwwiiippp. Twwwiiippp.*

A red ladybug crawls over my toes. She stretches her wings. Open, shut, open, shut. She lifts her wings and flies away. Her house must be on fire. If I had wings, I'd go with her. I'd rather be anywhere but here, with my hands on my knees and my panties stretched out between my ankles.

Heavy on their branches, the purple lilacs hang down over my shoulder. They smell like my grandmother.

My father wraps the belt around his hand. I'm getting the strap side. I can tell because the buckle isn't jingling anymore. That's good. It's hard to stand there, hunched over, waiting for the belt to come. I tell myself, *If I'm good and I don't cry, it won't last long.*

I close my eyes. I don't need to see to know it's coming. I can hear it. I dig my nails into my kneecaps. I clench my teeth.

Whack.

The tail of the strap snaps hard against my bottom. It burns. I gasp. I press my mouth together. The second blow comes quickly. I rock forward into the lilac bush. Three. Four. Five. It might as well be fifty. I'm skinned-knee sore. Something wet runs down the back of my leg.

He must have seen, because he stops. I look down at my feet. It's important not to move too soon. He doesn't like assumptions.

"Fucking cunt," he says. He always says that afterward.

He walks away.

I pull my panties up. Welts rise up off my skin. I'm glad. I'll look at them later and be proud of myself. Proud that I didn't cry. I think about our steers. I feel sorry for them. I know what it feels like to be branded.

I take a deep breath. I'm going to do it. I'm going to help Buddy. I've been in prison all my life anyway. A mind prison. My father's the warden. He's always in there, terrorizing me. Saying I'm not good enough and that I'm stupid. Telling me who to see, what to say, where to go, and how to feel. I'm not sure, but I think I got a life sentence.

At least with jail I'll have a release date.

I decide not to tell Rayna about Buddy's call. If the police get suspicious and ask her questions about me, I don't want her to have to lie. Rayna's not a liar. I don't want to turn her into one.

A few days pass. I open my mailbox. Inside is a letter. It's from Audrey. I can tell by the swirly handwriting. The postmark says "Omaha, Nebraska."

There's a note and a letter to forward.

Dear Kelly,

I can only trust you! So please send this letter as soon as possible. Kelly, everything is somewhat great. I'm so happy for Buddy.

I love you,
Audrey

I take a train to the village, drop the letter in the first mailbox I see, and go home.

Two days later another letter comes. Four fifteen-cent Oliver Wendell Holmes stamps form an uneven row across the envelope's upper right-hand corner. An escaped convict sending letters with a Supreme Court judge's stamp as postage. For some reason that's funny to me.

Dear Kelley,

Thanks so much for being there. Could you please drop these off in the mail? I hope everything is going great for you. Hope you're working lots. A friend of yours wants to know if you're making any lime pie lately.

Things are still crazy, but fun. What more could you ask for but health and freedom?

Talk to you soon.

Love,
Audrey

Every few days I get another envelope filled with letters to forward. I make sure I never mail them from the same place twice. I feel like I'm in a James Bond movie. It's kind of exciting.

In the meantime, the reporters don't wait outside the door for me anymore. They're too busy trying to figure out where Buddy is. Some think he's in Canada. Some say Mexico. Others bet on the Caribbean or even Central America. And then there are the ones who think there's a possibility he's still in the city. Every day it's a different story.

I keep my postmarked letters to myself.

The detectives can't find Audrey. They think she's with Buddy. But then again, they're not sure. Melanie, Judge Kapelman, and other witnesses for the prosecution are under police protection. There's talk of phone tapping.

With the way the district attorney keeps showing his hand, it's not much of a poker game. All Buddy has to do is read the papers and he'll know what not to do.

There are photos of Buddy with his mustache next to an artist's drawing of him without it. He looks better with the mustache.

In interviews Evseroff calls the escape "stupid" and asks Buddy to "give himself up." He believes they'll win their appeal on the grounds that some of the jurors were coerced into voting for a guilty verdict.

The *New York Post* says, "Authorities hunting Howard (Buddy) Jacobson ruefully admitted today that the crafty escaped murderer has given them the slip. 'We are up against a blank wall. We have no idea where he is.'"

David and Doug refuse to talk.

I convince myself that if I like what the papers say, then it's true. If I don't, then it's a lie.

It works for me.

Everywhere I go, I hear people talking about Buddy's amazing escape. How he got out clean. How nobody got hurt. I hear the admiration in their voices.

Buddy calls me every couple of days. He doesn't have much to say. He asks me how I am. Am I working? How's Rayna?

Advertising executives gather around me at my Fotomat shoot.

One clears his throat. "Did you really drive the car Buddy Jacobson escaped in?"

The camera hasn't rolled yet. If I say, "Oh. That's not me. That's another Kelle," they might change their minds and hire another girl to do their commercial. For all I know, the only reason they hired me was to ask me that question.

I make my eyes big. Like the answer might make me cry. The last thing they want is an actress messing up her makeup ten minutes before she's due to go on camera. "Excuse me?" I say. My lip quivers.

"Nothing," he says.

The wardrobe girl hands me a short blue tunic. "Put this on," she says.

"Where's the pants?" I ask.

"No pants. You're just being shot from the waist up."

I hold the tunic up. "It's not going to fit over my dress. What do I wear under it?"

She looks at me as if to say, *That's your problem, not mine.* "We've all seen a girl's legs before," she says, and leaves the room.

So there I am, in her crotch-length Fotomat tunic and my vintage blue polka-dot heels. I'm quite a sight.

A young guy knocks on the dressing-room door. "Kelle, we're ready," he says.

In the middle of the studio floor is a real yellow-roofed, blue-trimmed Fotomat drive-through booth. As I walk toward it, the men look me up and down. The women give me dirty looks. I feel like I'm walking the plank.

I step into the one-person booth and sit down. Claustrophobia never felt so good.

Between shots I think about Buddy. I hope he calls me tonight. I want to tell him about my day.

He'll know how to make me feel better.

He always does.

I'm beginning to worry.

Buddy and Audrey haven't sent any letters or called in a while.

Maybe they're afraid my phone is tapped. Maybe the police are monitoring my mail.

I keep checking my mailbox. Nothing. Nothing. Nothing.

And then finally—something.

This time it's a small, fat envelope addressed in Buddy's scratchy handwriting.

I wonder why.

I open the envelope. There's no note inside. Audrey always writes little hopeful things to me. I miss that. On the inside flap Buddy's written, "Please mail these." "These" are two letters, both addressed to a town in Long Island. Both say "Att. Audrey Barrett" on the bottom.

Oh, Buddy. Has Audrey given up on you?

I search the envelope for clues. He's used Frances Perkins stamps on my envelope. Audrey's envelope has a sideways American flag stuck on it. Everything Buddy does, he does for a reason. I think he's sending me a message. I look up Frances Perkins. She was the first female presidential cabinet member. She was known as fearless, tactful, and politically astute.

I wonder if he's trying to tell me something.

The next day I get three more letters. The inner flaps say "Thank You" and "Please." The third one says nothing. They're postmarked Portland, Portland, and Marina Del something. All are sealed with masking tape.

My phone rings.

"Hello," I say.

"Babe."

It's Buddy.

I don't say his name.

"Hold those things you picked up."

He hangs up.

I stare at the phone like it's let me down.

The phone rings again. It's Rayna.

"Kelle," she says. "Audrey's turned herself in."

I drop down on my couch. "Oh, no," I say.

She reads to me from the *Daily News*.

"'Investigators revealed that Jacobson and his twenty-two-year-old girlfriend, Audrey Barrett, made a daring cross-country auto trip, tempting arrest by stopping police to ask for directions. As part of the disguise, the car was filled with camping gear and Jacobson was wearing a baseball cap over a wig.'"

"Did you know Audrey was only twenty-two?" I say.

"No. I always thought she was older," Rayna says. "Here's more. . . .

"'Barrett balked at an attempt to set an elaborate trap for Jacobson which called for her to contact him and beg to meet him at a secret rendezvous, sources said. The Brooklyn district attorney has clamped a tight lid of secrecy on the case as law enforcement agents inch closer to Jacobson in his on-the-lam struggle for freedom. Barrett's attorney, Lewis Cohen, has called his client a victim of Jacobson's psychological torture. Barrett is being held on three hundred fifty thousand dollars' bail at an unnamed hotel.'"

"Torture!" I say. "That's ridiculous."

"Last bit," Rayna says. "'Detectives said that Jacobson drove away from the jail in Brooklyn in a late-model Dodge Aspen that had been rented by Kelly K., a defense witness at the murder trial and a girlfriend of Jacobson's son Douglas.'"

Oh, Buddy. Poor, poor Buddy.

I get a loaf of bread out of my freezer, slide Buddy's folded, Glad-wrapped letters in between the frozen slices, twist the top closed, and put it back in the freezer.

Buddy calls me every day. Little short calls. He doesn't ask me for anything. He just wants to hear my voice. I miss him. I'm happy to hear from him until he hangs up. Then I miss him even more. I wonder if I'll ever get used to it.

There's a knock at my door.

I open it.

It's Rayna. Her bottom lip shakes. Mascara-colored tears leak from her eyes.

"Rayna. What's wrong?" I pull her into my apartment. I hand her a tissue. She gives her little nose a dainty blow. I throw the tissue away and give her a fresh one.

She looks at me. "It's Buddy," she says.

My body tenses. "What about him?"

"They caught him."

"The police?"

She nods. "They caught him at a restaurant in Manhattan Beach."

"Is that on Long Island?"

"California."

Geography isn't my strong suit. "What else?" I ask.

"He ordered fried zucchini with Parmesan cheese."

Rayna's really literal when she's upset about something. "Go on," I say.

"While he waited for his order to come, he called David. The call was traced. The police had him handcuffed and manacled within minutes."

I look at the spot on my counter where Buddy squished the roach. Those were such good days.

Rayna spreads a newspaper out on the table. There's a photo of Buddy. He's handcuffed. A big chain circles his waist. His shoulders slump forward. He's looking down. The headline reads, A TASTE FOR ZUCCHINI AND A YEN TO TALK.

Rayna takes a deep breath. "They said on the news they're taking him to a prison near the Canadian border. The inmates call it Little Siberia. Nobody's ever broken out of there. Ever."

Buddy got twenty-five years to life. That's a long time to spend in a place called Little Siberia. Buddy's small and thin. He's not good in the cold.

I sit down. I can barely breathe.

Rayna and I stare at each other.

We've lost our words.

Forty days wasn't enough.

I think about the letters in my freezer. Rayna knows all my secrets. What's one more?

It doesn't matter anyway. It's over. The police got what they wanted.

They got Buddy.

I lay the frozen bread down on top of Rayna's newspaper. Tiny ice crystals scatter across Buddy's photo. I bet it snows a lot in Little Siberia.

I hand Rayna the frosty-cool letters.

She scrunches up her forehead. "What's this?" she asks.

"I've been forwarding mail for Buddy ever since he escaped. He wrote these to Audrey right after she left him." I stop. "Audrey! What's going to happen to her now?"

"Oh, once they caught Buddy, they let her go." Rayna taps the letters. "Keep going."

"Oh, sorry," I say. "Anyway, when Audrey turned herself in, Buddy called and asked me to hold all his mail."

"Forwarding mail. Holding mail. Phone calls!" Rayna shakes her head. "How did I not know about this? Why didn't you tell me?"

"I wanted to protect you. If we both went to jail, who would I have to visit me?"

Rayna smiles. I smile back.

She traces Buddy's writing with her fingertip.

So close. So far away.

"Why'd you put them in the freezer?" she asks.

"If my place got searched, I didn't want the police to find them."

She nods her head and grins. "I'm going to remember that one," she says.

I always keep a six-pack of Coke in my refrigerator for Rayna. Whenever I look in and see the bright cherry red carrier in there, I think of her. I pop one open, stick a bendy straw in it, and hand it to her.

"Thanks," she says. She straightens the straw a little and takes a sip. Rayna likes her bendy straw angled just so.

"Evseroff thinks he'll win the appeal. There was a fistfight in the jury room during the deliberations. He's all over that," she says.

"A fistfight. Cool," I say.

There's a soft tap on my door.

I look at Rayna.

She looks at me.

"That better not be a reporter," I whisper.

We tiptoe over to the door. I look through the peep-hole.

I spin around. "How's my hair?"

Without missing a beat, Rayna pulls my hair out from behind my ears. "Good," she says.

I open the door.

My face is hot. My heart pounds.

"Hi, Viggo," I say. "Come on in."

He looks down at his feet. "I just wanted to give you this," he says. "I heard what happened."

He hands me a little bouquet of soft yellow butter-cups. The ends are wrapped in a wet paper towel.

"Viggo. This is my best friend, Rayna."

I look at Rayna. "Viggo's in my acting class."

Rayna gives him a little wave. "Hi," she says.

He waves back.

"I better go," Viggo says. "I'm going to be late for work."

He's got a cool little scar right above his lip. I want to kiss it.

"See you tomorrow in class?" he asks me.

I lean my cheek against the door. "Yeah. Thanks for the flowers."

Viggo blushes. "You're welcome."

I watch him walk away.

I close the door. I fan my face.

Rayna beams. "I take it that's the blond boy?"

I nod.

"Oh my gosh, Kelle. He's gorgeous! What's that accent?"

"He's Danish."

"They sure know how to make 'em," she says.

"I really, really like him," I say.

"I bet you do!"

I look at Rayna's sparkly green eyes. She's so happy for me.

She's so hopelessly hopeful.

I don't know how I ever got so lucky. She makes up for everything that's hard in my life.

When I need a hand, she offers both.

When I feel left behind, she says life's not a straight line, it's a circle.

When I'm mad, she says I never stay mad long.

When I'm lost, she says she's good with directions.

When I'm weak, she gives me something to carry to prove that it's not true.

When I forget who I am, she says she remembers.

She's Rayna.

She's my best friend.

$\mathcal{I}$ *never saw Bagel Shop Vince again.* Not in person, anyway. I see him all the time in my mind, though. Kindhearted people bring him right back to me. There's a little bit of Vince in all of them. Same with Lobby Watchman Leonard. I think of those big angel arms of his closing around me, and I know that there is light in this world.

And the New York Public Library Stair Step Saint who found me that day, so hopeless and filled with despair. Did he know that Patience and Fortitude would save my life? Did he know what our brief encounter would come to mean to me?

Everywhere I look, I see angels.

Vince, Leonard, my Stair Step Saint, they came into my life to show me how it's done. They were the experts.

I lost contact with David and Doug. I heard that David was a racehorse trainer. I was at the Santa Anita racetrack for a party a few years ago. Afterward I went to the track area to watch the horses run. One of the horses running had my name. I don't know why. Maybe it was one of David's. I read somewhere that Doug was a real estate developer.

The apples didn't fall far from the tree. I'm glad.

Nicola's Restaurant is still open. According to the Internet, it attracts the "movers and shakers from the political and art world." At least some things stay the same.

In 1982 Buddy wrote to tell me that Audrey's brother had passed away. Buddy never heard from her again. I think about her a lot. So sweet. So good. I miss her.

The last time I heard anything about Melanie was in 1989. Buddy had just died. She was mentioned in his obituary. It said that she had moved out of the city and that she had a daughter. I've always wondered if she married the Christmas tree guy.

I have no idea what ever became of the Boys Who Should Have Known Better: Ken, Perry, Brant, Lloyd. I suppose in a way I should thank them. They taught me to trust my instincts, to ask for more, to stand up for myself, and to fight for what I believe in. Like a backhanded slap that isn't soon forgotten, their lessons were clear. They were not going to save me. I had to save me. They taught me to say enough is enough— and mean it. I wasn't going to make them like me or love me or respect me or even be kind to me. I wasn't going to change them. All I could do was wish them luck and love, and move on. Sort of like my parents.

My brothers and my sister are happily married. Like me, they "got away." They found their half-mates, the ones that complete them. We're like ducks. We mate for life.

I never found out what happened to my beloved pony Muffet. Like my sister's frozen cat, Nicky, sometimes it's better not to know. Every once in a while I'll be driving somewhere or making the bed or something, and the words "Muff Puff Cream Puff" breeze through my mind. I'd like to think it's Muffet sending me her love from heaven. When I was little, I decided that Muffet was actually an angel who came to Earth to watch over me.

I still believe that.

The cute blond boy stuck with the acting. He's a big star now. He was a great guy. But he wasn't "the one."

Randy was.

I auditioned for a role in *Dynasty*. He was the casting director.

I didn't get the part.

I got him.

On May 16, 1989, Buddy died of bone cancer that had spread to his spine. He was fifty-eight years old.

I was right. He wasn't good in the cold.

We stayed in touch. Sharp and funny to the end, he said things like, "Drop in anytime. I'm always here." He died swearing by his innocence. He never gave up. His spine crumbled, but he never did. Proving that there's more than one way to stand strong.

And then there's Rayna.

We're still best friends.

As amazing as she used to be—she's even more amazing now.

A voice deep inside of me told me that the life I was living wasn't good enough.

I listened.

I wanted to get away and make it right.

I believed that I could.

I wished for a knight in shining armor.

I got more than one.

I hoped for love.

I found it in my friends' eyes.

It wasn't always easy. It's not supposed to be.

For me, the things that start out the hardest are usually the things that end up being the most satisfying. It's all about earning it.

And when things aren't good enough, the best thing I can do is . . . something, anything—'cause doing things is what changes things.

I put some good music on and I get busy.

I act like my life depends on it.

Because it does.